Praise for *Ne*

"A step-by-step guide on how to overcome the self-doubt and paralyzing fear of failure instilled in us from our very beginnings by a world that still doesn't welcome women into leadership. Piper and Samarasekera draw a map for women who are determined to beat the odds and take the risks necessary to grasp the brass ring. And then, once you have it, how to use your power for good. I couldn't put it down."

—Honourable Christy Clark,
Premier of British Columbia (2011–2017)

"Part memoir, part leadership book, *Nerve* takes us on the lifelong journeys of Martha Piper and Indira Samarasekera, culminating in their respective presidencies of two world-class institutions, the University of British Columbia and the University of Alberta. The compelling real-life stories of pitfalls and triumphs make *Nerve* definitively inspiring and empowering for future leaders."

—Sara Seager, OC, Professor of Planetary Science,
Astrophysics and Aerospace Engineering at MIT and
bestselling author of *The Smallest Lights in the Universe*

"Martha Piper and Indira Samarasekera rank with Canada's most accomplished leaders of their generation, having led at the top-most levels in higher education, government policy-making and corporate boardrooms with legendary results. Now they tell us, with compelling stories and wise advice, how they did it to inspire women to answer the call to lead and follow in their footsteps. These are great lessons not just for women but for all of us who can learn to lead from their remarkable example."

—Rob Prichard, President Emeritus, University of Toronto

"*Nerve* is a timely contribution to our collective knowledge about women and leadership. The authors' shared learnings, moving personal stories and reflective questions offer all of us—leaders and those who aspire to be—a powerful set of lessons. And yes, a reminder that above all, it is vital to find joy and 'gather the sweet nectar out of life.'"

—Barbara Grantham, President and CEO, CARE Canada

"This book is a gem. *Nerve* could easily be titled *Grit and Grace*, two entwined values dramatically explored through its pages. It tackles the unique challenges facing women leaders with compelling practical advice and the imaginative resilience of two extraordinary women. It is a valuable manual for anyone—female or male—interested in the anatomy of leadership."

—David Johnston, Governor General of Canada (2010–2017)

MARTHA PIPER &
INDIRA SAMARASEKERA

NERVE

Lessons on leadership
from two women who went first

Foreword by The Right Honourable Kim Campbell, PC

Purchase the print edition
and receive the eBook free.
For details, go to ecwpress.com/eBook.

This book is also available as a
Global Certified Accessible™
(GCA) ebook. ECW Press's ebooks
are screen reader friendly and are
built to meet the needs of those who
are unable to read standard print due
to blindness, low vision, dyslexia, or a
physical disability.

Published by ECW Press
665 Gerrard Street East
Toronto, Ontario, Canada M4M 1Y2
416-694-3348 / info@ecwpress.com

Editor for the Press: Jennifer Smith
Cover design: Made by Emblem

LIBRARY AND ARCHIVES CANADA CATALOGUING
IN PUBLICATION

Title: Nerve : lessons on leadership from two women
who went first / Martha Piper & Indira Samarasekera,
foreword by The Right Honourable Kim Campbell, P.C.

Names: Piper, Martha C., author. | Samarasekera,
Indira Vasanti, 1952- author. | Campbell, Kim, 1947-
writer of foreword.

Description: Previously published: Toronto: ECW
Press, 2021.

Identifiers: Canadiana 20220226091

ISBN 978-1-77041-673-4 (softcover)

Subjects: LCSH: Piper, Martha C. | LCSH:
Samarasekera, Indira Vasanti, 1952- | LCSH:
Leadership in women—Canada—Case studies. |
LCSH: Leadership—Canada—Case studies. | LCSH:
Women college presidents—Canada. | LCSH:
Directors of corporations—Canada.

Classification: LCC HQ1233 .P57 2022 | DDC
303.3/4082—dc23

ALSO ISSUED AS:
ISBN 978-1-77041-601-7 (hardcover)
ISBN 978-1-77305-815-3 (ePub)
ISBN 978-1-77305-816-0 (PDF)
ISBN 978-1-77305-817-7 (Kindle)

This book is funded in part by the Government of Canada. *Ce livre est financé en partie par le gouvernement du Canada.* We also acknowledge the support of the Government of Ontario through the Ontario Book Publishing Tax Credit, and through Ontario Creates.

PRINTED AND BOUND IN CANADA   PRINTING: MARQUIS   5   4   3   2   1

*To our grandchildren, Charlotte, Henry, Elliott, Anila,
Finnegan, Jacob, Benjamin, Priya.*

*Our hope is that you will live inspired lives
and make a mark in the world.*

CONTENTS

———

FOREWORD

Martha Piper and Indira Samarasekera describe themselves as "two women who went first." Piper was the first, and to date only, woman to serve as president of the University of British Columbia (UBC), and Samarasekera was the first and only woman to serve as president of the University of Alberta (U of A), both institutions in the Big Five of Canadian research universities. Although my days at UBC as a student and lecturer long predated Piper's presidency, I knew her reputation as an outstanding leader. By the time she finished her second term at the helm of UBC, she was seen to have completed the process begun by her predecessor, David Strangway, in putting UBC on the map as one of the leading universities of the world.

In 2013, Indira Samarasekera approached me to speak to a group of U of A supporters about a new project—the Peter Lougheed Leadership Initiative. Before long I would agree to come to U of A to create one part of that vision—the Peter Lougheed Leadership College. As she describes in this book, that initiative was a perfect illustration of the difficulty of leading in a university. One of my colleagues at U of A described being a department chair in a university as "being given a gun with no bullets." The description of a university faculty as "a collection of independent contractors, brought together by a shared grievance over parking" accurately reflects the reluctance of university faculties to be "led." As a woman who shares membership in the "Went First" club as Canada's Minister of Justice and Attorney General, Minister of National Defence and Prime Minister, I want to emphasize that no matter how difficult and challenging political leadership is, it is an extraordinary achievement that these two women were not only named presidents of their respective institutions but also had the nerve to stay the course and that they succeeded beyond their greatest critics' wildest fears!

Nerve is often used for a brand of courage to which the woman in question is not deemed to be entitled as in, "she has a lot of nerve." Nerve is not just courage per se, but, specifically, the courage to *do* something—thus, "I just didn't have the nerve to do X." The two authors describe the unwillingness of many women to take on leadership roles as their "lack of nerve." Women feel the need to exceed the requirements of any job for which they might be considered, a frame of mind that is not often found in men, whose nerve has been described as the masculine propensity for "positive illusion." I think an important factor in explaining the frequent lack of nerve in women is their understanding that, for them, failure will not necessarily be just a part of a process of learning and growing in their leadership role but could just as likely end it.

A number of years ago I participated in a program with most of the 10 women who had led provincial and territorial governments in Canada. The program was entitled "No Second Chances," and I was surprised at the number of participants for whom the leadership experience was unhappy and demoralizing. Often, their chance to lead came when their parties were in bad shape, and the electoral prospects were dim. If they succeeded, their male colleagues worked to edge them out since the top job was now attractive. If they were unable to turn the party fortunes around, the result was put primarily on their shoulders. The risks of leading are greater for women than for men. That being said, I have no regrets about my own experience. My observations of national leaders such as Jacinda Ardern of New Zealand and Germany's Angela Merkel are that they love what they do. They are among the most respected leaders of either sex in the world today.

The late UC Berkeley philosopher Joseph Tussman liked to say, "The unit of human understanding is the story." In exploring their routes to leadership, Piper and Samarasekera tell the stories of their lives.

Their decision as friends and colleagues to do this together is much to their readers' benefit as the parallel storytelling allows us to take note of the differences and similarities in their paths. As skilled teachers, the authors reflect on what they describe and draw out the lessons to be learned from their leadership experiences. I found that this structure encouraged me to compare my own life as a female "first." The observations of Piper and Samarasekera form an excellent framework for discussion and personal reflection for anyone, man or woman, who is interested in women and leadership. There is also a good dose of solid research incorporated into the discussion. One of the major developments in the understanding of leadership since my own youthful days is the growing body of scholarly research on why gender barriers occur and also on the skills and competences that women bring to leadership roles. Far from confirming the stereotypical assumption that men are more "natural" leaders, research shows that women often exceed men in the skills required to lead successfully.

Both Piper and Samarasekera describe their post-presidential experiences sitting on corporate boards of directors. Numerous studies confirm the wisdom of these appointments—to the extent that many jurisdictions require gender diversity on the boards of publicly traded companies. Support comes in the form of studies such as one by Credit Suisse (not an organization one would think of as excessively socially progressive) that demonstrated that companies that include women in senior management and on their boards of directors are more profitable than ones that do not. The question is no longer, "How can we justify to our shareholders putting you (female) on the board when our concern must be for the bottom line?" Now the question becomes, "Knowing what you do about the value of women in management and on boards of directors, how do you justify to your shareholders that you do not have any?"

Finally, *Nerve* is a generous book because the authors share some of the missteps that almost derailed them. My experience is that when women speak honestly of their failings, this becomes an excuse for those who do not accept their presence in leadership roles to pile on rather than allow an exploration of how to learn from mistakes.

Piper and Samarasekera talk honestly about how it feels to be out of power—an inevitability for any leader. In my own life, I have helped to form two organizations of former presidents and prime ministers—the

Council of Women World Leaders and the Club de Madrid. The former consists of women who are or have been president or prime minister of their countries—a growing number that is changing the landscape showing who gets to do those jobs. The Club of Madrid, former democratically elected presidents and prime ministers of both sexes, is a forum that allows former leaders to use their knowledge, experience, access and clout to support democratic values and governance throughout the world. I believe that a forum for former university presidents could also assemble the talents of educational leaders in a constructive role of advocacy and advice. Perhaps one already exists. The two authors of this book would be valuable members of such a group.

Martha Piper and Indira Samarasekera have led wonderful, productive and challenging lives. They have known tragedy and disappointment, but none of their experiences would, I think, lead them to regret taking up the challenge of leading. They radiate the happiness that comes from finding ways to use your human potential to make the world a better place. That demonstration of the deep satisfaction that comes from a life that includes leading will, I hope, encourage many women to read this book and find the nerve to say yes to the opportunity to lead.

—THE RIGHT HONOURABLE KIM CAMPBELL,

19TH PRIME MINISTER OF CANADA

INTRODUCTION

---

*"It takes more than talent. It takes a kind of nerve . . . a kind of nerve,
and a lot of hard, hard work."*

—GEORGIA O'KEEFFE

Women are notoriously ambivalent when it comes to leadership. They often ask us, "Should I seek or accept this leadership opportunity, or should I forgo it?" or, "Should I take the leap or give it a pass, waiting for another, better time?" Obviously, the answers to these questions are complicated and must take into consideration the circumstances, timing, priorities and ambitions of the individual. But why do women so often doubt their ability, willingness or readiness to lead? Would men ask the same questions when faced with a leadership opportunity? Why are women so quick to reject the clarion call to leadership, no matter how prepared they are for the role?

The reasons underlying this ambivalence are varied. Some women worry that they are making the wrong choice, or that the choice they have made is inappropriate, poorly timed or has unintended consequences. Others feel guilty about putting their needs before others; still others lack confidence in their own skills and are overly modest in the assessment of their achievements and personal talents. Regardless of the reasons advanced, one thing is certain: rarely do you hear men voicing the same ambivalence when presented with leadership opportunities.

Why is this? Why is leadership viewed differently by women when compared with men? Do we lead differently, set different life objectives, confront different barriers when striving to lead or lack the drive, ambition or desire to take charge? Why is it there are still so few women leaders in today's world, even though many of the barriers, such as lack of access to education and unfair employment policies, are being removed around the world, albeit slowly in some countries? Why has Canada had only one woman prime minister and the U.S. still has not elected a woman president? Why is it that within the corporate world we are still debating the need for more gender diversity in higher levels of management, as well as on boards of directors?

These are the questions we pondered over the past several decades as we navigated our own leadership journeys. Born on two different continents into two distinct ethnic cultures, we worked together as academic colleagues at the University of British Columbia (UBC), with Indira Samarasekera serving as the Vice-President, Research, when Martha Piper was president. Indira went on to assume the presidency of the University of Alberta (U of A), resulting in our being the first women to serve as presidents of two of Canada's largest universities. Subsequently, we have assumed leadership positions in corporate boardrooms and in the nonprofit sector. Our career paths have been uncannily aligned—from being Vice-Presidents, Research, to becoming presidents of universities, serving as directors on large market cap corporate boards and having two children and four grandchildren living close by. Over the years, we have developed an enduring friendship based on trust, respect and mutual admiration. These interconnections account at least in part for our interest in working together to better understand how women develop into leaders, how they lead and how they live after leading.

We never thought we would write a book together. But as time passed, and we continued to hear from women who for various reasons were reluctant to lead or who sought information and advice on leadership, we reached the conclusion it was time to speak up, recount our experiences and share the lessons we have learned, in the hope that we would encourage other women to find the nerve to step up and lead.

Drawing upon our wealth of experience, we review the similarities and disparities in our respective childhoods, educational backgrounds, early career decisions and serendipitous events we believe helped prepare us to lead. In addition, we address the significant challenges, as well as the highs and lows, women leaders face on a day-to-day basis. Finally, we recount our efforts to redefine our life's purpose after stepping down from our leadership positions. Focusing on the three aspects of the leadership journey—what comes *before* leading, what comes *with* leading and what comes *after* leading—we share our personal stories and outline the lessons learned as we navigated our careers as women leaders, revealing along the way the decisions, attitudes and experiences that female leaders frequently encounter, as well as the personal characteristics common to women in leadership roles.

Throughout this conversation, we conclude that, for women, there is a recurring thread connecting these three phases of leadership: *nerve*—developing your nerve to lead, drawing upon your nerve when leading and finding the nerve to reinvent yourself when you no longer are leading. Nerve is the personal attribute that we believe is not only required to lead but also is often missing in women, even in those who aspire to leadership roles. Nerve to be true to yourself, nerve to take a path less traveled, nerve to go first, nerve to act decisively, nerve to redefine yourself. Women are good at most things: we know how to work hard, we often overprepare for whatever task we are performing, we are proficient at collaboration, consultation and compromise—all important traits for a leader. But if there is one characteristic that we must actively work on developing and consciously draw upon as we chart our course as leaders, it is *nerve*. Not easy, not obvious, not immediately part of our repertoire.

We propose that nerve not only needs to be acknowledged but also actively cultivated by women leaders. Without nerve, women become captive to tradition and tend to succumb to living their lives constrained by what's deemed appropriate by society. Without nerve, women worry about being liked and keeping everyone happy. Without nerve, women are prone to avoiding the tough decisions and to forgoing their principles in the face of adversity. Without nerve, women are more likely to recoil from the chance to lead, deciding that it is too difficult, that they are not adequately qualified or that the timing is not right.

Without nerve, neither of us would have answered the call to lead, nor would we have succeeded at a time when there were very few role models for women in leadership—and very many obstacles for women at the top and on the way there. This book is a reflection on leadership, how it differs for women and men, and what it takes for women to excel as leaders. It is also part memoir—telling the stories of how we developed the nerve to lead, how we led with nerve and how, in the years after leadership, we are attempting to reinvent ourselves with nerve. It is our hope that by sharing our experiences as women leaders who went first, we will encourage the next generation of women to find the nerve to step up and lead with confidence, strength and conviction.

PART I

Developing the nerve to lead

CHAPTER I

Born or bred to lead?

"Some are born great, some achieve greatness,
and some have greatness thrust upon 'em."

—WILLIAM SHAKESPEARE, *TWELFTH NIGHT*

Little girls rarely, if ever, dream of becoming *leaders*. Mothers, doctors, teachers, even astronauts or zookeepers, yes; but not what we tradition-ally think of as a public or high-profile leadership role. While anyone in these kinds of positions may end up leading, it is not the *leadership* aspect girls are thinking of when they cite these life aspirations. And yet, girls do lead. They lead on the playgrounds, in the schoolyards and in the local gymnasiums. They lead their siblings, classmates and friends. They are leaders in the creative arts and in their places of worship and communities.

The questions are, "How does this happen if girls don't aspire to leadership and if society in general does not expect it of them? Are some girls born to lead, rising to the top and becoming the leaders of whatever group they are associated with regardless of their individual backgrounds or talents? Or does leadership occur as a result of environmental influ-ences, necessity, good fortune or learned behavior? In any case, what role does gender play in creating or cultivating leaders?"

As two women who have led similar organizations, we were interested in better understanding how we both became leaders, each of us breaking new ground by being the first woman to lead our respective academic institution. Why and how did we shatter the glass ceiling at a time when it was rare to see females in these kinds of senior positions anywhere—in academia, business, boardrooms or politics? Was this inevitable? Did we share certain experiences in our upbringings and early childhoods or in our professional backgrounds that would clearly explain our similar outcomes? Was it that our circumstances or environmental opportunities were aligned in such a manner that would explain our decisions to lead? Maybe it is just coincidental that two academics, in entirely different fields, who just happen to be women, were chosen to lead similar universities in neighboring provinces . . . but maybe it is not. Maybe there is a more objective explanation, one that can be studied and replicated.

The explanations that are frequently offered to explain why some women naturally become leaders—such as being an only child or firstborn, having only sisters for siblings or being educated in an all-girls environment—do not seem to apply consistently in our cases. Neither of us is an only child; one of us is firstborn, the other, third, both from families of four children. Neither of us is the only girl in our respective families, and we both have brothers. Neither of us attended elite, private universities, and only one of us attended an all-girls school. We were both blessed to be raised by two loving parents who created warm, trusting and secure environments, while at the same time setting high personal expectations. To our knowledge, our parents neither actively encouraged us to lead nor held aspirations for us to become leaders. And yet, we each have recollections of leading as children, even though we don't remember either thinking about leading or yearning to lead.

Birth Order or the Desire to Please

We are consistently amazed by how often we are asked if we are the eldest child in our families. Clearly, that is not the case for both of us, and there are far more influences at play than birth order to explain why some women choose to lead. We believe it's more likely girls are raised to be leaders than are born into the role; however, the myth of the firstborn leader persists, likely because it is so attractive in its simplicity.

Multitudinous studies have been conducted over the years to determine the role birth order plays in affecting personalities, accomplishments, attitudes and abilities.[1] In the 1920s, Alfred Adler theorized that birth order helps shape one's personality, with firstborn children being more likely to have a "taste for power." This obsession for control, and hence to lead, is largely derived from the long-term effects of being adored and pampered by parents. Whereas middle children, as a result of having to compete more for their parents' attention and love, tend to be more creative and competitive, Adler's theory holds that the extra undivided attention bestowed on firstborn children prepares them to thrive and lead.

Firstborn children are more likely to stay in school longer, be more successful and have higher IQs, and they are 30 percent more likely to be CEOs or politicians than their younger siblings.[2] Unfortunately, this study only examined the experience of boys, thereby raising the question as to whether the same holds true for firstborn girls. When comparing a sample of male versus female presidents and prime ministers, another study found more firstborn children among women leaders (34.2 percent) than among their male counterparts (28.2 percent).[3]

In their classic 1976 book, *The Managerial Woman*, Margaret Hennig and Anne Jardim review retrospectively the experiences of 25 women who rose to leadership positions in the corporate world, attempting to explore whether there was a discernible pattern in these women's lives. They note that all of them were eldest in families of all girls and theorize that in the absence of sons, fathers directed their attentions and aspirations onto the firstborn daughter, encouraging her to act more like a man than a woman, thereby resulting in increased ambition for power. In this study, gender and birth order interact, and the absence of male siblings is a key factor, permitting the father to devote his attention to his first-born daughter.

It is difficult to know whether we would find the same unique role for the father-daughter relationship in today's women leaders. Young women now often have mothers who have had opportunities that women 50 years ago did not have, including outstanding educational backgrounds and professional careers. In addition, family structures in the 21st century have expanded to include single parents, extended families and gay couples. We are confident that younger women are now as likely to find their mothers or other elders, in addition to or instead of their fathers, playing a prominent role in their lives and providing role models as leaders in their communities.

Yet, the father-daughter relationship continues to be highlighted as instrumental in the development of some women leaders.[4] And our experience within our own family structures suggests that our fathers were instrumental in encouraging us to excel and inspiring us to lead. The relationship we both had with our fathers helps us better understand our underlying ambition to be the best we can be, to compete with others and to find the nerve to take on leadership responsibilities that we might otherwise have forgone. Our mothers were extremely important in our lives in terms of developing creativity and providing us with happy and secure childhoods, but for both of us, it was our father whom we most desired to please.

PIPER:

I was neither firstborn nor born into an all-girl family. I was born third, sandwiched between two brothers, with my older sister being the eldest child in our family. Those two factors, an older sister and two brothers, individually and collectively would disqualify me for my father's undivided attention. And yet, I do know this. I wanted more than anything to live up to his expectations.

My father had exceptionally high standards and a well-developed sense of purpose, never accepting any excuse for not doing our best or not making the most of our talents. He believed that you alone were responsible for your fate and that hard work would lead to success.

While I never believed as a child that he singled me out among his children with regard to his love or his favor, it was only after he died that I learned from others how much he believed in me and gloried in my success. Was I his favorite child? I do not believe that for a minute. But were my talents and achievements a source of pride to him? I believe the answer is, categorically, yes: that pride, that encouragement, that interest in my being the best I could be—from my father, the most important man in my life as a child—must explain, more than my birth order or gender, some of my determination to lead or take control of my destiny.

SAMARASEKERA:

What lessons did I learn in my formative years that have molded who I have become? Perhaps the most obvious stemmed from my being the oldest of four siblings, which led naturally to a tendency to exercise authority. My sister, two years younger, complains of having been "bossed" around; she laments that I called the shots on what games we played and when the game would end.

While being firstborn most likely has had an impact on my ability to lead, I now also recognize that my father was an important figure in my early development. My mother married at a young age and did not attend university, but she impressed upon my sister and me that we should aspire to higher education and careers. My father was in many ways a man ahead of his time; his aspirations for his daughters were truly remarkable. He would regale us with the achievements of Olympic athletes and Nobel laureates, great painters, singers and writers. His message was clear: he expected us to excel in whatever field we chose, and we were to aim very high. It would require nerve.

From where did my father draw his inspirational ideas about women? Years later, I realized his progressive views on women were shaped by his aunt, Mary Irwin, a Canadian physician and missionary. She married my father's granduncle, Samuel Rutnam, and made Sri Lanka her home. She was a pioneer in her time, a leader who transformed conditions for the women of Sri Lanka, advocating for their right to vote and access to quality education and family planning. A woman who personified nerve by taking on conservative colonial Sri Lanka to upend deeply embedded biases that limited opportunities for women. As a young boy, my father spent some time in the home of Mary Rutnam, "Aunt May," as he called her, when his parents were working in India. There is no question in my mind—my father's enlightened aspirations for women were rooted in Mary Rutnam's extraordinary achievements as an exceptional leader and have had a lasting impact on my own personal story.

When I decided I wanted to study engineering, he did not say, "Are you crazy? Women don't become engineers. Be something appropriate, like a teacher or a nurse." Instead, he encouraged my ambitions. He had wanted to be a physicist, and his parents discouraged him, thereby ensuring he studied medicine, instead. Accordingly, he wanted me to have the chance he never had to pursue his own dream. Even when I had cold feet after being admitted to engineering, afraid that I would be the only woman, he allayed my fears. He suggested we visit the Council for Higher Education to ask how many women had been admitted to engineering that year. To our surprise, there were 12 of us entering the program (of 150). So I had no excuses left!

Looking back, I now know that I consistently sought my father's affirmation, and I always wanted to make him proud. Every crucial decision in my life was made with his input or guidance. When I was appointed president of the University of Alberta, he and my mother traveled from Sri Lanka to attend the installation. They were both overjoyed. It was an extraordinary moment for our family.

Crucible of Family

The saying goes that it takes a village to raise a child; by extension, it seems increasingly clear that one might also say it takes a village to raise a leader. Early childhood experiences have consistently been shown to have long-term impacts on a child's development and self-esteem.

And leaders appear to emerge from environments where there are strong role models, elders who express hopes, aspirations and ambitions for these young people—and who show confidence in their ability to achieve the goals they set.

To date, just two presidents of the United States, Franklin Roosevelt and Gerald Ford, and four of the 41 women presidents or prime ministers in the earlier mentioned study of political leaders were only children. What does that say about the key role siblings might play in developing leaders? While many studies have demonstrated that only children become leaders, siblings may also play an important role developing in children the qualities essential for leadership: cooperation, sharing, getting along and compromising.

We believe it is more than coincidental that we both were raised in families with loving parents and, interestingly, three siblings. We both have one sister and two brothers. While our birth orders differed, our families were strikingly similar. In the end, we have concluded that our parents and siblings provided us with our values, our nerve, our determination and our desire to live better lives.

As important, both of us had grandparents who individually shaped our thinking in meaningful ways and had a profound impact on our lives. Though it's unusual in today's world, where families are often separated by significant geographic distances, we had the luxury of having grandparents who lived nearby—interacting consistently with us and providing a perspective on life different to that of our parents.

In short, our families, both nuclear and extended, played a significant role in our development in a manner not easily reproduced by the school, broader community or place of worship. What role family plays in the long run in producing women leaders is still unclear, but we are both able to trace many of our characteristics and attributes back to our families and the relationships we had with our siblings, parents and grandparents. Indisputably, the broad influences we enjoyed in our familial experiences shaped us in a way that, if nothing else, prepared us to lead.

SAMARASEKERA:

My sister loved make-believe games, while I had my nose buried in a book. Our differences in personalities and interests caused no end of squabbles, as she would pester me to participate in her imaginary world, which I engaged in reluctantly. My parents would reprimand me for being unkind to my sister when these games did not end amicably. I learned early on that getting my way did not lead to a favorable relationship with my sister nor a pat on the back from my parents. My sister claims that she was instrumental in imparting interpersonal skills, essential to me as a leader.

My brothers' arrival, eight and 10 years later, required that I take on the role of helper from a young age. My two baby brothers drew my sister and me closer together as now we had common cause. We weren't always kind to the boys, but by and large had to be, or else our parents came down on us like a ton of bricks! Having younger siblings nurtured in me a sense of responsibility for others. I enjoyed the role of big sister to my siblings and the numerous cousins who were all younger than I.

PIPER:

I had what most would describe as an idyllic childhood: two loving parents; a creative, intelligent mother; a respected and successful father;

and a large three-story house with a rambling backyard right on Lake Erie.

More than anything, I adored my older sister. She was my role model for what a girl should be: pretty, fashionable, popular, kind and smart. Even though there were only five years between us, she was old in my eyes, always doing things that I could only yearn to do. She was experimenting with makeup while I was still wearing pigtails. She was dating while I was reading all of the Nancy Drew series. I did not play with her; I only admired her and wanted to be beautiful and popular like her when I grew up.

My brothers, on the other hand, were my playmates and partners in crime. I was positioned between them, with only 18 months separating each of them from me. I did whatever was necessary to obtain their approval—doing the tasks that they wanted done, in order to be able to keep up with their antics and activities.

My older brother was a bit of a daredevil, always seeking thrills and excitement. One summer, he and his buddies decided to build a homemade water-ski jump. It was made of plywood floating on large barrels, with a steep incline that made the approach extremely treacherous. There was one slight problem: The surface of the jump was canvas. It needed to be watered down with a mixture of lake water and Ivory soap flakes just before the boat approached. This task fell to me. I was required to swim out to the raft holding the soap box in one hand, climbing on just before the boat and skier ascended to soap up the ramp and then jumping into the water quickly and hiding under the raft to avoid being hit by the boat. Not exactly a leadership job!

And as if my older brother's antics were not enough to beat any leadership tendencies out of me, my younger brother controlled me economically. He was a financial wizard and had various schemes to make money as a kid. Whether it was sharing a paper route with him or being his associate in his "Worms and Night Crawlers" summer business, I was always his sidekick—not the other way around.

Was this a gender issue? Was I deferring to the males in my life, or was it my position within the family due to my birth order? One might argue that being surrounded by males so early in my life, being acculturated by them and having to learn how to keep up with them, contributed to the development of my nerve to lead in a variety of circumstances.

Who knows? For whatever reason, I do not recollect leading as a child in my family or in my neighborhood; however, my experience suggests that I was cultivated by my brothers to be fearless, to compete to be heard and to work hard in order to keep up. So perhaps they helped set me on the path to leadership, unbeknownst to me at the time.

SAMARASEKERA:

"It takes a village" has a metaphorical as well as literal meaning for me, since I spent most of my childhood in an extended family setting that could qualify as a village. My maternal grandmother, a central figure in my life, was one in a family of 10 children, and as adults she and all her siblings lived next door to one another in a neighborhood called Cinnamon Gardens in the capital city of Colombo, Sri Lanka.

There were deep-rooted family traditions, such as attending church at St. Michael's followed by Sunday lunch. My mother's siblings and their families came to my grandparents' house weekly for a sumptuous Sri Lankan meal, which was always the same and of which we never tired: yellow rice, chicken curry, eggplant badun, lentils and popadam. As children we became acquainted with the accomplishments of extended family members who were leaders in their chosen fields—surgeons, lawyers, accountants, artists and civil servants. I came to realize that excelling and breaking new ground were deeply valued. Many relatives married outside our ethnicity, traveled overseas for education and work and demonstrated a penchant for risk taking.

As happy and interesting as our family was, we were not spared tragedy. One of my grandmother's siblings lost his only son in a car accident, and I recall the funeral vividly as a 16-year-old, the family rallying to support his young widow a few months pregnant. A nephew developed schizophrenia and was found hanging from a tree in their garden. My uncle developed epilepsy, and my grandmother had to rush to the U.K. when the landlady found him unconscious in the bathroom. I learned that tragedy and triumph were part of the human condition. I also realized that human strengths and flaws gave color to the village.

My maternal grandmother, who was the family matriarch, had the greatest impact on me. Her mother was one of the founders of the Women's International Club in Sri Lanka, a place where women gathered to play bridge and mah-jongg, listen to an interesting speaker or watch a performance. My grandmother became president of the club, like her mother before her, and was constantly engaged in one community-building activity or another, pursuing her interest in history, the arts and culture. Her love and support of her siblings and their families in tough times and her unquenchable zest for life left a deep impression on me. Did my grandmother's example of resiliency and nerve influence my leadership journey? I will never know, but I am convinced that the "village" of elders was the crucible in which my personality and character were molded, preparing me for leadership.

PIPER:

In my early teens, my paternal grandmother died, leaving my grand-father a widower. He was still working as a judge but was unprepared to live alone; hence, he came to live with us, moving lock, stock and barrel into my family's home. I thought nothing of it. It seemed natural at the time for us to be a three-generational household. I now know how brave it was of my mother to take on responsibility for her father-in-law while still raising four children. As for my grandfather, I can only imagine how his life changed—from a quiet existence with my grandmother, to a crowded, chaotic, noisy and crazy life with four active grandchildren.

What I also now realize is how my life changed dramatically with his arrival. His presence had a transformative effect on me; he was always there, sharing stories, imparting wisdom and giving me his undivided attention when my parents were often preoccupied. We would listen to the Cleveland Indians baseball games on the radio, and I learned how to mark every play and every pitch using a scorecard. I learned the value of a university education as he regaled me with endless stories of his love for the University of Michigan. And as he aged and suffered a stroke, I learned how to care for others with disabilities, perhaps laying the foun-dation for my future professional choice of physical therapy.

One of the lessons he imparted to us came in a piece of often-repeated advice: "Always, always carry jumper cables in your car!" While my grandfather drove a Cadillac, he was very aware that not everyone on the road had the luxury of driving such a fine vehicle. He saw it as his duty to assist those who were less fortunate; to give someone a boost when they required one; to lend a hand to someone in need.

To this day, I always carry jumper cables in my car. But I also know that my grandfather's admonition was more than good advice for road safety—that what he really meant was it was our duty and our responsibility to assist others from time to time, to share our privilege with others and to give back to our communities.

Adversity and Nerve

Resiliency is often identified as one of the most important traits of strong leaders: the ability to recover from a disappointment or failure, the skill of picking yourself up when you are down, the knowledge that you will recover from a disappointment or disaster. Life is never easy; it is filled with obstacles and difficulties. Some people react with despair and mental anguish, resulting in career setbacks or severe discouragement; in others, however, adversity appears to breed resilience and nerve—nerve to continue, nerve to take on difficult tasks, nerve to make tough decisions. Can nerve be acquired through events experienced early in life? Can it be learned, or is it an innate trait in people who are born to lead? What role does adversity play in cultivating nerve and the ability to lead?

SAMARASEKERA:

My early childhood was spent adapting to constantly changing circumstances. When I was three years old, my family sailed from Colombo (it was called Ceylon at that time), to London, U.K., where my father pursued fellowship training as an ENT surgeon. We lived in a typical British flat, three stories high, damp and dreary in winter, with an entrance onto the road. My sister and I spent a lot of time on the street outside, riding a two-wheeled scooter or pushing a doll carriage. Hyde Park, Regent's Park, the Tower of London and other historic places were frequent destinations, framed in my mind's eye to this day.

We returned to Sri Lanka when I was five and my formal education began in Galle, on the wet southern coast. Coconut trees were abundant, and the city was distinguished by a magnificent Dutch fort, complete with ramparts, where we would play for hours. But because my family is Tamil, we fled after the race riots of 1958 to Jaffna, a hot and dusty town in the dry zone at the northern tip of Sri Lanka. Dotted with palmyra trees, with a clock tower in the center and the famous Hindu Temple, Jaffna was mainly populated by Tamils who, following independence from the British in 1948, were experiencing discrimination in employment and opportunities, relative to the Singhalese, who were 75 percent of the population.

I began my education in Singhalese in Galle and switched to Tamil when I moved to Jaffna. My first year in school, split between Galle and then Jaffna, was traumatic to say the least since I spoke only English, with a "cockney British accent." I remember sitting on my school suitcase outside the classroom in protest, desperately wanting to return to London. I have often wondered whether all the disruption I experienced as a child—learning three languages, moving countries and cities, experiencing race riots, all before grade 1—increased my resilience and gave me the nerve to accept change.

My father suffered from depression, and I recall his situation getting much worse, which I found painful to watch; I missed the father I knew. When he was depressed, which would sometimes last weeks at a time, he struggled to work as an otolaryngologist; yet despite this affliction, he was a wonderful father. My mother was extraordinary in her support of him, telling us frequently that he was not responsible for his ill health. As I grew older, he became more despondent from time to time, which distressed and weighed heavily on me, as the eldest. Over the years, I learned to cope with the consequences of having a parent who was not always well and developed a deep admiration for my parents' resilience in the face of adversity.

Were these challenging early years foundational in honing my capacity to succeed in the face of obstacles? Was I conditioned to take risks and venture into the unknown because I had been thrown headlong into such situations as a child and survived? Leaders have to respond to disruption and challenge, and childhood adversity can build character and confidence as long as there is a loving and supportive family to provide security, which I had in spades.

Taking Stock

Teenage girls who are still struggling with their sense of purpose and gender identity frequently engage in intense self-reflection. Who can they follow on social media, and who is following them? Who went out of their way to talk to them? Who made an impression on them as their next potential boyfriend or girlfriend? Who, if anyone, would they like to see again or hear from?

It is our belief that this type of review (albeit asking very different questions)—a scanning of one's past to see what leadership opportunities one has had—is helpful for women thinking about leading. By reviewing their specific background and circumstances—when, if ever, they have been asked to lead or have assumed leadership positions—women are able to consider and learn from the experiences that have equipped them to lead. By taking stock of the past—their family situation, support network, pivotal developmental experiences—women may gain a better understanding of their leadership skills and be more prepared to think about potential leadership positions when they arise in the future.

What does your past tell you about your own leadership abilities? Are there recurring examples of your taking on leadership roles or being asked to lead in school, sports organizations, your workplace, programs or your community? By ignoring the value of these experiences, women may underestimate their innate or developed leadership qualities, their qualifications or their desire to lead. By reflecting from time to time, by acknowledging their own past records of leadership, women can prepare themselves with a better understanding of, and appreciation for, new opportunities to lead. You may already be more of a leader than you think you are!

PIPER:

My mother once told me that my kindergarten teacher shared with her that I was a "natural leader." I, of course, have no recollection of that conversation or what inspired it, but my mother depicted me standing in front of the class, waving my arms frantically while the other children sang. I remember neither the songs nor the arm waving, but something clearly resonated with me whenever my mother recounted that story.

If I look back over my life, there is a pattern. I was chosen as the patrol leader for my Girl Scout troop; I led almost every high school club that existed; I was the president of my sorority and later assumed the role of Panhellenic president at the University of Michigan. As a freshly minted PhD, I was selected to lead the School of Physical and Occupational Therapy at McGill University with no prior academic appointment.

While hindsight reveals this pattern, I was completely taken aback when I received the call from the headhunter about the presidency of UBC. Had I taken the time before that to reflect upon my past leadership roles and how they prepared me for larger leadership positions, I might have been less surprised by, and more accepting of, the invitation to apply for the presidency.

Lessons Learned

Although various theories have been developed to explain who is most suitable for leadership, we believe it is much more complex than any single hypothesis, particularly for women. Few people are truly born to be leaders, and nurture plays at least as important a role as nature. More often, leaders are forged by their experience, their upbringing, elders and other influences in their lives. A girl's family and her relationship with her parents, siblings and grandparents may play a more important role in cultivating leadership skills than whether she was first- or only born.

Similarly, the development of nerve may occur as a result of having had to deal with adversity sometime in your life—whether it be experiencing a divorce of parents, being uprooted from the familiar and moving to new and foreign locations or coping with life tragedies.

While none of these factors—birth order; relationships with fathers, mothers, elders or siblings; or having weathered an adverse situation—is singly predictive of who will lead in the future, when considered together they may provide a better understanding of how and why some women become leaders. Regardless, we believe there is merit for women not only to take stock of the many factors that play a role in their development as potential leaders but also to review from time to time the leadership opportunities they have encountered throughout their lives. Whether they are *born* or *bred* leaders, they may discover they are more prepared to lead than they realized.

1.   What were your most significant relationships with family members? What role did they play in the development of

your values and aspirations? What did you learn from them in terms of working with others, finding your voice, developing nerve, making decisions and striving for excellence?

2. How has your family, including your extended family, influenced your sense of purpose and self-confidence? How did you relate to your siblings, and what role did they play in determining who you are?

3. Reflect upon the experiences in your life that have been challenging, disappointing or represented failure. How did you react to them, and how do you generally react to adversity? Are there ways you might develop your nerve to be able to move more positively through difficult issues? Think about and learn from people who have faced adversity with courage and been able to thrive following their difficulties.

4. Take stock of the leadership experiences you have had, even if you didn't perceive them as such at the time. Is there a pattern? Have you been asked to lead or assume positions of increasing responsibility? If so, acknowledge that you are able to lead.

CHAPTER 2

The education of a female leader

"An investment in knowledge pays the best interest."

—BENJAMIN FRANKLIN

In 1929, Virginia Woolf published an extended essay entitled *A Room of One's Own*, based on two lectures she delivered at the University of Cambridge. Woolf makes the case, both literally and figuratively, that in order for women to succeed as authors in a man's literary world, they require both money and a quiet space to write, that is, a room of their own.

She continues by lamenting the historical absence of educational opportunities for women as the real culprit in preventing them from acquiring either money or a room of one's own, thereby undermining their attempts to compete on an equal footing with men. Woolf argues that because universities had for centuries denied women access to higher education, women were unfairly disadvantaged when it came to contributing to the literary and artistic fields.

Her message, however, ends with hope and a call for action. She notes that because Oxford University had begun to admit women in 1920, women no longer had an excuse for not making good in the world.

She admonishes women to take advantage of their newly acquired access to universities and to take their full place, as equals, in society.

Woolf understood implicitly the importance of education, and specifically higher education—privileges that men had always enjoyed—to women being able to pursue their life goals. She attributed the dearth of women writers and artists, along with lawyers, doctors and entrepreneurs, to the lack of education and believed fervently that with the opening of the doors of universities to women, true equity would be achieved.

Nearly a hundred years later, women are still grappling with their ability to compete in a man's world. While universities around the globe have over time admitted women (Harvard degrees were awarded to Radcliffe students for the first time in 1963; Princeton first admitted women in 1969), and while women have slowly but surely received degrees in the disciplines traditionally dominated by men (business, medicine, law, engineering, physics and mathematics), few women have broken through into the elite ranks of scholarly recognition. The rarity of female Nobel laureates, for example, has been attributed to their relative lack of access to higher education and the absence of women's networks to support nominations of other women. Although more women have been winning the Nobel Prize, the Fields Medal in mathematics and other prestigious international awards in recent years, the gender gap is far from closing. Only time will tell whether women will achieve equity when it comes to being recognized for groundbreaking thinking and discovery.

Even outside of the rarefied world of academic achievement, the playing field is still not level for women. They have yet to achieve equal access to the corporate boardrooms or the corner offices, let alone the halls of political power. We have yet to see a woman elected president of the United States and have had only one female Canadian prime minister; and less than 25 percent of corporate boardroom appointments are women.

What is holding us back? How do the educational paths we choose affect our ability to rise to the top of our fields or disciplines? Does it matter what we study, or are there other factors that must be considered when women compete for leadership positions? As two women who had remarkably different educational paths, were there some commonalities in our experiences that might explain our ability to become leaders? If so, what are they and how might they interact with our educational background?

Curious Learning

On the subject of Nobel Prizes, why are more awarded to Americans than to the Chinese? Is there a bias in the selection process that tilts the balance, or does it reflect significant differences in the educational systems of the two countries? Some have argued that while the Chinese dominate the Americans on standardized educational tests, they fall short when it comes to creative problem solving and innovative thinking. Critics have attributed this disparity to the major differences in educational philosophies between the two countries, with China emphasizing rote memorization of facts and the U.S. favoring an approach of independent, problem-based, student-driven learning.

More educational experts are now recognizing that competitiveness in the 21st century will be determined by innovation, creativity and entrepreneurial endeavors—that is, creating novel solutions and products to serve a knowledge-based society—rather than by reciting answers to a multitude of questions formulated on a standardized test. No longer will we be able to compete based solely on replicating procedures or methodologies; rather, our competitiveness will rely on our ability to be innovative and creative in the development of new products, services and processes, adding value to established areas of inquiry.

One might extend this thinking to the practice of leadership as well, for great leaders are innovative and creative when crafting their organization's vision for the future, developing solutions to persistent problems and inspiring others to perform at their highest levels. Great leaders need to know more than the answers to repetitive questions; they will be judged by the questions they ask rather than the preordained answers they have learned. We firmly believe it is this type of learning, which we have named *curious learning*, that forms the educational backdrop for outstanding performance as a leader.

SAMARASEKERA:

My earliest childhood memories are of the dreary gray evenings in our London flat where my mother would read me poems from Robert Louis Stevenson's *A Child's Garden of Verses* and A.A. Milne's *Now We Are Six* long before I was six years old. I had many favorites, but the words from "The Lamplighter" resonate with me to this day: "But I, when I am stronger and can choose what I'm to do, / O Leerie, I'll go round at night and light the lamps with you!" As a result of this early exposure to language and my mother's dedication, I learned to read around the age of four, much to her delight. I reveled in the imagery and imagination of beautiful children's stories, whether they were *Grimm's Fairy Tales* or Hans Christian Andersen's stories. Through reading, I escaped into other worlds and cultures and discovered a love of curious learning.

We returned to Sri Lanka not long after my fifth birthday, sailing on an ocean liner through the Suez Canal and stopping at Port Said in Egypt. The memories of its lively and exotic city street life and markets filled with strange and interesting things stimulated my curiosity. These experiences were kept alive by the ottomans and cushions my parents brought back from Port Said, which retained the peculiar and pungent smell of the market they came from. I will never know the exact impact of experiencing life in London, or traveling through the Middle East, or returning to Sri Lanka, an island in the Indian Ocean imbued with the culture of the Portuguese, the Dutch and the British, all before my sixth birthday. We do know that scholars are in agreement on the powerful influence that experiences in early childhood have on human development. I believe that change and novelty such as I experienced early in life foster curious learning.

On returning to Sri Lanka, we initially settled in my maternal grandmother's home, a two-hundred-year-old sprawling Dutch colonial bungalow aptly named Fairy Hall. I remember being enthralled by the stacks of old leather-bound *Books of Knowledge* in my grandparents' home: books on plant, animal and human life; books on literature and fine arts; books on men, women and famous people; a book of Golden Deeds; a book of poetry; a book of "things to make and do"; and, finally, my favorite, a book filled with questions such as, "How deep is the sea?" and "How does a soap bubble hold together?" and "Why does a bee make a humming sound?" I developed an insatiable appetite for an incredible breadth of information through my exploration of these books.

Although I majored in mechanical engineering in university, I never lost my interest in reading widely and broadly. I love wandering through bookstores, selecting multifarious books because their titles, subject matter and dust covers intuitively appeal to me. Of all the skills I drew on as a leader, perhaps the most important was the ability to absorb diverse subjects and find common threads in uncommon themes. Looking back, I see that I was always inspired by people who broke new ground, made momentous discoveries and took risks to achieve their goals—people with nerve. I learned that it takes curiosity and nerve to advance frontiers.

Nancy, Hillary and Eleanor

Single-sex education. The debate continues on the merits of single-sex education and whether students who have attended such schools perform better than their coeducational counterparts. The evidence is mixed, depending on what you read and what data are collected, but one thing is certain: the focus on the benefits of all-girls education has been enjoying a recent renaissance, as we attempt to understand why some women find their voice, become leaders and innovators, and others don't. To understand how formal education at its best can encourage curious learning and help young women to find their place, let's look at the experience of three prominent women leaders.

Nancy Pelosi's high school and college days provided a host of leadership opportunities often denied to young women of that era. She attended the Institute of Notre Dame, an all-girls high school under the care and tutelage of the sisters of Notre Dame in Baltimore, and served as vice president of student government. At Trinity College, a women's college in Washington D.C., she was active in the International Relations Club and the Political Affairs Club. Elsewhere, the number of women studying political science was on the decline, and more generally academic settings had witnessed "the great withdrawal" of professional women. But in the protected environment of a women's educational institution, the study of politics and practical leadership experience came with women as role models and without the stigma and limitations of coeducational settings.[5]

When Eleanor [Roosevelt] was fifteen, her grandmother enrolled her in Allenswood, an exclusive girls' school on the outskirts of London, led by Mademoiselle Souvestre. An inspired teacher, Souvestre inspired her students to open their minds and imaginations and think for themselves. She would often discuss politics and public affairs, subjects that had never been mentioned by Eleanor's grandmother's circle of friends. Eleanor wrote, "Mlle. Souvestre shocked me into thinking, and that on the whole was very beneficial. Never again would I be the rigid little person I had been before." Eleanor would later call her years at Allenswood "the happiest of my life."[6]

Hillary Clinton, who specifically chose to attend an all-girls college, Wellesley College, is a strong advocate of public schools offering single-sex education. When arguing in 2002 for innovative single-sex schools and programs, she said: "We know that single-sex schools and classes can help young people, boys and girls, improve their achievement."[7]

While many women leaders have been educated in different learning environments, it is interesting to note that some of our most famous contemporary women leaders share the all-girls educational experience and attribute many of their leadership qualities to having been educated in a single-sex classroom. The arguments for all-girls education are numerous, including the view that it provides an environment where anything can be achieved, with few, if any, of the barriers women commonly confront, and it represents a learning experience that permits creativity and exploration while instilling confidence and courage. The counterview is that single-sex learning environments are unnatural; they do not provide competition with their peers of the opposite sex, which they most surely will face in the future. Some object to all-girls schools because they harken back to the finishing schools of old, where instead of instilling courage and strength they encouraged girls to defer to men and lead traditional lives.

Most likely it is not any single educational factor or environment that nurtures girls to become leaders by acquiring a voice, courage, confidence, inquisitiveness or ambitious career goals. But we were particularly interested in exploring our own early educational experiences and how they might have influenced our later career decisions. Given that one of us (Samarasekera) was educated in an all-girls environment, while the other (Piper) received all of her education in the public, coeducational system, we thought it might be informative to compare and contrast our early learning environments and how they may have helped shape our later lives.

PIPER:

The city I grew up in, Lorain, Ohio, is now part of the Rust Belt in the northeastern United States, but was a thriving steel town when I was a child. Located on Lake Erie, Lorain was a working-class city, with slag from the steel mills polluting the harbor, river and lake. While the coeducational public schools were not known for their academic excellence, almost everyone attended them, believing they were more than adequate to equip them for the future they would likely face. If a family desired something more academic or wanted a single-sex education for their children, the private schools in Cleveland were the closest option. Interestingly, Toni Morrison, the Nobel Prize–winning author, is a product of the Lorain public school system, demonstrating that raw talent flourishes almost anywhere.

I was fortunate to grow up in a family that valued education. I always knew that I would go to university. My paternal grandfather, a county judge; my father, a prominent attorney; and my mother were all university graduates, and it was an unspoken assumption that I and all of my siblings would go to university. It was not debatable; it was never in question; it was a given.

That was the easy part—knowing with certainty that my education would continue. The more challenging issue was figuring out what I would study and what career I might choose. I remember feeling confused, uncertain and perplexed about the choices I had to make, knowing there was an unspoken expectation that I would select something traditional, like teaching or nursing, rather than something more unusual for a woman of that time, like law or medicine.

Looking back, I believe two issues affected my educational choice. First, my father was a "man of his time"—a nice way of saying that he would be considered sexist today. While he always wanted the best for his two daughters and took enormous pride in our accomplishments, his idea of "best" for us was clearly couched in his beliefs that the appropriate role for women in the 1950s and '60s entailed marriage and motherhood, and in that order. Education was important, but for women, the real value of a university education was to find the "right" man to marry and to be able to support yourself and your children in the event, God forbid, your husband died. Education for his sons, on the other hand, was critical in terms of providing them with the skills and knowledge necessary to support a family, have a fulfilling professional career and become a well-respected member of society.

My mother's own example was foremost in my mind; she had a university education, was extraordinarily intelligent and talented, but she had given up her teaching career as soon as she married to become a stay-at-home mother. My siblings and I were clearly the benefactors of her undivided attention, wonderful creativity and her devotion to parenting and family, and as such, I viewed her as the example for how I should live my life. It was in this context that I vividly remember rejecting the notion of becoming a medical doctor. It was clearly a male profession at the time; it required many years of study and sacrifice, only to be forgone when you married. Why would any woman who saw herself as wife and mother first choose that path? So, I found myself selecting studies in another health-related field: physical therapy. At the time, this was clearly a female profession that only required four years of study and thus would allow me to work until I was married and had children, at which time I would become a full-time wife and mother. This choice clearly satisfied both my father's criteria for educating his daughters and my mother's example of what an educated woman's proper place was in society.

The second issue that affected my educational choice was the role my male peers played in my coeducational high school environment. Intelligence was not seen as an attractive feature in a girl; to be popular, you could not be smarter than the boys in your class. Instead, you needed to play dumb, to fail to assert yourself academically and to allow the boys to lead at every level of the school. The thought of a girl running for class president was unimaginable, just as a boy becoming class secretary was unthinkable. And, if you wanted to be really popular, you had to assume all of the "female" roles in high school, such as being a cheerleader, playing the flute in the orchestra and serving on the prom decorating committee. Roles throughout my high school years were clearly gender stereotyped, and I found myself torn between aiming to be the best and doing what was required to be liked.

I cannot help but wonder whether my high school years would have been dramatically different had I been exposed to an all-girls educational environment. Would I have been able to counter my father's expectations had I been in a school that allowed girls to be who they are, inspired them to be the best they could be and not be encumbered by limitations imposed upon them by their gender? Would my career path have been different? I will never know for certain. But I am now coming to appreciate that my decisions around career choice may have been influenced not only by my family but also my high school experience.

SAMARASEKERA:

My formal education began in Jaffna, where I attended two all-girls schools founded by American missionaries. The two schools were academically rigorous and had superb teachers. Vembadi, where I spent five years, was publicly funded, so students came from families that ranged from poor to prosperous. The school, whose motto was "Dare to Do Right," had spacious grounds, but rudimentary facilities. I recall one of my early classrooms where bats slept in the rafters during the day. They made me nervous, as I was convinced that one of them would land on my head, but that never happened. We all wore a white uniform with a green tie, which leveled our economic differences, except for our shoes. I vividly remember children with no shoes, but as far as I was concerned, they were just like me in every way.

It was an idyllic time in my life, where achievement was highly prized. I was a very good student, always coming first or second in my class. In the absence of boys, one was free to excel in what might have been considered masculine subjects, such as mathematics and science. When I was 12 years old, my parents enrolled me at Ladies' College in Colombo, which was founded in 1900 as a sister school to Cheltenham Ladies' College in England. It was a "posh" school, and the students were from well-to-do, influential families. The classrooms and facilities were several notches above Vembadi—definitely no bats taking refuge in the rafters! Miss Hitchcock, the principal, who walked the hallways with a slight limp from having had polio, was stern and set high expectations. She knew us all by name and fostered an air of order and respect, as well as a culture of excellence and achievement.

We felt that anything was possible at Ladies' College, and the girls in my class, especially the top students, aspired to become doctors, lawyers, accountants, musicians, artists, teachers and leaders. At the time,

Sirimavo Bandaranaike was prime minister of Sri Lanka, the first woman in the world to hold this position. So, my peers and I believed that all opportunities were open to us.

There was no female bias at my school in terms of professional choices, so given my talent in mathematics and physics, I aspired to become an engineer. My parents and my mathematics teacher at Ladies' College, also a woman, were resolute in their support of my career ambitions. In this nurturing environment, I excelled and blossomed.

Would I have had the nerve and confidence to pursue engineering had I not gone to an all-girls school? Would I have developed the leadership skills as a school prefect and as a member of debating and athletic teams if I had been distracted by the presence of boys or influenced by their opinions on a daily basis? Would I have aspired to high achievement had I not lived in a society where there were successful role models, including a female prime minister and many remarkable professional women? All these years later—after moving to North America and watching my daughter navigate high school, with the daily pressure to look and act in a certain way in the presence of boys in her class—I can't help but feel fortunate for my experience in an all-girls setting.

Dirty Dozen

Although career choices and opportunities for women are vastly greater today than 50 years ago, with more women than ever choosing to be physicians, lawyers, scientists, business leaders and entrepreneurs, still, few women strive to be engineers, computer programmers and physicists. The question that needs to be asked is why certain fields have opened up to women, while others remain largely dominated by men. Enormous resources have been put into attracting more women into the STEM disciplines, with mixed results. And yet, other areas in the biological sciences, such as pharmacy, microbiology and medicine, are now commonly selected by women.

Similarly, certain fields still remain largely the domain of women despite attracting more men than in earlier years: nursing, the humanities, food science and dental hygiene, for example. Is this because women are "better" at certain tasks than men, or enjoy certain subjects more than men, or is it only a matter of time until career choices will be truly gender blind?

And regardless of the field, how do all these educational and professional choices affect women who choose to lead? Is there a preferred path that better prepares women to lead? Do educational choices make a difference to the ability to assume leadership roles or to be chosen for them?

These were the questions that interested us as we reviewed our two varied experiences. Our initial career choices were dramatically different: one of us, schooled in a coeducational environment, chose a "female" career path in physical therapy; the other, coming from an all-girls educational experience, took a very different "male" path with engineering. What motivated our choices, and how did these educational experiences prepare us to eventually become leaders? Was there a discernible pattern that future women leaders might learn from? And if so, what was it?

SAMARASEKERA:

I always wanted to be an engineer, although I have no idea when I started thinking about this or why. Was it because I excelled in mathematics and physics? Or was it because inventing and building marvelous machines that made everyday life easier appealed to me? There were no engineers in my family, so there was no obvious role model.

The Faculty of Engineering at the University of Ceylon was established with Cambridge University as a model. With only 150 spaces each year, free tuition and close to ten thousand applicants, admission was highly competitive. Twelve women were admitted, including me, and we were nicknamed the "Dirty Dozen" by our male colleagues. There is no doubt in my mind that it took nerve for each of us to enroll in engineering. Living on the same floor in the residence hall, constantly in each other's rooms asking for advice, seeking assistance with tutorials and discussing our male professors and colleagues, we bonded from the get-go.

I have often wondered how the 12 of us succeeded in a male-dominated discipline. I believe it was the strong bonds we formed and our commitment to supporting one another that made the difference and provided us with the nerve required to succeed. Of the four first-class degrees awarded on graduation, two were to women, including myself—a point of great pride. To have been educated in such an exceptional setting, with the brightest young women (and men), was the gift of a lifetime.

PIPER:

To pursue my decision to study physical therapy, I attended a large university, the University of Michigan, where among thousands of undergraduates I entered a very small program of approximately 25 women and one man. Despite being essentially a female profession, the program was extremely difficult to be admitted to and was extraordinarily competitive academically.

How then did that environment affect my future? I was surrounded by a group of exemplary women—women determined to make a difference in a health-care field that was academically demanding. For the first time in my life, I was inspired and influenced by only women: my student peers, the faculty and professional mentors. Women whom I admired and respected. Women who allowed me to find my voice, and women who motivated me to strive to be an exceptional therapist. Being smart was valued; being the best you could be was encouraged; excelling at what you did was rewarded.

I cannot help but wonder whether this unique educational experience at a world-class university mirrored in some way an all-girls educational environment. I was not competing with men, I was not trying to please men, I was not being held back by men. I thrived in this environment. I didn't have to be popular; being smart was not only good, but also it was something to be proud of.

I joined a sorority and became the president of my local chapter and eventually the president of the Panhellenic Council at the university. I lived with women, learned from women and developed friendships with women who to this day have supported me through all of the ups and downs of my life. I learned to lead by being among other women who encouraged me to be whoever I wanted to be, who affirmed my values and my intellect and who permitted me to be their leader.

Best-Laid Plans

Women are great planners. We are known for making lists, thinking ahead, keeping our schedules, organizing events, remembering birthdays and anniversaries, and contemplating all the possible outcomes before making up our minds, whether we are buying a new dress or renovating a home. We are the ones who plan the menus for the family picnics, make sure we have enough toilet paper in the house, call the doctor for appointments, send the thank-you notes and schedule the playdates for our kids. Our planning skills are notorious, thought to be emblazoned on our DNA.

We believe we can plan our lives if we just think about it long enough: our careers, when to study and when to work, when to marry (or not to), whether to start a family, when to take time off to care for our children and when to remain at home or return to work. We lull ourselves into thinking that we are in control—that peace, order, personal fulfillment and wellness can all be planned. If we work hard enough and demonstrate enough discipline, we will succeed in fulfilling all of our desires and lead a productive and happy life.

Of course, planning can only go so far, until the unexpected—illness, divorce, geographic moves, children and financial concerns, to name a few—throw women off course, demanding they change their carefully thought-out goals. There are so many examples in the lives of our families, friends and associates that suggest that the inevitability of the unexpected makes planning difficult. Still, women tend to believe that by planning carefully, they will avoid life's pitfalls; that they can simply adapt to changing circumstances, planning anew for different conditions; and, most importantly, that if they are good planners, they can have it all.

Despite our belief in the power of planning and the preparation of our formal education, women are notorious for not planning for an important opportunity that might present itself in their lives— the opportunity to lead. Women worry that because they have never envisioned being a leader, because they have not aspired, studied, contemplated or been encouraged to lead, they are unprepared or not ready to answer the call. In these cases, what at first appears to be a strategic strength—the ability to plan and prepare—can become an obstacle for some women, casting self-doubt on their ability to move in a different direction than they had imagined for themselves.

Is this a woman thing? Are women less likely than men to think about or carefully plan their educational decisions and career paths with leadership opportunities in mind? Are men more focused on their life choices with leadership as the end goal? Having observed many of our male counterparts who have assumed leadership positions, we doubt that men, in general, ever experience the same conflicts that women do when being asked to lead. Is it because men have always aimed to lead, or is it because they have systems in place that diminish the conflicts women often experience?

Many of the concerns women face when confronting leadership opportunities are associated with forgoing the traditional roles they have assumed for centuries—bearing and raising the children, caring for partner and household, and being the chief nurturer in family and society. And while most of these responsibilities may be addressed by engaging help and developing support systems, many women believe for some reason that it is *their* duty to do them. The choice to lead feels like forfeiting what they think of as their best-laid plans, leading to enormous guilt and internal conflict.

How often have you heard a man state that he feels guilty about putting his child in day care? How often do male leaders think about the fact that they are hiring help or giving up some of their familial or societal responsibilities? How often do men turn down leadership positions because they need to spend more time with their children? And, perhaps more important, how often do men develop best-laid plans that entail part-time work and full-time marriage and parenting as the end goals?

PIPER:

I have often wondered when I either dreamed of being, or planned ahead to become, a leader. I think that I never consciously considered leadership to be a career goal; my deliberate life plan entailed first becoming a physical therapist and, second, marrying and becoming a wife and mother. Those were my best-laid plans. Full stop.

As a child I did not play "being a leader" or "business owner." No, instead I played "house" and "school." I have memories of sweeping the porch of our house, mimicking my mother; setting up a school with my stuffed animals as the students; treating my dolls who were sick. My brothers, on the other hand, were always "taking charge"—picking who was going to be on their neighborhood baseball team, being the lead cowboy or enforcing the rules of Monopoly.

Leadership opportunities, whether I was a young girl, university student or wife and mother, always seemed to be thrust upon me, rather than something I consciously sought or desired, let alone planned for. As such, when leadership opportunities arose, like many women, I consistently struggled with the obvious conflicts between the chances to lead that I encountered or stumbled upon and the goals I had consciously chosen. How could I find the time to lead as the president of my university sorority when my goal was to study hard and do well in my courses? How could I possibly lead an academic department or program when I should be focused on my responsibilities as a wife and mother? Why couldn't I be satisfied with working part-time and spending more time with my children? Why did I feel I had to choose between the roles I thought I should assume versus the roles that were presenting themselves to me? What would be the consequences to my children and marriage if I chose not to follow my "best-laid plans" and push ahead on the leadership track?

In each case, whether it was in university or later in life, I struggled with the decision to even explore, let alone accept, the call to lead. My stomach would twist and turn, I would lose my appetite and find it difficult to sleep and feelings of guilt would often engulf me as soon as I contemplated accepting a leadership position. My plans were being sidelined at best and shattered at worst. Was I doing the right thing? Would I regret my decision? Why should I have to choose a new path, different from the one I had earlier mapped out so carefully in my head?

As I look back on my educational decisions, I wonder, if I had chosen to study business administration or law rather than physical therapy, would I have been better prepared for my eventual life of leadership? While one is never able to relive those decisions, I must conclude that my educational choice did not detract from my ability to lead. Having the nerve to throw my "best-laid plans" to the wind to pursue another path may have been instrumental in my becoming a leader.

SAMARASEKERA:

My goal in life was to become an engineer, perhaps eventually to teach. Becoming a leader was not on my agenda, although my first taste of leadership, as a school prefect, was exhilarating. I should have realized at the time that leading was inherently satisfying, but I was too focused on my "best-laid" plans of becoming an engineer to notice that another path was possible for me.

While I attained my goal of practicing and teaching engineering, becoming a single parent at the age of 32 put to rest any thought of leadership. I knew that I had to be home by 6 p.m. every day to ensure the children had their dinner and were read to and put to bed and that the flexibility I had as an academic would be lost if I took on additional responsibilities as a department head or dean.

When my daughter was finishing high school, a senior female colleague in engineering, who was a close personal friend and a department chair, decided I needed a change and nominated me for the position of Vice-President, Research, a position I never thought I would be appointed to due to my lack of academic leadership experience.

Looking back, I now realize that the so-called best-laid plans are almost always upended by unexpected events in life, over which one has little control. Almost as often, encouragement from colleagues and mentors opens doors that would have remained closed without their intervention. I have learned that we must avoid rejecting new opportunities that present themselves just because they do not align with the plans we formulated for ourselves earlier.

Lessons Learned

The educational choices women pursue may not be as important in the long run in preparing them to lead as one would think. Our view is that it really does not matter whether you choose to become an engineer or a physical therapist, as long as you are pursuing a career that you find interesting and challenging. In addition, our experience suggests that it is more important to discover *how* you learn rather than *what* you learn. Finding ways to feed your curiosity and foster creative learning is more likely to prepare you for leadership opportunities than studying for a specific profession or a particular subject.

Similarly, seeking out and identifying with a group of women you trust and respect, regardless of their age or background, is instrumental in giving you the confidence to lead. Women support other women; women permit other women to be the best they can be; women encourage other women to step forward. Groups of women, whether it be in an all-girls educational environment or later in life, foster self-confidence, nurture excellence and provide essential support through all of the trials and tribulations of your life.

With all the planning that women engage in to map out their educational, career, marriage and motherhood choices, it is clear that even with the best-laid plans, things happen. Best-laid plans often need to be abandoned in order to explore and assume leadership opportunities that present themselves. Flexibility and the willingness to embrace a new plan, rather than a rigid adherence to an earlier well-thought-out formula for life, should become the new norm for women.

1. Pick a career path that interests and excites you rather than something that others, including family members and male peers, consider right for you.

2. Explore creative learning opportunities wherever you can find them. Attend to the things that you are passionate about, whether it be movies, music, carpentry, astronomy, flying airplanes or hockey.

3. Focus on learning how to ask the important questions, rather than worrying about the correct answers.

4. Seek out other women who inspire and support you. Appropriate groups of women can be identified in your educational, work or recreational environments. Focus on supporting other women in their leadership efforts, helping them find the nerve to lead.

5. Understand the limitations of individual life plans and that best-laid plans are often displaced by life events and unexpected opportunities. Willingness to be open and adapt is a key leadership trait.

6. Resist identifying all the reasons why you cannot consider new opportunities that do not align with your current life plans. Realize many of these excuses are based on your earlier beliefs of how your life should unfold, rather than justifiable reasons to forgo a new opportunity. Consider how well prepared you are by your educational path and career experience. Think of all the ways in which you have what it takes to grasp a new challenge or developmental path.

CHAPTER 3

Marriage and children: Can we have it all?

"I've yet to be on a campus where most women weren't worrying about some aspect of combining marriage, children and a career. I've yet to find one where men were worrying about the same thing."

—GLORIA STEINEM

As Gloria Steinem notes, young women consistently question whether they can possibly have it all—a satisfying career, a rewarding marriage and happy children. This, probably more than any other issue, differentiates men from women as they contemplate their career paths and leadership opportunities. Very few, if any, men worry about balancing their career with the desire to marry and have a family. They automatically assume it will work and rarely give it much serious thought or concern. Women, on the other hand, worry incessantly not only about whether they can be wives and mothers as well as leaders but also how they will possibly manage the balancing act.

Any woman who has married and had a career can tell you that managing both aspects of their lives is not always easy. Marriage, or any long-term relationship, is fraught with demands, personal sacrifice and the need to sometimes replace one's own priorities with those of another. A successful marriage, whether traditional or common-law, same-sex or heterosexual, takes enormous work, dedication and commitment to another person's well-being, leading some to question its viability in today's self-centered society. This commitment to someone else's happiness, coupled with the desire to advance one's own career, provides challenges for even the most organized and determined individual.

Yet, happy marriages can represent the most special relationship two people will ever experience, filled with shared hopes and dreams. Within a harmonious marriage or long-term relationship, each partner is able to grow as an individual while supporting the other to be the best they can be. Couples who live happily together enjoy each other's company, consider the other to be their best friend and truly celebrate the successes and accomplishments of their partner. As such, many women leaders will point to the unique relationship they share with their partner as being an essential component to their personal achievements. Others believe that a deep commitment to another person poses specific issues that can be viewed as deterrents to their ability to lead.

Similarly, while women are now able to control if, when and how they will become pregnant, often delaying the decision until they are in their mid to late thirties, the large majority of women are still deciding to have children. Regardless of whether they are pursuing a career or decide to marry or not, women continue to choose motherhood.

This choice is a lot different today than it was in previous generations, when women were likely to forgo any career goals once they became pregnant, if they even had them in the first place. Today's women often have serious careers and have already experienced professional recognition before deciding to become a parent. They believe, rightly or wrongly, that they may have both—careers and children.

Anne-Marie Slaughter, in her controversial 2012 article "Why Women Still Can't Have It All," put the cat among the pigeons when she suggested otherwise; that is, women who are in leadership positions may not always be able to balance the responsibilities of motherhood. While Slaughter had always believed that she could manage a top-level career with being a mother, her two-year experience in Washington working in a senior position in the White House suggested otherwise. She encountered rough waters in managing both roles and, as a result, wrote an opinion piece that aroused a heated debate in feminist circles—one that continues today.

Can women truly have it all? We believe that it depends on the woman and the specific circumstances surrounding her leadership, her support systems and priorities, coupled with the timing of the events. And, although we are convinced that women can lead while still raising their children, in our opinion, it is not a matter of having to decide between a career and motherhood, but rather that women often place unrealistic demands on themselves when pursuing both. As women, we are hard on ourselves, expecting to be perfect at everything we do, and thus setting ourselves up for disappointment and regret. Why do we think the house has to be immaculate, healthy meals cooked and the children's science project perfectly designed—and as Slaughter states, "thin and beautiful to boot"?

We do it to ourselves. By attempting to be perfect at everything we take on, we place ourselves in an untenable position. If having it all means that we cannot or will not give up some of these unrealistic tasks and expectations, we will most certainly disappoint not only ourselves but also those around us.

By being clear about what *must* remain your responsibility while delegating other tasks to someone else, we believe you can manage child rearing with leading. But we also believe strongly that you can't, in fact, have it *all*. You must be prepared to limit unreasonable demands on your time, saying no at certain times in your career and looking the other way on others. Only by being clear about your priorities and time management will you be able to juggle all of the obligations associated with leading *and* mothering.

Partners

Some women clearly state that having a supportive partner throughout life has been one of the most important factors in their professional advancement. They note that leadership can be a very lonely experience, and having a loving, trusting companion and best friend at their side helps them to be the best they can be, rejuvenate and refresh on a regular basis and pursue their leadership goals.

Other women have had the opposite experience, and recount that their partner actively discouraged them from taking on more responsibility, suggesting that they should be happy with a diminished career role and avoid leadership opportunities. Whether it is competition or jealousy that fuels the perception that the woman is more focused on her job than her relationship, these circumstances may result in the partnership becoming an obstacle to a woman's desire to lead, and vice versa.

As two women who married in their early twenties and have had different experiences, we believe our perspectives on the role a committed relationship plays in helping or hindering a woman's career is worth examining. One of us has been happily married to the same person for over 54 years; the other decided early in her marriage that the better route for her and her family was to dissolve the union. We take this occasion to reflect upon the role a significant partnership may play in a woman's quest to lead.

PIPER:

I have been married to the same man for 54 years and counting. As a young woman, I was fortunate to find my future husband, Bill. He was kind, sensitive, intellectually gifted and dedicated to helping others through his professional career choice, clinical psychology. We shared interests, outlooks, opinions and concerns, as our youth was consumed with the issues surrounding the Vietnam War, the military draft, race riots, Jim Crow laws, the shootings of John F. Kennedy and Martin Luther King Jr. and questions about our religious and spiritual beliefs. I was extraordinarily lucky to have found someone who could share the burden of these momentous issues and stretch my thinking to better define the purpose of my life.

Perhaps most important, we supported each other when support was needed, being generous with our time and concern and reveling in each other's personal fulfillment and success. Bill has always believed in me and provided me with the encouragement and support to pursue my career goals. He has been there consistently, through all the ups and downs of my leadership journey, cheering me on when others have faltered and picking up the slack at home whenever it is required. While he has actively pursued his own career, our professional lives have been a combined joint effort—solving problems together and filling the obvious gaps that occur when both people in a relationship have fulfilling and demanding careers.

I am often asked how I managed a marriage and a career; wouldn't it have been easier for me if I had been single? While each woman is different and must make her own decisions, my experience suggests that one of the reasons I could take on the leadership roles I did was because I had my partner's support and commitment. He provided me with the fortitude to act with nerve, believed in me when things got tough and was the first to cheer me on. In my mind, my leadership goals were enhanced through the partnership I've had with Bill. Indeed, the partnership was not a deterrent, but rather a genuine asset.

Difficult Marriage, Dream Divorce

North American divorce rates rose rapidly in the 1970s, and in the 1980s were at an all-time high of close to 45 percent. People married at a younger age in the preceding decades than they do now, and couples rarely lived together before marriage. And, because the feminist revolution was in full swing, many women who married found that their partner was less responsive to the independence they were seeking within that union. Since that time, divorce rates have declined as more women are delaying marriage, entering into common-law unions and forming relationships based on a better understanding of what contributes to a meaningful partnership.

Nevertheless, unhappy marriages do occur and can have a pervasive impact on both partners in terms of self-esteem, personal fulfillment and career pursuits. While divorce is never easy, increasingly women are recognizing that sometimes it is better for everyone if the union is dissolved. It takes nerve to reach the decision to divorce, but often it is the best option when staying in an unhappy marriage can do more harm than good.

SAMARASEKERA:

A good marriage is based on the development of emotional intimacy— an intimacy founded on trust and respect, friendship and intellectual companionship, providing both partners unconditional support to pursue satisfying careers. I married my husband, Sam, when I was 23 years old, two years after graduation and days before we left for the U.S. to pursue postgraduate education. We had much in common, or so I thought. We were both mechanical engineers and graduated from the same Faculty of Engineering in Sri Lanka, where we had met. We enjoyed each other's company and were intellectual equals.

Unfortunately, after 12 years of marriage I was faced with a difficult conundrum. The emotional intimacy that I had hoped would develop in my marriage, and the support for my career, had deteriorated to the point where I was deeply unhappy. What was I to do? Should I separate and seek a divorce or stay for the sake of our two small children, aged seven and four? How would it affect them if we divorced? Should we first seek counseling? What about enlisting the assistance of family and friends? How would I endure the stigma of being divorced? How would I cope with the shame I would bring on our families? This was a very painful time. I would lie awake at night, in tears with inescapable fears of what would happen to our family if I walked out.

My husband had been enormously supportive while I completed my doctoral degree. However, once the children were born we argued over how hard I was working, as he believed that I should spend more time with the family. We also did not seek help for cleaning the house and other chores, so the conflict spilled over to "who did what" after a long day's work. These sorts of differences are typical in any marriage, but we had a flawed approach to conflict resolution. Following a disagreement, there would be a period of stony silence, without a satisfactory attempt to make amends, to say sorry and to offer and receive forgiveness. In the absence of an effort to negotiate a truce, every interaction became more adversarial, and resentment built. If I were to identify the one thing that caused a breakdown in emotional intimacy, this would be it.

I decided to fly home to Sri Lanka to seek my parents' counsel. I remember the occasion like it was yesterday. My mother, father, grandmother and I were discussing my marriage dilemma in the front verandah of my grandmother's home, Fairy Hall. I told them that it was either marriage or career, and my father said, "You can choose to walk away from your career and nothing will change. Your marriage will not improve and conflicts will emerge elsewhere. You have worked hard to get a doctorate degree and have a great future; you should leave your husband." My grandmother then chimed in saying how unhappy she had been in her marriage and that had she been presented with the opportunities I had, she would have left. Their words gave me the nerve I needed.

Staying in an unhappy marriage is often far easier than finding the courage to leave. I am grateful for my father's wisdom, my mother's support and my grandmother's advice, without which I would not have had the strength to face an uncertain future as a single parent. Had I stayed, my career would have suffered and I might have had to abandon my calling to pursue an academic career for a less demanding job.

I returned from Sri Lanka and filed for divorce. Looking back, it was the best decision for me, as I could not find a way to be happy in this marriage, pursue a rewarding career and give my children the home they deserved. In the ensuing three decades, Sam and I have experienced what I would describe as a "dream divorce." We both love our children deeply, and he is a wonderful father. Neither of us denigrated the other to our children, nor did we expect our children to take on our fights or pick sides. We had an amicable division of responsibilities: he was in charge of sports and the weekends, and I was responsible for schoolwork and parenting during the week. This enabled me to make the necessary investments of time and intellect in my career, while providing the children a stable, happy home.

Three decades since divorcing, we share a pride in our children and who they have become. Neither my husband nor I remarried, so it makes it easier to have a cordial relationship without the complications that could arise from having new partners. We are both present at family birthdays, and we go on holidays together with the children and their families. He has also shown pride in my accomplishments and attended my installation when I was appointed president of the University of Alberta.

I would be remiss if I did not say that the hardest thing an individual faces in an unhappy marriage is the decision to leave. It takes enormous courage to end a committed relationship, given the uncertainty associated with the children's well-being (if you have them), personal finances and being alone. If I could summarize what I learned from my own experience, it would be the following: First, find the inner strength to suppress the fear of the unknown and believe that life can be happier. Second, seek the advice of those who know and love you, such as parents, siblings or close friends. Third, consider the alternatives, what could happen if you stayed, including the negative consequences for the children's mental health and well-being and for your career aspirations.

Pregnancy: Just Do It

As difficult as it is for young women to relate to today, it was not that long ago that women had very little, if any, control over their own bodies when it came to pregnancy. The available contraception was largely ineffective and generally viewed as socially unacceptable. With few safe or efficacious options available to either prevent or terminate unwanted pregnancies, large families were the norm. Our own grandmothers expected to be pregnant most of the time during their fertile years. The idea of planning when they would be pregnant, or ending an unwanted pregnancy, was foreign to them.

Just a few short decades ago, most women stayed home after having children, becoming full-time mothers and homemakers even if they had already started a career, often having to relinquish their jobs as soon as it became known they were pregnant. No small wonder that few if any became leaders in business, education, health or government. Women today have the exact opposite experience. With the advent of the pill and other effective birth control measures, women not only assume they will plan if and when to become pregnant, but they also believe they will control every aspect of the pregnancy, whether they are married or not: becoming pregnant when they so desire; relying on IVF, surrogate pregnancies and other alternatives if they need to; and resuming their careers at some time after the child is born. While some women will choose to give up their careers after having or adopting children, more and more women plan to have some form of childcare that will allow them to resume their professional ambitions once their maternity leave has ended.

Clearly, a major cultural shift has occurred over the past decades, upending centuries of experience surrounding the timing of childbearing and the acceptable role women assume as mothers. How is this major cultural shift working out for young women as they establish their careers? Are they able to delay childbearing without having their biological clock run out? Can they plan both the timing and the number of their pregnancies in such a manner that their careers are not disadvantaged? Are they succeeding in assuming leadership positions without sacrificing or compromising the joys of motherhood?

As two women who planned their pregnancies and had two children while juggling the demands of their careers and the responsibilities of being a mother, and as mothers who have observed their own daughters and daughter-in-law wrestle with the same issues a generation later, we believe our observations and reflections are useful in identifying some of the key issues young women face as they pursue their desire to both have children and a satisfying professional life.

PIPER:

I was lucky—twice I became pregnant almost immediately after I had planned to. My first pregnancy was planned around my husband's career trajectory; by the time we were ready to try again, the planning was centered on my career ambitions. Our eldest child was born when my husband was completing his PhD and entering the U.S. Navy as a commissioned officer, permitting us for the first time to have a steady income that was not mine. Our second child arrived when he was a full-time academic, and I was a PhD student at McGill University, providing me with more flexibility to care for my two children than I would have had if I had been working full-time. My career was far from being established, and I was young by today's standards, having had both of my children and completing our family by the time I was 30.

In comparing my experience with that of my daughters, both of whom have had two children three to four decades later, there are some stark differences. Their pregnancies were also planned, but their childbearing years began, rather than ended, in their thirties. Both had completed all of their advanced education, and their careers were relatively established rather than just beginning.

But there were similarities, too. In addition to timing our respective pregnancies, all three of us planned everything we thought we would need. Maternity leaves were negotiated; cribs were purchased; rooms were painted; strollers were researched; books were read; courses were taken. Most important, nannies were interviewed and hired, as we each intended to return to work after having children. We had considered every possible need, every potential requirement for the arrival of this new person in our lives.

Or at least that is what each of us thought: we had planned everything and were ready for any and every eventuality. Enter our infant babies—beautiful beings, miracles of life, love objects in the flesh. Helpless and dependent on our breast milk, beautifully formed with inquisitive eyes and beating hearts. We each in our own way fell hopelessly in love with these little creatures. Suddenly, the thought of leaving them in anyone else's care was unthinkable; the importance of our careers soon took second place to our newfound maternal instincts. The certitude of all our planning now seemed so insignificant, and in some instances downright wrong. Clearly, we had failed miserably in our planning; we had not even considered, let alone recognized, the emotional pull of motherhood and the inevitable conflict we would feel as we began to navigate the turbulent waters of juggling careers with kids.

Over time my daughters and I, along with our partners, have worked tirelessly to resolve this conflict—managing both being a mother and pursuing a career. But it was not, and is not, easy. What is now clear to me—despite all of the advances women have experienced over the past decades with regard to contraception, securing extended maternity leaves, fathers actively helping with childcare and the availability of day care—is that the emotional aspect of having a child can neither be planned nor ignored with all the best intentions. We often do not envision the emotional vulnerability that accompanies having a child, and by neglecting this universal emotional response, we tend to underestimate the internal conflicts career women will face when starting a family.

I have come to believe that by focusing on the typical concerns of pregnancy—should I breastfeed, what type of mobile should I buy, should I find out the sex of the baby before its birth—women often ignore, at their peril, the emotional roller coaster they will experience once the child is born. Unfortunately, planning can only go so far. Women need to know that all mothers who continue their careers experience the tension between the emotional pull of motherhood and their desire for a professional life.

Mary Poppins Does Not Exist

For years, women have grown up watching Julie Andrews play Mary Poppins in the film adaptation of P.L. Travers's book by the same name. Whether as young children or grown adults, women have been exposed to this amazing image of what constitutes the quintessential nanny. And, once confronted with the task of arranging for childcare, women often fantasize that the person they hire will emulate this fictional character. As such, they tend to believe that while the umbrella and the magic may be missing, the admirable character traits will most certainly be present, ensuring that their children will be well looked after when they are not present. Mary Poppins, for better or for worse, has become the idealized version of the perfect caregiver.

Of all the responsibilities working mothers contend with, arranging childcare tops the list in terms of triggering anxiety, guilt and unrealistic expectations. Mothers come to believe that if they are able to come up with the "perfect" solution, all of their personal guilt surrounding leaving their child will dissipate. That if they can hire a Mary Poppins, all will be well.

How realistic is this? How likely is it that they will they be able to identify, afford and engage the perfect nanny or access outstanding day care? If so, will the chosen solution last the entire time childcare is required, that is from infancy to the teen years? And if plan A fails, for example, if their nanny suddenly leaves, do they have a plan B? Perhaps most important, even with the practically perfect solution, will they resolve the guilt they typically experience when leaving their child?

In our day, it was not common for mothers to work outside the home. We were seen by some as being different because we did, and others thought that by continuing to work we were putting our children at risk. We not only had to grapple with finding acceptable childcare arrangements but also had to confront the social norms of the day. Looking back, we believe that the decision to continue working after having children, at a time when that was not commonly done, played a significant role in preparing us to be leaders. Having the nerve to do things differently and to deal with criticism are traits that often distinguish leaders from followers.

The practically perfect solution does not exist, and while the guilt of leaving your children when you work may lessen, it is never totally alleviated. Unfortunately, society still tends to blame any problems experienced by children of working mothers on the fact that the mother "worked outside the home"; whereas, if children of stay-at-home mothers experience the exact same problems, it is interpreted as being just an unfortunate random situation. The perils of over-parenting are now being studied and may prove to be as detrimental to a child's development as under-parenting, not to be confused with neglect.[8] Either way, there are numerous factors that go into raising children, and it is far too simplistic to attribute a child's behavior, performance or outcomes solely to the amount of mothering they have received. We believe that if working mothers accept this premise, their job of finding appropriate childcare will be considerably easier and less worrisome.

PIPER:

Over the course of approximately 18 years, from the time my children were infants until they were in high school, I had many nannies. They varied in age, nationality, experience and strengths. Some were creative; some liked to play with the children outside; some preferred doing the laundry; others were excellent cooks. I engaged grandmothers and young women; I used agencies, and I went it alone; I hired and fired. They came and went over the years. One thing was certain, however: I never had a Mary Poppins.

I look back on those years and I recognize that if you are balancing your role as a leader with your obligations as a mother, you need to keep two things in mind. First, no matter who you hire, there will be times when you will question whether you should continue working or become a full-time mother. Things that were never planned happen; circumstances change; no system is fool proof. When these unexpected events occur, it is critical that you do not make any rash decisions and that you draw upon others to support you in these times of need. My example of a "bump in the road" occurred when my youngest child was two years old, and I had just accepted a significant leadership position at McGill: director of the School of Physical and Occupational Therapy. After three days of attending day care, my previously robust and healthy toddler was extremely ill and lethargic. She lay in her bed moaning, with her little hands pressed against her feverish forehead in pain. Upon admission to Montreal Children's Hospital, she was diagnosed with bacterial meningitis, a very serious childhood illness that had recently been linked by public health professionals to infant day care. The story ends happily in that she fully recovered after several weeks of hospitalization with no residual brain damage.

I was, however, so distraught and consumed with guilt from this occurrence I thought I should quit my leadership position, stay at home and care for my recovering child. Enter my husband, who said something like this: "If you stay at home, you will go crazy, and you will drive me and the kids crazy. Go back to work!" I am forever grateful to him for his resilience and support of my desire to work; I know my career path would have been significantly deterred had I made a different decision.

My second observation is that when you are juggling children with leading, there is no end to the need for help. When I was a dean at the University of Alberta, we hired an older woman, Margaret, who would come to our house around 3 p.m. and stay with the children until we returned later in the day. It worked well; both our kids loved Margaret, and she provided a warm, secure environment for them when they returned home from school. As they entered high school, I thought we no longer needed Margaret's services . . . surely they were old enough to be alone for the few hours after school until either I or my husband arrived home. In discussing this decision with them, I was caught off guard when they objected vehemently to the idea of no longer having someone in the house when they arrived home from school. It was a stark message, emphasizing to me that the need for childcare does not end when children age. Perhaps it becomes even more important through the teen years; that being alone, regardless of whether they are capable of looking after themselves, is not a great option. Needless to say, Margaret continued to come every day after school until our youngest graduated from high school.

SAMARASEKERA:

My search for childcare was an exercise in navigating uncharted waters. When my son was born, I enlisted a close relative to care for him while I completed my doctorate. When that arrangement ended when he was

18 months of age, I put him in day care where he was utterly traumatized, screaming vehemently when I dropped him off, and starting to cry about 10 minutes before I arrived, according to the caregivers. How did he know when to time such a performance?

Distraught, I consulted our family doctor, a man, who suggested that I consider staying at home for a few years—until he was older. I was astounded. In the end, with my husband's support, I summoned the nerve to ignore the doctor's advice and leave my son in day care. I have often wondered what would have happened to my career trajectory had I stepped away. I am fairly certain that it would have set me back in my career, and there was no assurance that I could have recovered from the setback.

Once the children were in school, I hired a series of live-in nannies who provided what I was looking for: oversight, meal preparation and some supervision of their activities. I also needed an adult to be at home when I traveled to conferences or on consulting trips, which was essential to the progression of my career. Nevertheless, I always worried about whether the children were being properly cared for and whether my absences were detrimental to them.

I remember calling home from Texas where I was working for a few days, and my son answered the phone. Before I could ask him how he was, he said, "Mom, what's for dinner?" I chuckled and said, "I have no idea. I am in Texas." He laughed and confessed that he had forgotten I was away. We mothers worry far more than is warranted.

Even so, once the children were in high school, I turned down the invitation to be a candidate for dean of engineering, since I knew that the demands on my time would preclude me from reliably being there for the children at dinner. Instead, I took on the presidency of the Metallurgical Society, a role that came with the responsibility of organizing the Conference of Metallurgists in Vancouver. At the time, my son was 16 and had a summer job, but my daughter, who was 13, needed more activities than a nanny could provide. What was I going to do? I remember calling my sister in the U.K. to lament. She said, "Send her here for the summer. She will be good company for my two girls!" So off to the U.K. she went with the nanny in tow! The Conference of Metallurgists was well received, and being president was an important milestone in my leadership journey.

Menoposse: The Strength of Moms in Numbers

The teen years can be difficult for both girls and boys, as adolescents are no longer considered children, nor are they young adults. In a stage of transition, their bodies and brains are undergoing profound biological changes, which make them particularly volatile and unpredictable. They can go from moody to excitable, inattentive to talking back, bored, impulsive and sometimes reckless. They can sleep for hours, listen to music endlessly and are reluctant to forge good study habits. Worse, teenagers are especially vulnerable to influence and pressure from their peers and prone to experiment with drugs, sex and alcohol. Disciplining teenagers and establishing limits becomes a challenging and frustrating exercise for parents.

For any working mother, navigating this phase of their children's lives is demanding. For one of us, a single parent, supportive networks of other women became a lifeline in times of stress, a source of companionship and joy.

SAMARASEKERA:

On her first day of high school, I noted that my daughter spent more time than usual getting dressed, looking in the mirror to ensure she made a good impression. She was a confident girl, but I was apprehensive about how the years ahead would unfold for her. After several months, I began to hear her refer to a group of five girls whom she had befriended as the "Posse." The six of them spent considerable time together, shopping and playing soccer and softball on the same teams.

I got to know their mothers well, and we became a support group for each other. Given that our daughters had named themselves the Posse, we coined the term *Menoposse* to describe ourselves. We kept close tabs on where our daughters were and what they were doing, keeping one another informed. When the girls would develop some hair-brained scheme to go to a party where alcohol was likely available or go to a rock concert dressed in outlandish clothes, we would agree on expectations and common curfews and would coordinate rides home.

This group of supportive women became my lifeline during those difficult years. I recall being in Brazil consulting for a steel company when my phone rang in the middle of the night. It was my nanny reporting that my daughter had a dangerously high fever and wanted to know whether to call 911. I told her to wait a moment while I called one of the other mothers I had on speed dial. I was grateful when she rushed over to the house and assessed the situation, gave my daughter some Tylenol and averted a trip to the emergency room. I could not have engaged in consulting for the steel industry around the world had I not been able to rely on my women's network, my surrogate family.

Lessons Learned

The issues women leaders face when juggling marriage, children and career are extremely personal and complex in nature. Young women consistently ask both of us questions about how to manage these various roles: How did you manage to have children and become a leader at the same time? What advice do you have for dealing with the demands of work and family responsibilities? Although each woman must craft her own solutions that speak to her personal priorities and family values, there are some invaluable lessons we have both learned firsthand about balancing family commitments with leading. In the end, however, it is a juggling act—one that requires an honest and frequent appraisal of the things you deem most important in terms of your daily decisions and chosen activities.

1. If your marriage or partnership is successful, celebrate the role your partner plays in supporting your career goals. Recognize how your partnership is a true asset in terms of allowing you to excel and seek leadership positions.

2. If your marriage or partnership is not successful, and you have taken all of the steps you and your partner are prepared to take to make it better with little affect, seriously consider calling it a day. Staying in an unhappy relationship is not always the best option. Seek the help and guidance you need from trusted people in your life to assist you in making your decision about whether to end the partnership. Understand that it takes a great deal more nerve to leave an unhappy relationship than to remain together and that divorce is not

a sign of failure, but rather represents a thoughtfully considered decision that is in everyone's best interests.

3. When contemplating having a child, whether you are single or in a relationship, understand that with all the planning in the world, your best-laid plans may not unfold. Realize there is a limit to how much you can prepare for a new person in your life, that you will not be able to truly understand the emotional attachment you will have for your newborn until you actually experience it.

4. When considering childcare options, keep the following in mind: 1) no childcare option is either perfect or permanent; 2) unplanned events may occur that will lead you to question whether you should forgo your career goals—if this happens, try not to make any rash decisions, but rather seek support from trusted people in your life; 3) oversight and support of teenagers are as important as physical care of infants; 4) regardless of how comfortable you are with your childcare arrangements, you will continue to experience some guilt, which is normal and okay.

5. Remember that mothers should not bear sole responsibility for how their children develop. While the amount of parenting may play a role in how a child develops, there are many other factors that contribute to a child's emotional, mental and social well-being.

6. As you navigate balancing your family and children with leading, recognize the importance of developing relationships and friendships with other women who have children the same age as yours. These women will support and assist you in times of need, and they will stand firm with you when imposing limits on your teenagers. Together you will be better able to confront the challenges and inevitable twists and turns that all parents face when raising children.

7. Whether it is the timing of your decisions to lead or deciding which activities do not need to be done or could be done by others, acknowledge your own limitations when it comes to setting your expectations for balancing the demands of your career with the responsibilities of child

rearing. Determine clear priorities as to what is important to you and stick to them. By realizing that you cannot have it all, you will be more effective in managing your career and motherhood.

CHAPTER 4

Serendipity: happy surprise

*"The coincidences or little miracles that happen every day of your
life are hints that the universe has much bigger plans for you than
you ever dreamed of for yourself."*

—DEEPAK CHOPRA, *THE SPONTANEOUS
FULFILLMENT OF DESIRE*

Serendipity. Some call it luck, others identify it as chance, but neither definition is correct. The word *serendipity* was coined by an Englishman, Horace Walpole, who became enthralled by a Persian fairy tale about three princes from the Isle of Serendip, now known as Sri Lanka, who were always making remarkable discoveries they were never in search of. Walpole suggested that this fairy tale held tremendous insights about human genius and the gift of making fortunate discoveries by accident.

In a 2016 *New York Times* article, Pagan Kennedy writes about a study of a hundred people, designed to find out how they created their own serendipity, or failed to do so. The study identified three kinds of people: "non-encounterers," individuals who stuck to their to-do lists and rarely did anything that wasn't pre-planned; "occasional encounterers," who stumbled into moments of discovery now and then; and "super-encounterers," who appeared to have special powers of perception and intuition and the ability to identify clues, resulting in unexpected discoveries or happy surprises.

So what does all this have to with leadership? Leaders don't wait for good things to happen to them or for leadership opportunities to appear unbidden; they pursue a plan or vision, but not to the exclusion of everything else. They remain open to possibilities, finding the nerve to act when others may be deterred. Knowing how to read a situation, no matter how subtle or nuanced, and when to respond to unexpected events or changing conditions are two marks not only of a super-encounterer but also of a great leader.

Kennedy believes that you become a super-encounterer in part because you believe that you are one; that you enjoy exploring the unknown and listening to your gut rather than always allowing logic to blind your decisions. We believe the best leaders are prepared to take risks, trust their instincts and are good "clue readers," piecing together bits of information in a manner that is unique, and often arriving at a happy surprise.

We both have had unplanned and unexpected experiences and encounters that could have been ignored, but instead were welcomed and resulted in major impacts on our respective career trajectories. Are we super-encounterers? Who is to say? But we do believe the Persian fairy-tale lesson has merit; that good things can happen if you allow yourself to recognize opportunities when they present themselves serendipitously.

SAMARASEKERA:

When my husband and I were graduate students at the University of California, Davis, 44 years ago, we received an invitation to lunch at the home of my father's friend. At first we were reluctant to go since we had so many unfinished assignments, but we accepted the invitation.

We met a gentleman, Mr. Kulbir Singh, who was visiting from Vancouver, Canada—a place we had never heard of in a country we had yet to visit. In the course of a casual conversation, he learned that my husband was seeking employment. Although a complete stranger, he invited us to visit him in Canada and said that he could arrange for a job interview for my husband at the company he worked for.

I remember asking my husband several questions: "Is this offer genuine? Why would a complete stranger extend such a gesture? What was the likelihood of an interview leading to a job?" Vancouver was a long way away from Davis, California, and we had neither a car nor much money.

However, the offer of an interview and a possible job and the prospect of a life in Canada were enticing. We decided we would accept Mr. Singh's invitation, and we bought a small used car for five hundred dollars to drive from Davis to Vancouver. It was a wonderful West Coast road trip, and upon arriving in Vancouver we went directly to Mr. Singh's home in Surrey, where he had graciously invited us to stay with him and his wife and their two young daughters. Their generosity and hospitality were heartwarming.

My husband interviewed for the job and was offered a position at the company. We returned to California and applied for permanent resident status in Canada. At the interview, the Canadian immigration officer asked me what my occupation would be once I moved to Vancouver. I had plans to start a family, so I said, "Housewife," which was recorded for posterity on my entry document to Canada!

To this day I marvel that a truly serendipitous encounter led to a job for my husband and 44 wonderful years and counting in Canada. A stranger's hand opened a door that altered the course of our life completely. If we had turned down the lunch invitation and stayed at home that day to work on our to-do list, or if we had not had the nerve to visit Vancouver, we would have missed the most momentous meeting of our lives. We had chosen to be super-encounterers, and the dividends were immeasurable.

PIPER:

Upon completion of my PhD in epidemiology and biostatistics, I was excited about my career possibilities. I wanted more than anything to be an epidemiologist working in a department of public health and applying mathematical modeling to determine the risk factors, incidence and prevalence of certain diseases. This is what I had trained for; this was what I desired to do.

And then the phone rang. It was the dean of Medicine at McGill, Richard Cruess, who was recruiting for a new director of the School of Physical and Occupational Therapy. I did not know Dr. Cruess; he did not know me. But he did know one thing about me. I was a rare bird at the time, one of the few physical therapists in Canada who had a PhD, and he wanted desperately to move the school forward academically by hiring a director who had, in addition to professional credentials, research training. I fit the bill.

At first, I completely rejected the notion of taking on an academic administrative position in a field that had nothing to do with epidemiology. I no longer identified myself as a physical therapist. I was an epidemiologist. I was not interested in administering a school; I wanted to conduct groundbreaking epidemiology research.

And then the clues began to make themselves known. Perhaps I could make a bigger difference in changing the two professions, physical therapy and occupational therapy, than I ever could through the research I might conduct as an epidemiologist. Using my unique combination of skills and qualifications, perhaps I could bring the rigor and discipline of evidence-based practice to the world of rehabilitation medicine and change the way it was researched and conducted. Perhaps by working with other outstanding scholars in the Faculty of Medicine at McGill, people whom I had admired from afar, I would learn more about research excellence than I ever would in a government-run public health department. Perhaps, just perhaps, I could initiate graduate programs in the two health disciplines that would educate more therapists to become researchers, who in turn would transform the professions.

Some call it just plain good luck that I received the phone call from Dr. Cruess. I call it a happy surprise, for I now know there was more to it than luck. I wasn't selected as part of a lottery; I was picked for one reason only—I was a physical therapist with a PhD. I was selected because of the path I had chosen, the decisions I had made about my career and the work I had already done. I could easily have said no. Instead, I summoned the nerve to examine my experience and my future goals; risk my career ambitions; identify what made this opportunity different and inviting; and meet this serendipitous event head-on.

That happy surprise and my decision to accept the offer changed the course of my entire career. I moved from that position to a deanship and then a vice presidency at the University of Alberta and finally became UBC's president—all because I was prepared to think differently about how I might apply my graduate education.

Mentors

Most leaders are able to identify several people who have mentored them at some point in their lives, specific individuals who made a difference in their career decisions or actions. While many of these interactions are carefully planned, some occur unexpectedly, out of the blue, and under unusual circumstances. The trick in those situations is to be able to recognize the importance of the specific interaction and to be able to act upon the advice and counsel you have received. Indeed, the art of serendipity.

Mentors come in all shapes, forms and sizes. They can be people you know well or people you hardly recognize. They can be people in your work environment or people who are retired. They can be friends and associates or people you know only by reputation. But they are always people you trust and respect, and people who are generous with their guidance and expertise. When they speak, you listen. When they advise, you take them seriously. You are comfortable confiding in them, knowing they will not breach your trust. You value their time, their experience and their assistance. You are grateful to them for their generosity and look to them for support and understanding. Mentors build your confidence when you lack nerve, offer empathy in tough times and expect very little in return. They hold a mirror up to you, empowering you to push your awareness and understanding, and challenging and supporting you to be the best you can be professionally and personally. They can help change your career and your life.

PIPER:

When I was contacted by a headhunter about applying for the presidency of UBC, I was conflicted. I was relatively happy in my role at the time, Vice-President, Research, at the University of Alberta, and not seeking a presidency; we enjoyed living in Edmonton; and I was uncertain whether I really wanted to lead a university. On the other hand, I recognized the amazing opportunity that UBC represented, being one of the premier universities in the country. I was uncertain about what to do.

My husband was little help. He basically said the decision was mine and that he would support me in whatever I decided. Clearly, he did not want to be responsible for urging me to apply if that was not what I wanted to do; similarly, he did not want to stand in my way if I decided I wanted to be president of a university.

This invitation to apply was highly confidential, so I thought it was inappropriate to discuss it with either my friends or colleagues. I gradually realized I was on my own. Enter my unexpected mentor, Don Mazankowski, a Member of Parliament for 25 years who served as a cabinet minister under two prime ministers and as deputy prime minister under Brian Mulroney.

I had gotten to know Don in his role as a member of the Board of Governors at U of A, and I was in awe of his intellect, judgment and overall wisdom. I had watched him deal with controversial issues, financial concerns, community engagement and university affairs, and I admired and respected his capacity to identify the core issues and craft solutions to difficult problems. In my mind, he was very smart, very wise and a very special Canadian.

One night as we were both leaving a university reception, Don offered to walk me to my car as it was extremely cold, dark and late. As we made our way to the parking lot, I decided to confide in Don, to seek his opinion on what I should do about my conundrum. I am not certain why I let my guard down, but I did. I trusted him and, more important, respected him and genuinely wanted to hear what he would recommend. He listened carefully to my dilemma and then quietly said something like this: "With most opportunities that come your way, you can find reasons to delay, thinking that the timing is not exactly right, or your kids are too young to move, or you are happy doing what you are currently doing. If you are lucky, maybe once or possibly twice in your life, an opportunity will come along that will never come again. If you want to be president of UBC, not president of any university, but president of UBC, the time is now. This opportunity will *not* come again, as the next time the UBC presidency becomes available, you will neither be the right age nor a favored candidate."

His words hit me like a ton of bricks. He was mentoring me on one of the most important decisions I would ever make. He had given me his best advice and provided me with wise counsel. He didn't tell me what to do; he gave me a new perspective. He was right—this opening would not come again, and I needed to recognize that if I wanted to lead UBC, I needed to embrace it and apply for the position now, not several years later. What a happy surprise. Seeking advice on the spur of the moment and receiving wise counsel from someone I admired and respected. Serendipity at work.

Mentors need not always be people who give advice—they might be role models, displaying behaviors that influence your future actions. Such was the case of Nannerl Keohane, the first woman president of Duke University. While I had never met her, I had read many of her publications and looked to her as a role model, as a woman leading a preeminent university at the same time I was leading UBC.

Because I respected her as a woman leader, I jumped at the invitation to meet her at a dinner hosted by Gordon Giffin, the U.S. ambassador to Canada during the Clinton years. It was a lovely, intimate affair, with only eight guests around the table. I was in awe and listened intently to everything Dr. Keohane said. Today, try as I may, I cannot recall even one of the things we spoke about. It was through her actions, rather than her words, that I learned a lesson that has remained with me to this day.

As dinner was ending, Dr. Keohane stood up and graciously thanked the hosts for a lovely evening. She then recognized each guest by name, commenting on something personal about her interactions with us, and announced that she must be leaving as she had a very busy schedule the next day. Automatically, as if it were pre-planned, we all stood, responded appropriately and thanked our hosts. The dinner was over—and most important, we were now all free to leave.

Nannerl Keohane, my new mentor, had given me a most precious gift: the example of how to leave a dinner or meeting graciously without offending anyone. Amazing. No more drawn-out conversations around the table after dinner ended. No more uncomfortable moments wondering when it would be permissible to exit a meeting. All I now had to do was a *Keohane*—stand, be gracious, thank the hosts, acknowledge the other guests and depart.

In both of these examples, as wildly different as they were, I experienced a happy surprise that taught me an invaluable lesson. By seeking advice from someone I admired and by observing the actions of someone I respected, I encountered serendipity in action. It was now up to me, to take what I had learned from these mentors, put the pieces of the puzzle together and move forward.

SAMARASEKERA:

Within months of arriving in Vancouver and despite starting a family, I decided I would apply to the doctorate program in engineering at the University of British Columbia. I am a knowledge seeker and enjoy solving intractable problems, so pursuing a doctorate sounded like the right path.

I remember riding the bus to UBC and being awestruck by the beauty of the campus and the sheer size of the place. As I walked around, I wandered over to the metallurgical engineering department. Canada was a major metals-producing country, and I thought that pursuing research in an area of national importance would better position me for a job after graduation. I met the head of the metallurgical engineering department and obtained his permission to meet with the professors in the department to find a PhD supervisor and identify a project for my dissertation. This was long before the internet, so I could not google individual faculty members to determine their research reputation or what they were working on. I was flying blind.

I knocked on several doors without much luck. Then I walked into the office of the youngest professor in the department, who could have passed for a graduate student. My immediate reaction was, *Does he have the experience to be a good supervisor? Should I find someone older, wiser and well established?* Despite my initial misgivings, he surprised me with his energy and passion. His research was mathematical modeling of metals processes, utilizing computers, which were just becoming powerful enough to solve large-scale problems.

When I asked him about a potential project, he pulled out a napkin from his desk drawer on which he had recorded a conversation he had in a bar with someone from the steel industry. Although I knew nothing about the steel industry or the issues they had discussed over a drink, the topic lit a spark in me. I was surprised but daunted.

Was I going to spend the next three years researching an idea that had been drawn on a napkin in a bar? Had anything been done to date on the topic? There were no long lists of papers I could review, and I realized that if no one had done much in this area it could prove to be a gold mine. Sure enough, this unconventional approach to finding a supervisor and a research project resulted in exciting discoveries that advanced the frontier of the steel industry worldwide.

Looking back, I see serendipity was at work. There was nothing logical about my approach, but it was my willingness to open many doors and trust my intuition that guided me to the right path. Keith Brimacombe, my mentor, became preeminent in his field, but at the time I met him he was early in his career. I took a chance, and the result was entirely serendipitous!

Sponsors

The concept of a sponsor has not been as widely understood or studied as the notion of a mentor. However, a sponsor can have an enormous influence on one's career trajectory, often more than a mentor. "How?" you might ask. Sylvia Ann Hewlett's book *Forget a Mentor, Find a Sponsor* explains the difference in detail. Mentors are people who take an interest in you, listening to your issues, offering you a shoulder to cry on, while giving advice and guidance. They expect very little in return. A sponsor, according to Hewlett, is a senior person who believes in your potential and is willing to take a bet on you; they advocate for your next promotion, encourage you to take risks and have your back. And they expect a great deal from you, namely stellar performance and loyalty. According to research conducted by Hewlett and colleagues based on the experiences of ten thousand workers and leaders in Fortune 500 companies, sponsors can put you on a trajectory that results in pay raises, high-profile assignments and promotions.

Some sponsors work in mysterious ways, undetected by the individual they are sponsoring. Sponsors advocate for and promote individuals they believe to be winners, suggesting them for appointments, career advancements and leadership roles, without the individual they are sponsoring being actively involved. Often the person they are sponsoring has no idea this is the case, only becoming aware of the role their sponsor has played after the fact. Sponsors are truly happy surprises, creating serendipity through their actions.

So how do you find a sponsor? You attract a sponsor by delivering professional performance in exceptional ways, by gaining a reputation for being trustworthy and loyal, and by having a distinct personal brand and skill set. In addition, you may attract a sponsor by increasing your external visibility through joining a nonprofit board, running for office in a professional association or community organization, attending conferences, volunteering your time to advance a cause and figuring out how to be a speaker, panelist or facilitator.

SAMARASEKERA:

My story of sponsors begins with my two Marthas, Martha Salcudean and Martha Piper, both of whom have been pivotal to my career trajectory. I met Martha Salcudean when she arrived at UBC in the mid-1980s to become the first female head of the Department of Mechanical Engineering. At the time, there were only three women professors in engineering at UBC. We became good friends over the years, and she took a great interest in my career. When the position of Vice-President, Research, became available at UBC, she told me that she would like to nominate me for it.

At first I laughed at her suggestion since I had no senior administrative experience, never having been a dean or department head. I could not muster the nerve to see myself in this role. She persisted and told me that I was an excellent researcher, had a broad range of experience on national committees and professional associations and would be a successful Vice-President, Research, should I be appointed. Her sponsorship of my candidacy, along with the support of the head of the Department of Materials Engineering, which she solicited, gave my candidacy credibility.

Enter my second Martha, Martha Piper, who had been appointed president of UBC two years earlier. I did not know her but admired her from afar for her vision and vigor. I will never forget the one-on-one breakfast I had with her before my formal interview, where she asked me why I wanted to be Vice-President, Research, and what made me think I could do the job, given how little formal administrative experience I had.

I was prepared for the question and succeeded in being offered the position. Without Martha Piper's willingness to take a chance on me, and without her continued sponsorship while I was vice president, I might have fallen short. She was one of Canada's most outstanding university presidents, and I was fortunate to have worked with her; that experience served me well when I assumed the position of president of University of Alberta five years later. Sponsorship matters, and matters a great deal.

Another story of sponsorship involved someone I did not know at all. Given my research in steel processing and its impact, I had been appointed to the Dofasco Chair in Advanced Steel Processing at UBC. I don't recall having much to do with the CEO of Dofasco, Mr. John Mayberry, but every year I sent him a Christmas card and thanked him for the company's support of my position. Many years later, he surprised me by accepting my invitation to attend my installation as president of University of Alberta. Three years after that, my phone rang; it was John Mayberry, now former CEO of Dofasco and incoming chairman of the board at the Bank of Nova Scotia, who happened to be in Edmonton. Over coffee he informed me that he planned to nominate me for a position on the board. I nearly fell off my chair.

He told me that Scotiabank was looking for an individual, preferably a woman, who had demonstrated excellence in their career and was leading a large and complex organization in Alberta, and that I qualified. Over the course of two days, he introduced me to the members of the Governance Committee and the bank's CEO, Mr. Rick Waugh. A few months later, I was appointed to the bank's board. Here was an individual, John Mayberry, whom I hardly knew, sponsoring me for an appointment on a major corporate board. He was a senior Canadian leader who believed in my potential and who was willing to take a bet on me. Serendipity.

PIPER:

My sponsor was Paul Davenport, who, before serving as president of Western University in Ontario, was president of the University of Alberta when I was dean of the Faculty of Rehabilitation Medicine; thus, I was able to work with him and get to know him personally. I valued his leadership and respected what he was doing for the university. But it is the support he provided me that became the defining feature of our relationship; and it was because of that support that he was forced to give up the position of president at U of A and move on to the presidency of Western. That is correct.

How did all of that happen? Paul believed in me when others did not. He had recruited me to be U of A's Vice-President, Research, at a time when being a physical therapist was not seen as a viable qualification to take on the lead administrative research position at the university. Others, including the chair of the Board of Governors, preferred a male biochemist for the role, but Paul was having none of it. He was determined to appoint me as his vice president, and as a result of his sponsorship, he confronted the board and some of the powerful academic leaders of the university. Although he prevailed in having my controversial appointment approved, he sacrificed his presidency at U of A in the process.

Paul's sponsorship was critical to my career trajectory; without it I would have never progressed as I did. And because he fought to advance my career over the objections of others, he risked his. I have never forgotten the courage he displayed and the principles he honored. As a result of this experience, I became fully aware of how important sponsors are in advancing the interests of others. No one achieves success on their own. Everyone needs individuals who truly believe in them and who are willing to advocate for them, defend them when they are criticized and represent them fairly and fully when they are unable to speak for themselves. Paul Davenport was such a person in my life.

Lessons Learned

Life is full of twists and turns that can either derail personal goals or provide amazing opportunities. Few, if any, leaders would suggest that they attribute their achievements solely to their pre-planned actions or undertakings. Instead, the record shows that serendipity or happy surprises have often contributed significantly to their critical decision-making and career choices. While we both recognize that no one can ever depend solely on serendipity to launch them into leadership roles, we also acknowledge that there are always unexpected events and encounters that will make a difference in your quest, or your good fortune, to lead.

Similarly, key individuals in your life make a difference—sometimes more of a difference than you could ever envision. Whether it is through mentorship or sponsorship, certain people play a significant role in guiding, counseling, advising, encouraging and supporting leaders as they move forward. These people invariably live in the shadows of the leaders they support, never seeking the limelight or acknowledgment and often working in mysterious ways. But their impact can be wide and deep. Mentors and sponsors are respected and admired individuals who provide sage advice and influence others to take notice of the leader in waiting. One never knows when or where these mentors or sponsors will make themselves known, but being aware that they exist and are willing to step up for you because they recognize your potential to lead is a critical component of your journey.

1. Be aware that serendipity does exist and that unexpected and unplanned things will occur throughout your life that you will need to recognize for the springboards they present. How you piece together the breadcrumbs or clues will determine your reaction to these serendipitous events and where your career goes from there.

2. Remember Alexander Graham Bell's words: "Don't keep forever on the public road, going only where others have gone . . . Leave the beaten track occasionally and dive into the woods. Every time you do so you will be certain to find something that you have never seen before. Of course it will only be a little thing, but do not ignore it. . . . one discovery will lead to another, and before you know it, you will have something worth thinking about to occupy your mind."[9]

3. Trust your gut, find the nerve and don't always allow logic to blind your decisions. Knowing what you want from life will allow you to recognize opportunities when they present themselves serendipitously.

4. When someone you respect and admire offers guidance, advice or counsel, or demonstrates certain behaviors, listen and observe carefully. Their wisdom may be just what you are looking for to direct your decision-making.

5. Recognize that sponsors are as important as mentors. While they often work behind the scenes and are unknown to you at the time, sponsors are clearly aware of your strengths and potential. Their influence on your career, while sometimes indirect, can be propitious in determining the opportunities that unfold.

6. In order to secure sponsors, be the best you can be at whatever you are currently doing. If you excel at your job, you will be noticed by the people who can sponsor you and influence others to recognize you, thereby making a difference in your life.

CHAPTER 5

Answering the call: leading

"You must do the thing you think you cannot do."

—ELEANOR ROOSEVELT

A well-known headhunter once remarked that when she approached potential candidates for leadership positions, she noticed a distinct difference in their response according to gender. Women consistently were surprised to receive her call, were reluctant to engage and needed to be courted and strongly encouraged. Men, on the other hand, were expecting her call, welcomed it with glee and had their application in yesterday's mail, as it were. The headhunter was intrigued by the blatant differences in the responses to her overtures and quickly learned that in order to bring candidates to the table, she had to employ gender-based strategies, different approaches for women and men. Whether this is a good or a bad thing is open to question, but we believe women need to confront their reluctance to consider a leadership role and work actively to counter it with a more positive response.

Women are notoriously ambivalent. "What outfit should I wear to a special event? Should I buy or lease my car? Should I speak up in a meeting or remain silent? Is it really proper for me to ask for a raise or is it inappropriate to promote my own interests?" This ambivalence regarding both small and important decisions leads to relentless questioning about what is the "right" thing to do. And if that is not enough of a problem, women are also known to continually revisit their actions, second-guessing many of their decisions and interventions. How many men spend sleepless nights recounting a conversation with a colleague or a point they raised in a meeting, wishing they had said it differently or wondering whether they have offended someone or left the wrong impression?

This indecisiveness is also seen when women are confronted with leadership opportunities. Invariably, when asked to think about leading or actually offered a chance to lead, women identify all the reasons why they should not or cannot step into the role. Unlike men, who almost uniformly welcome such invitations, women often enumerate every reason under the sun as to why they are neither able nor qualified to become leaders: their partner cannot move, their children are too young, they are happy where they are, they are not experienced enough. Most of these pretexts are just excuses that mask an underlying fear of leading.

Who Me? You Must Be Kidding

As two women who have had to battle many of our own demons when it came to answering the call to lead, we are increasingly aware that women are often more reluctant than their male peers to assume leadership positions. Why do women harbor so many reservations when it comes to contemplating leading? Why do women often identify all the reasons why they should not consider a leadership position, while men are more likely to see themselves as being prepared to pursue these opportunities? Is it because women are less confident than men, or does it reflect their underlying view that they should never appear to want something too much or to actively promote themselves? Have women been taught to be modest and restrained when it comes to assessing their own strengths and qualities, thereby undermining honest self-appraisal?

The apparent confidence gap between women and men has been explored by Katty Kay and Claire Shipman in their book *The Confidence Code*. Through numerous interviews with influential women over two decades, they claim that there is a "dark spot," namely female self-doubt, which is holding capable women back. They point to a Hewlett

Packard study that found women working in the company applied for a promotion only when they met 100 percent of the qualifications, while men did so when on average they met 60 percent of the requirements. Perfectionism, the enemy of the good, is at work in many women. Are women more prone to being perfectionists? It certainly appears so. Does this tendency hold women back? Do women who have achieved high positions suffer from self-doubt as a result of their desire to be "perfect"?

Kay and Shipman recount a lunch with one of the most powerful women in the world, Christine Lagarde, a French politician who rose to become head of the International Monetary Fund and is now president of the European Central Bank. Lagarde revealed that she, too, had suffered self-doubt as she rose through her career, getting anxious before presentations, having to find her nerve to raise her hand to make a point. She also shared that she had commiserated with Angela Merkel, chancellor of Germany, about her experiences as a woman leader. The two discovered they approached their positions similarly by over preparing for every possible eventuality, working the file "inside, outside, sideways, backwards, historically, genetically and geographically." They both believed they often lacked confidence in their abilities to fulfill all of their responsibilities.

Can you imagine two male leaders of the stature of Lagarde and Chancellor Merkel commiserating over their own lack of confidence? Do women require more nerve to lead? Here were two of the most powerful and remarkable leaders in the world, overcoming but never fully outgrowing self-doubt, working harder to compensate for what they perceive they are lacking and reaching for a standard close to perfection. Our hope is that the experience of these female leaders and others will show women that they can overcome their feelings of inadequacy and not succumb to the impossible standard of perfection.

SAMARASEKERA:

In July 2004 I decided it was time to do some much-needed sprucing up of my house in Vancouver. I was preoccupied with the task at hand when the phone rang. Jim Edwards, chair of the University of Alberta Board of Governors, was calling to say the university was launching a search for the next president and was exploring whether I would be interested in being considered for the position. My brain was engaged in painting and interior decoration, so without a thought, I replied that I really was not interested. He asked me to think about it and said that he would call again.

Six weeks later he called back, and once again I expressed little interest. He was persistent and suggested he visit me in Vancouver. Over dinner, he asked me to meet with the search committee, not as a candidate, but for an informal discussion about the position. Knowing that U of A was one of the top universities in the country, I felt embarrassed that I was being so dismissive. Even if I was convinced that I had no interest, surely I should at least visit out of courtesy and then decline.

I met with the search committee in early September, and lo and behold it snowed in Edmonton that day! The search committee assured me that it did not always snow in September, and I remember saying that if I became interested in the position, weather would not be a deterrent. I was very impressed with what I learned during the informal visit, but was still not ready to throw my hat in the ring. Given my continued reticence, Board Chair Jim Edwards and Chancellor Eric Newell agreed to give me another six weeks to think about it.

Looking back, I cannot fathom why I was so cavalier about a life-changing opportunity. I came up with all kinds of reasons why it wasn't right for me. *I had lived in Vancouver for 28 years; how could I possibly move to Alberta and start a new life and leave my family and friends? Taking on the presidency seemed like such a daunting challenge; was I really ready for it?* Fortunately for me, the six weeks I was given to consider the position led me to the conclusion that this was absolutely the best fit for me and for the institution.

When I finally interviewed for the position, it was with enormous enthusiasm and conviction. The potential to make a difference at another great institution was exhilarating. I wanted the job, so I prepared extensively, and it obviously came through in my interview. Upon reflection, I realize how close I came to forfeiting the chance of a lifetime, all because I was not ready to "answer the call."

PIPER:

One of the things I hate to admit, and quite frankly continues to surprise me, is that after 10 years of leading a large institution I still am reluctant to take on new leadership roles. Do you never outgrow this problem? Why is it that even after leading I am still resisting invitations to lead?

I had been a corporate board member of TransAlta Corporation for several years after stepping down from UBC, serving on the human resources (HR) committee, when I was asked by the CEO and board chair to assume the chairmanship of the board's HR committee. The past committee chair was retiring after serving admirably for a number of years, and I was being asked to replace him.

I remember vividly my meeting with the CEO when he asked me to take on this leadership responsibility. My response was classic. I openly questioned my ability to assume this position: I wasn't ready; I had neither the expertise nor the required experience; there were others more qualified. I even went on to suggest that I would consider doing it only if I could take a course on board governance with a focus on HR issues. What was I thinking? Did I really believe what I was saying? Was I only looking for reassurance that I was qualified to do the job, or was I just plain scared of the role?

Whatever the reason for my deference, he was having none of it. He was a busy man of few words and was not going to either beg or cajole. He was not used to having to convince his male board members to assume the chairmanship of committees, as they were always eager to take on leadership roles. I either wanted the job or not—and clearly the answer was "not." I didn't crave the position. On to the next candidate.

I remember feeling rebuked. It took time to get over this rejection and even more time to realize that I was the cause of my own demise. Fast forward several years to when I was serving on the Shoppers Drug Mart board and was approached by the chair to assume the very same role, chair of the HR committee. This time I was prepared to respond appropriately. I was not going to make the same mistake. While I must admit I was still fearful and lacked self-confidence, I did not hesitate in responding. I was honored to be asked to chair the committee and took on the responsibility of leading with determination and discipline.

Fear of Leading

Leadership is scary. While leading can be exhilarating and energizing, it can also be hard and complicated. When leading, it is normal and appropriate to fear the consequences of your decisions; to fear the uncertainty of the environment you find yourself in; to fear being criticized; to fear failure. The issue is not whether it is okay to be scared; the issue is whether you have the strength, fortitude and nerve to overcome the fear and not allow it to deter you from doing the job.

Are women leaders more fearful than their male peers? We aren't sure, but we doubt it. What we do think, however, is that women are more likely to acknowledge their fear than men. Where women have always been able to admit their vulnerability or express their anxieties to others, it is neither easy nor, often, socially acceptable for most men to acknowledge they are afraid of anything, let alone have a fear of leading.

PIPER:

After I had accepted the presidency of UBC, but before I assumed the position, I was relating to a friend how frightened I was by the enormity of the job. What had I been thinking when I accepted the position? I was not really prepared to take on the duties of being president, and I was terrified by the responsibility I was assuming. Surely I had overreached and the job was beyond my capability.

My dear friend looked at me and said something like this: "The search committee knew exactly what they were doing. They have chosen you for who you are, not for who you think you should be. Don't despair. Don't worry about trying to be someone you aren't. Just be Martha!" Those three words, "Just be Martha!" were the most reassuring words I had ever heard. They affirmed that I should be true to myself, not try to be someone else, and should have confidence that if I did what I thought was right and lived by my principles, I would be okay.

As a parting gift, my friend gave me a small framed piece of calligraphy that reads, "Just be Martha!" I immediately hung it over my desk at UBC. I cannot tell you how many times I looked at it and found the nerve to dig deep and confront whatever issue I was facing by relying upon my principles and values. That wonderful piece of artwork has remained with me from that day forward and still hangs over my desk at home. While the fear of leading never really leaves you totally, by addressing it honestly, you are able to keep it from interfering with your ability to lead effectively, or to lead at all.

Never Look a Gift Horse in the Mouth

A gift horse is first and foremost a gift, no matter what shape the horse is in. The idiom admonishes the recipient of the horse not to look at its teeth to see how old it is, but rather to graciously accept it. In other words, don't evaluate a gift by only assessing its faults, but rather recognize it as the generous offering it is, even if it has some negative features.

So it is with the gift of leadership. All prospective leaders should survey the landscape and understand what they are getting into before proceeding; but when considering the call to lead, you need to think about its potential for greatness, rather than focusing solely on its drawbacks.

Every organization, regardless of its current difficulties, has strengths and positive attributes. It is important to identify those strengths when you are thinking about leading and to build upon them as you consider the "gift" of leadership you are being offered. By so doing, you will be able to leverage the unique qualities of the organization and address its shortcomings by acknowledging its various strengths.

SAMARASEKERA:

My initial reluctance to consider the presidency of the University of Alberta stemmed partly from my ignorance of the status of the university and, more importantly, of its potential. Although I knew that U of A was ranked among the top five universities in Canada and that it had a history and tradition of excellence, the institution's public reputation was not commensurate with its standing. And, because of its location in Edmonton, a smaller northern city, compared to Vancouver, Toronto and Montreal where UBC, U of T, McGill and University of Montreal are situated, respectively, it was more challenging to attract outstanding students, faculty and staff from elsewhere to join its ranks. What efforts would be required to elevate its stature in Canada and around the world? What would need to be done to overcome its northern location in order to be more of a magnet for top talent?

During the six weeks between my scouting visit to Edmonton and when I formally became a candidate, I was enormously impressed by what I learned about the university. The first president, Henry Marshall

Tory, had been a visionary and was determined to build a great university on the banks of the North Saskatchewan River by recruiting the best talent from top universities across North America. Alumni had won a Nobel Prize in Physics, been elected prime minister of Canada, been appointed chief justice of the Supreme Court of Canada and served as dean of the Harvard Medical School, to name a few impressive accomplishments. Over nearly a century, discoveries from U of A had an enormous impact on the frontiers of agriculture and engineering, medicine and astrophysics, carbohydrate chemistry, the humanities and fine arts. There was no question in my mind the University of Alberta was a gift, and I realized I would be risking the opportunity to lead by looking that gift horse in the mouth.

Lessons Learned

Women, for a variety of reasons, are reluctant leaders. As many have noted, they are the first to doubt their qualifications or abilities when considering leadership positions. Some suggest this reluctance is based on being perfectionists, which makes them question their ability to lead until they have convinced themselves that they can do the job flawlessly. Others attribute the reluctance to lead to a lack of confidence, which causes women to identify all the reasons why they are not able to step up. Still others see the hesitation to assume leadership positions being related to the overall fear of leading and, hence, the fear of failure. And some chalk up women's ambivalence towards leadership to their determination to assess and evaluate the situation to death—emphasizing all the negative aspects of the position while ignoring the positive attributes of the opportunity.

We believe this "reluctant bride" syndrome is probably a combination of all of the above: inability to see themselves as leaders, lack of self-confidence, fear of leading and an inclination to see the pitfalls rather than the potential. We also believe that this tendency to forgo leadership positions persists even after leading successfully, as women often hide from or excuse themselves from leadership opportunities. While men may share some of the same concerns, they are more likely to ignore them and move forward quickly and firmly when leadership options present themselves.

Women can and must learn to confront all of the reasons they perceive as barriers to leading. By recognizing them for what they are, just excuses as to why they should not lead, women will be more likely to answer the call.

1. Recognize that the self-doubt you experience when approached to lead is a normal reaction of women and not something unique to your particular experience.
2. Understand that confronting your lack of confidence by identifying all of the reasons you can lead rather than all the reasons you can't, is the first step to taking action.
3. Be prepared to take a risk and draw upon your nerve. Even when it is uncomfortable to do so, recognize that all leaders are risk-takers and that no matter how much you analyze, evaluate and prepare for a leadership position, it will never be risk-free.
4. Recognize confidence is as important as competence and that you need to focus as much on developing your self-confidence as you do on establishing your skill set.
5. Understand that many of your male colleagues look at leadership through a different lens and have a hard time identifying with women's concerns. As such, when working with male colleagues use caution in expressing your lack of confidence or reluctance to step up.
6. Be aware that your defensive reaction to leading does not disappear over time. When it recurs, recognize it for what it is and confront it head-on before rejecting a new opportunity to lead.
7. Yes, leadership is scary, but in answering the call to lead you will experience one of the most exciting times in your life. By taking on a leadership role, you will have both the responsibility and privilege to make a significant difference to the organization, institution or agency you choose to lead.

PART 2

Leading with nerve

CHAPTER 6

Early days: assuming the mantle

*"If more women are in leadership roles, we'll stop assuming
that they shouldn't be."*

—SHERYL SANDBERG

For all leaders, the early days in the role are both energizing and challenging. Regardless of whether you are new to the organization or have spent your entire career working there, new leaders face unique situations, problems, issues and opportunities in their first months of leadership. Books have been written, lectures delivered, coaches hired— all to assist new leaders navigate the first year of their tenure. You are no longer a member of the team, an associate or colleague, but rather the leader. This is no regular promotion, but a huge adjustment—demanding and exhilarating, lonely and scary—and the biggest development opportunity of your life.

The First Hundred Days, or the Honeymoon Period

Taking over the reins of the organization means having to define your vision and goals, rise to the expectations of others and place your mark on the organization. How a leader orients herself to her new leadership role and responds to these early demands will define, to a large extent, her tenure as leader. What then are the key things a new woman leader must do? How should she best spend her time and determine her priorities?

Many leadership experts emphasize the importance of setting personal objectives for the first hundred days of leadership—outlining very specifically the goals the leader intends to accomplish within this relatively short time. Franklin Roosevelt originated the idea of the first hundred days in 1933, and almost 90 years later we are still adhering to this dictum. Arthur Schlesinger notes in *The Coming of the New Deal*, volume two in his Age of Roosevelt series, that FDR during his first hundred days in office "sent 15 messages to Congress, guided 15 major laws to enactment, delivered 10 speeches, held press conferences and cabinet meetings twice a week, conducted talks with foreign heads of state, sponsored an international conference, made all the major decisions in domestic and foreign policy, and never displayed fear or panic and rarely even bad temper."

How realistic in today's world is it for a new leader to meet the high bar that was set by Roosevelt in his first hundred days? And are women leaders best served by trying to emulate a male leader who lived almost a century ago? Are there other less task-oriented goals a woman leader might set for her first hundred days that emphasize different aspects of leadership? For example, how do you develop trust within the institution and who do you rely on to assist you in navigating your first months of leadership?

Leaders are introduced to their organization in the early days of their leadership by means of receptions and dinners, meetings, town halls, focus groups and visits to various units and departments. In all of these events, the leader is most often greeted warmly, treated as being important and welcomed to the community. In the majority of instances, this is a time for the leader to enjoy herself, meet new colleagues and anticipate the future with optimism. Some people call it the honeymoon period; others refer to it as the time where the leader gains traction and has an opportunity to present a positive image of herself. In general, communities are excited about having a new leader, are quite generous in their support and are eager to embrace the leader, warts and all. But be aware that this initial glow won't last forever; you will have to get up to speed quickly and make important decisions about how you will move the organization forward and how you will make your mark. Given that the expiry date is relatively certain, leaders are advised to use this gift of time to their advantage, building up as much political and social capital as possible while the community is still enamored with and curious about their new leader.

When we assumed our respective presidential roles, we were new not only to the organizations we were being asked to lead but also to our communities in general. Neither of us had ever lived in the cities we found ourselves in; we were unfamiliar with the history and culture of the universities we were joining and we knew few, if any, of the players. And if that weren't enough, we were both the first and, to date, only women to lead our respective universities. All this novelty meant that we faced intense scrutiny. Our first hundred days did not mirror Roosevelt's in any way; instead, we attempted to balance the fascination with our gender with our determination to orient ourselves to the people and the culture of our respective institutions.

PIPER:

My first hundred days were awful. I had inherited the decision made by the previous president that UBC would host the extremely controversial Asia-Pacific Economic Cooperation (APEC) Leaders' Meeting, which was to take place within my first few weeks. I remember distinctly that when I was informed that this meeting was to take place my first reaction was, "What is APEC?" Needless to say, I learned very quickly—APEC is an international meeting of leaders, at that time including Clinton and Chrétien, along with Jiang Zemin from China and Suharto from Indonesia, to name a few, of countries in the Pacific Rim. Some of the leaders slated to attend were facing accusations of human rights violations, and the university community was in an uproar. Students were protesting, faculty were angry and security was tight.

I was overwhelmed, discouraged and confused. I had not agreed to this controversial event, but I was responsible for overseeing it. Instead of being warmly welcomed, I had protests at my house, sit-ins in my office and tents being erected by professional agitators on the grounds of UBC's Museum of Anthropology where the leaders were to meet.

And yet, in the midst of all this turmoil and dissent, I took comfort in knowing that I would have one day of celebration—my formal installation as president. These ceremonies are grand affairs with people from every constituency attending, including faculty, students, staff, alumni, family and friends, government officials and colleagues from around the world. They are beautiful events, full of pomp and circumstance, with academic regalia, floral arrangements and inspirational music. They are meant to be joyous undertakings and highlight not only the individual who will lead the institution but also the institution itself—emphasizing its history and overall excellence. They provide a significant platform for the leader to speak broadly to the community about her goals, desires and ambitions for the university she will lead into the future.

I had spent endless hours crafting my installation speech, knowing that it was a unique moment not only to introduce myself to the broader community but also to say something of significance about UBC. In my desire to have an impact, I sought to identify an overall theme for my speech, something that people might remember when they reflected upon UBC and its role in the world. After considering a few ideas, I landed upon the simple phrase "Think About It"—the idea was to encourage people to consciously think about UBC—its history, its excellence, its potential—and the role they could play personally in shaping its future.

As I contemplated this theme and began to write the speech, for some crazy reason, I decided to introduce *thinking caps* as a symbol of the thought process I was seeking to inspire—something that I will always wonder why I had either the nerve or stupidity to do. I remember the moment when I discussed my idea of the thinking caps with the protocol officer responsible for the traditional installation ceremony. He looked at me with incredulity and said something like, "Are you sure you want to give people *thinking caps*?" I reassured him that it would lighten the ceremony and make a clear statement of inclusion and celebration. He nodded reluctantly and like a good foot soldier went out and ordered hundreds of ball caps with "Think About It" embroidered on the front.

The day of the installation was gray and dreary. To make matters even more ominous, APEC protesters were amassing outside the auditorium where the ceremony was to take place. Security was everywhere, ensuring that bull horns could not be taken into the auditorium, and with a clear plan in case any disruptive behavior occurred. I was excited and nervous, but happy—confident that my speech was well written and carefully crafted. The venue was filled to capacity, and the ceremony proceeded as planned. As I rose to speak and introduced the theme, "Think About It," the auditorium became silent . . . you could hear a pin drop. Concluding the speech, I calmly removed my academic mortar board and replaced it with my *thinking* ball cap, waving it quickly to the crowd and securing it firmly on my head. The student choir in the balcony behind me erupted in a jazzy "Think About It" refrain that had been written especially for the ceremony. And, as we exited the auditorium, thinking caps were given to all attendees and "Think About It" banners unfurled on lamp-posts throughout the campus. While the APEC protesters continued to make their presence known, shouting at attendees as they left the auditorium, they did not succeed in disrupting the proceedings. I was pleased, relieved and happy that the ceremony had been so well executed.

Little did I know the turmoil that was to greet me. The academic community was aghast—at the message, at the baseball caps and at the irreverence of the overall theme. They were appalled at my apparent disregard for the solemnity of the traditional ceremony and the lack of academic rigor I had displayed. The fallout from my speech and the baseball caps was immediate. The majority of the faculty quickly expressed major misgivings about their new president as not being "academic enough" to lead the institution. Within a very short time, my bubble of happiness and celebration was broken by the criticism I was receiving from the very community I had been chosen to lead.

Who was this woman? Didn't she understand that she was being outrageous by introducing something as ridiculous as baseball caps at her own installation ceremony? How in the world could she be a serious academic leader for an institution of the stature of UBC?

I should have expected this reaction. Academic institutions are hidebound in centuries of tradition, and I had broken the cardinal rule and shown disrespect by introducing a new style, a new way of doing things to an age-old custom.

To make matters worse, the external community, alumni, donors, media and members of the business community, absolutely loved the message. The *Vancouver Sun* ran a front-page story the next day with a photo of me in my thinking cap that heralded the "fresh air" the new president was bringing to the campus. Donors wore their caps proudly, as did many alumni. These external accolades, interestingly, made the internal dissent worse. If the corporate world liked it, that only underscored to my academic colleagues how unacceptable the speech had been.

I was confused and disappointed. I had so wanted to have one day where I could put the APEC protests behind me and revel in my appointment as UBC's president. Instead, I was greeted with criticism and disregard by my own academic colleagues. It made me question myself, my judgment and my leadership. It took me many months, even years, to demonstrate that you can be different and impose your own sense of self while still honoring the values of the institution. And while I continued to be viewed by some as lightweight, frivolous and not academic enough, I do believe that over time people began to accept me for who I was and to judge me not on my style but on my performance. Still, I often wonder if I had to do it over again whether I would take the same approach. I tend to think I would, as that is who I am and how I am comfortable communicating and leading. One thing is certain: few male university presidents would ever have done such a thing.

SAMARASEKERA:

Martha Piper was named president of UBC when I was a professor there. I decided to attend her installation as my colleagues and I were surprised by, and curious about, her appointment. First, her discipline of physiotherapy was not considered to be one of academic heft, especially compared to that of the previous president, who was an internationally renowned geophysicist. Second, UBC tended to look to U of T and McGill for their leaders; this president was from the University of Alberta and unknown to many of us.

As she stepped up to the podium and began to speak, I was struck by her energy and her unusually bold message about UBC's potential. But when she traded her academic mortar board for a ball cap, with the choir singing "Think About It," I was appalled; it was the last thing any of us expected at a solemn installation ceremony. Academics dislike corny slogans, and her choice of "Think About It," worse still, emblazoned on ball caps, did not go over well with us. My engineering colleagues and I wondered out loud whether the university had made a mistake and appointed a cheerleader instead of a serious scholar. She was bold and unconventional, which was refreshing, but did she understand that being president of UBC required serious discourse about its future direction, and "Think About It" as a mantra simply did not cut it? Looking back, I have no doubt that what she did that day took nerve. How many people would have had the courage to stage something so unconventional at one of the most conventional of traditions, the installation of a new president?

When I returned to my office, there was a message on my answering machine from a female engineering colleague who knew Martha Piper very well, as they had served as Vice-President, Research, for their respective universities in the preceding five years. Her message as I recall was, "I know what you are thinking! Please give her a chance. She is brilliant and strategic!" She was right, and I am grateful that her message stopped me from prematurely concluding that we had appointed a lightweight as president.

Reflecting on Martha's presidency, I can unequivocally say that she was one of the most outstanding university presidents in the country. She earned enormous respect during her tenure, from academics, students, government, business leaders and alumni, for her creativity and for her unique approach to leadership. The centerpiece of her aspiration for UBC was her innovative vision entitled Trek 2000. Building upon the historical Great Trek in 1922—when UBC students marched from their crowded downtown Vancouver campus to the chosen site on Point Grey, demanding that the government of the day build the university there—she outlined an enlightened vision for UBC that emphasized the importance of preparing students to be global citizens.

Martha's vision broke new ground with concepts that few, if any, Canadian universities had embraced before, focusing on learning as opposed to teaching, and connecting learning to the research mission of universities. Using that vision as the driving force, she propelled UBC further into the ranks of the best universities in the world, silencing her critics and surprising even those who already believed in her ability. She paved the way for women to chart their own course as academic leaders rather than emulate the generations of men who had gone before.

Going First

Women who choose to lead are often the "first": the first woman to head the organization, the first woman to be named board chair or CEO, the first woman elected to represent a constituency. We all owe a great deal to women leaders who have gone first—Margaret Thatcher, Angela Merkel, Beverley McLachlin, Indra Nooyi, Nancy Pelosi and Kim Campbell, and now Kamala Harris, to name a few. These outstanding and remarkable women have helped pave the way for all of us who follow in their footsteps. Yet, despite the fact that the numbers of women leaders in all fields are increasing, being "the first woman" is, unfortunately, still all too common. Breaking the glass ceiling remains an issue. What does being *first* mean to a woman leader who is assuming the mantle?

Going first requires nerve. Whether it is jumping off the high diving board or speaking at a conference, having to go first is always anxiety-provoking. Increased attention, mere fascination and unfair criticism often accompany being first; in addition, unrealistic expectations often are associated with the first performance. People watch, listen and focus more on the first than on later entrants, and people often have opinions about what represents an outstanding performance.

Being the first woman to assume a leadership position within an organization, department, unit or institution is fraught with potential pitfalls and intense scrutiny. Unfortunately, too often, others' attention is focused on the leader's gender rather than the skills and attributes she brings to the position. "What does she look like and what is she wearing? Is she strong enough for the job? Does she have a partner and, if so, who is it? Is she a mother, and how are her children managing?" And, perhaps most disconcerting, "Was she appointed only because she is a woman?"

Few, if any, of these questions are asked about new male leaders. More commonly, the focus is on their experience, what background they bring to the position and the vision they have for the organization. Are new women leaders held to different leadership standards than their male peers? If so, what is the best way to address these double standards and move beyond the intense scrutiny that often accompanies being the first woman leader?

PIPER:

I remember when my appointment as the first woman president of UBC was announced. A well-known male journalist and UBC alumnus wrote a scathing article in a national publication that read something like, "Surprise, surprise, UBC appoints a woman as their president." His article insinuated that the only reason I had been appointed was because of my gender; that it had nothing to do with my qualifications but rather that UBC had been determined, no matter what, to appoint a woman, and I had been chosen regardless of how many qualified male applicants there had been.

I had been naive, as I believed I was definitely qualified to be president and that the search committee had selected me not because of my gender, but in spite of it. And, if public reaction was not bad enough, I received a congratulatory phone call from a female colleague who basically said, while women across the country were truly delighted with my appointment, I better not mess up, as women were depending on me to succeed. A back-handed compliment at best; a threat at worst.

I had not anticipated these reactions to my appointment, and they hurt. It was difficult to listen to the comments and not question my own suitability for the position. Would it have been easier if I had been the 10th woman president rather than the first? I am certain the answer would have been a resounding "Yes." Most men who become leaders are not the first or even the second; they are not unique; they are not unusual; they fit the mold; their appropriateness is not questioned; their gender is not an issue.

How then did I meet this "first" challenge? I tried to ignore the journalist's accusations and draw upon my nerve and my determination to succeed, regardless of what people were saying or how they were reacting to my appointment. I knew deep down that UBC would not risk its future by appointing someone who was unqualified to do the job. I also knew that in the end, I would be judged on my performance, not my gender, and as such I needed to focus on leading rather than attending to what my critics were saying.

Was I scared? Of course. A conversation with my mother summed up my concern. She was extremely proud of me and injected into every conversation with her friends the fact that I had been recently appointed as UBC's president. One day when talking with me, she shared with me her excitement and delight. I listened respectfully and then said something like, "Yes. I, too, am proud. But being appointed was the easy thing. I now have to do the job, and I am scared beyond belief."

Being chosen to lead is an amazing accomplishment, as is being the first woman in the role. But that is the easy part. Even with all the attention that often accompanies the appointment of a woman to a position that has historically been held by a man, the difficult part is doing the job. Knowing that and keeping your eye on that target are the most important tasks of assuming the mantle.

Fast forward. Nearly a decade after stepping down as president, UBC called upon me again, in a crisis, to return as interim president for a one-year period. It was a difficult personal decision, but I finally agreed to assist the institution that I so deeply cared about. Upon my return, a very good friend sent me a congratulatory note that said something like this: "Good on UBC. They have had two female presidents ... and you have been both!" As comical as her remarks were, they were also disheartening; I recognized that following my appointment, there had not been a single woman leader who followed. Instead, I had been succeeded by two male leaders, and then once again following my role as interim, another male president was named. I believe firmly that being the first is not good enough; that until we have the second, third and fourth women leaders, one after the other, we will continue to view women in leadership as the exception rather than the rule.

The Art of Listening

If there is one question new leaders are most likely to be asked, it is some variation of, "What is your vision for the organization?" All of the books that have been written on the early days of leadership suggest that this is the most important question to address, and it is critical to build your action plan around the answer to it. The emphasis is on acting— identifying specific goals and tasks to be accomplished in the first three months of taking office and then executing your plan.

These kinds of questions presume that the leader knows everything they need to know about the organization, including its strengths and its weaknesses, who's who in the organization and where it should be headed. This is a flawed presumption, even for leaders who are very familiar with the organization. The truth is that once you become the leader you will inevitably be exposed to people, issues, ideas and facts you were not aware of before assuming the mantle; there is a lot to learn. The trick is to avoid falling into the trap of trying to outline during your first months everything you plan to do as a leader. Instead, in addition to having and exhibiting enthusiasm and energy, new leaders need patience—patience to learn, patience to think and assimilate information and patience to listen—before drawing any substantial conclusions or instituting plans of action for the organization.

Listening is key to gaining new perspective and new insight—and it is hard work. It is neither a passive skill, nor one that comes easily to A-type personalities. To listen, to really listen, one needs to concentrate and focus attention on the speaker, to truly hear what the other person is saying and then to retain the nuggets of information one has received. Listening requires connecting the dots from one speaker to the next and putting together what you have heard into a matrix of ideas, concerns, passions, needs and plans. Brain imaging suggests that language processing, or listening, differs according to gender; men appear to listen only with one side of their brain, whereas women have been shown to use both sides—suggesting that while both men and women activate the speech and listening functions of the left temporal lobe, women also stimulate the non-auditory functions of integration and assimilation of the right temporal lobe.[10] Although it has not been shown that this gender difference affects either cognition or the ability to listen, it does suggest that women may have an edge when it comes to this skill. Regardless of gender differences, the most difficult thing any new leader has to do in the early months of leading is be patient enough to develop and practice the art of listening.

There is never a lack of people to listen to. To help make sense of all the input, it is sometimes useful to have a small advisory group of wise, respected persons who can make the most of the new leader's listening time by guiding her on whom she *must* hear from. In addition to the formal meetings with key people, the leader must listen to the white noise within the organization: What is the buzz happening around you? What are people saying who are not in your presence? And what are the lessons you can learn from those people who might not be viewed as being the important voices in the organization?

Experts suggest there are certain things a good listener can do to be an *active* listener, including making eye contact with the speaker; not interrupting, allowing the speaker to finish before saying anything; asking questions to clarify what the speaker has said, demonstrating you heard them; and listening without judgment. In short, by being a good listener in the first few months of your leadership, you will not only learn more about the organization, but also you will garner the respect and trust of the community you serve.

SAMARASEKERA:

The first September following my appointment was a time of great excitement for me. Surrounded by trees and resplendent in green and gold—the colors of the University of Alberta—the campus was humming with students walking in clusters and talking animatedly. I was participating in a campus tradition, riding in a golf cart around the central quadrangle to meet students and hand out U of A swag in exchange for answers to simple questions about the history of the university.

I will never forget my encounter with one student. In answer to the question about what year the university was founded, she replied, "1776." I chuckled, reminding her that Alberta was carved out of the North West Territories in 1906. The next question I posed was, "Who was Henry Marshall Tory?" She looked puzzled and said, "Who are you?" I replied, "Who do you think I am?" This was followed by a thoughtful pause, and the reply, "Student Union President?" I responded, "You have just paid me a great compliment! I am the president of the University!" Wide-eyed she said, "The whole thing?" To which I replied, "Yes." Clearly amazed, she looked at me and said, "Cool!" then walked away smiling but likely perplexed.

In listening to this student's answers, I had several epiphanies. First, just because I held the title of president I was not a recognized leader among the student body. I needed to raise the profile of the office by engaging the students, to better understand their expectations of a university education. I had to invigorate the campus community by initiating a conversation about the role of U of A in society and leading the articulation of a vision for the future. Only through acts of listening and engagement would I earn the reputation of being their leader.

My second epiphany related to the question about Henry Marshall Tory, the university's visionary first president. How could the student have known who he was when there was not a single visible monument on campus celebrating his leadership of the fledgling institution? Architectural monuments of historical significance commemorate important milestones; they honor and pay tribute to leaders while creating a sense of identity and pride. Having lived in Britain as a child and visited Oxford and Cambridge universities as an adult, I was impressed by the sense of history manifested in their spires, museums and monuments. I longed to see our history as the frontier of Western Canada displayed to inspire students and the public at large.

My encounter with that student sparked a discussion, and it gives me great satisfaction that those deliberations over many years led to the creation of a bronze monument depicting a conversation between Henry Marshall Tory, U of A's first president, and Alexander Cameron Rutherford, Alberta's first premier. The sculpture, by alumna and renowned artist Barbara Paterson, is called *Visionaries*. It stands at the center of the Presidents' Circle, with the expectation that the prominent new landmark would become a meeting point for students ("I'll meet you at the *Visionaries*"). This lasting tribute to two pioneering Albertans was thanks to a powerful lesson in listening.

I realized that the art of listening is not simply about hearing but also about reflecting. Listening stimulates deeper insights on how a leader can move the organization forward. I recall having several conversations over the first few months with students, staff and faculty, and I kept hearing how much the word *daring* resonated with the community. It spoke to the character of Albertans in general. As a result, we named our strategic plan "Dare to Discover," which served as the impetus for change. Good listening is a springboard for transformation.

Ignore the Culture at Your Peril

Numerous authors and researchers have focused on the critical role culture plays in shaping not only the organization's identity but also its performance. The definitions of *organizational culture* vary, but, in general, the term refers to the beliefs, values, practices and assumptions that have existed in an organization for a long time, and which can guide staff in knowing what to do and not do.[11] Leaders are often encouraged to place their own stamp on shaping the culture of the organization by being clear about what they believe and value, and by reinforcing behaviors they think will help achieve the vision and goals they have set for the organization. By prioritizing work and setting the agenda, leaders communicate clearly their values and as such, can transform the organizational culture.[12]

How does this perceived relationship between organizational culture and leadership behavior mesh with our experience as leaders of two culturally rich organizations? How do we think new leaders should deal with organizational culture and its impact on their leadership (and vice versa) in the early days of their tenure? Do women leaders view organizational culture through a different lens than men and, if so, how does that view affect their actions in the early days of their leadership?

Most new leaders, both men and women, internal or external appointees, harbor certain views on the organizational changes they would like to see transpire during their time in office. Similarly, most new leaders recognize the key role organizational culture, in terms of beliefs, values and assumptions, plays in successfully moving an organization forward. The issue, in our minds, is not understanding the role of culture, but rather the timing of a leader's efforts to affect the organization's culture. When and how do you confront cultural change? How do you transform an organization while still honoring its history, traditions and culture?

In writing about the first 100 days of leadership, Boston Consulting Group interviewed 20 CEOs in 2003 and asked them about their first months in office in terms of what they intended to do and what they did, as well as what they regretted doing and not doing. The advice they received included "Follow your instincts" and "Prioritize and act," both of which suggest that new leaders, early in their tenure, should clarify their ambitions, goals and priorities. This particular study suggests that a new leader should move quickly in informing the organization, either directly or indirectly, about the culture of performance they value.

Our experience suggests otherwise. We believe new leaders need to first listen to the organization, learn from it and its staff what values they hold dear and to respect, at least initially, the traditions and history of the institution before imposing their own views, vision and values. If nothing else, this slower approach sends a message of respect for the organization they are leading and an interest in learning how best to move forward from the members of the community. In fact, we believe new leaders ignore the culture at their peril; that by discounting the current culture, they leave themselves open to major criticism that may actually inhibit their ability to effect the change they desire in the long term.

PIPER:

As I walked the UBC campus after taking up the presidency, I was greeted by a closed and boarded up faculty club. Normally, this is a revered building on campus, where faculty and staff gather to meet, greet and eat. This one was a sorry sight; the parking lot was empty, and the doors were locked. It occupied one of the most beautiful locations on campus, adjacent to the flagpole plaza, overlooking the water with mountains in the background. What typically would have been a beehive of activity was quiet and desolate.

My predecessor had made the very controversial decision to close the faculty club because it was losing money—and lots of it—requiring it to be subsidized from an already extremely overstretched university budget. He believed it was indefensible to use dollars that should be spent on teaching and research to support a social gathering place for faculty and staff. Given the unpopularity of his decision, he decided to enact it just as he was leaving office, creating a fractured, demoralized work environment.

I had inherited a problem; a cultural icon on campus that had contributed significantly to a sense of community was no longer operating. While still in Alberta, I had received literally hundreds of letters at the time of my appointment, some congratulatory, some perfunctory, some welcoming, but there was no doubt that the large majority were letters from faculty and staff complaining bitterly about the closure of their meeting place. They were determined that I should be aware of this unreasonable decision and were, of course, looking to me to rectify it quickly. I remember vividly boxing all of those letters into my car and driving with them on the back seat as I crossed the mountains to my new home, keeping them close at hand to remind me of their concerns.

I had neither an instant solution nor a sincere interest in their complaints, as I largely discounted the issue as being insignificant to the future of the university. I understood the rationale for my predecessor's decision and appreciated the financial constraints it addressed, and given my experience at other universities, I believed that faculty clubs had seen their day, harkening back to a time when faculty, mainly men, had all the time in the world to socialize, eat and drink. One thing we no longer needed in a university was an exclusive club, and it had nothing, or at least that is what I thought, to do with moving the organization ahead strategically. The issue was clearly a nuisance.

It took me some time to fully appreciate how much the faculty club and its closure defined UBC culture. I slowly began to understand why I had transported all of those letters so carefully across provincial borders. I recognized that I would not be able to bring the community along and move ahead with strategic planning for the university without first addressing this issue. By closing a beloved gathering place, the administration had inadvertently given the message that the long-standing traditions and history of the university were no longer valued. As a newcomer, it became apparent to me that in order to gain the trust of the faculty and staff, I needed to listen to their arguments and concerns and find a solution that honored UBC's culture and met the community's needs.

We did craft a solution, and the building was reopened to great fanfare. While the faculty club concept was not resurrected in its entirety, the newly designed space served many of the same objectives as the original faculty club—serving good food, providing a space for meetings and gatherings and making available lodging for guests to campus. And rather than being heavily subsidized, a new financial model charged appropriate fees for the services offered in the building. Of course, the resolution did not please everyone, but by listening and understanding the culture of the university, we were able to create a financially viable model that also respected a long-standing tradition. By doing so, we gained the trust of the faculty, which was critical to building a strategic plan to move the organization forward.

Transition

A change in leadership is not just about the person assuming the mantle, their honeymoon period and the adjustment to a new organization and culture; it is also a time of transition, the passing of the torch from the old to the new. Numerous studies suggest that a smooth transition—that is, a carefully orchestrated hand off from the exiting leader to the entering leader—bodes well for the launch of the incoming executive. One study even suggests that leaders who undergo effective transitions "reach their potential nine months faster than those with an average transition."[13] The general thinking is that the more information and briefing the new leader has from the previous leader, the better equipped they will be in assuming the mantle.

Clearly, this is easier said than done. Various issues arise when planning the transition period, including differing goals, styles of leadership and ideas about where the organization should be headed. Often the selection of the new leader has entailed a conscious attempt by the board and others to identify someone who differs, sometimes substantially, from the previous incumbent, thereby resulting in potential tension between the two individuals. In cases where the leaders in question know and respect each other, perhaps even having worked together for periods of time, the incoming person often desires to put their own stamp on the organization and distance themselves somewhat from the exiting leader.

Methods to enhance the effectiveness of the transition period are numerous and include such things as the preparation of extensive briefing materials, personal meetings between the two individuals involved, discussions with key members of the executive team to understand the current issues in each portfolio and a comprehensive orientation to the governing board. Executive teams spend hours preparing and executing a transition plan, with the emphasis on ensuring the new leader understands the current status of the organization, its strategic directions and the people who are currently charged with delivering on the plan. What is rarely spoken of or addressed is the chemistry between the two leaders and how that alone can foil the best transition plan. This factor is exacerbated when the incoming leader is neither respected by nor is the preferred candidate of the outgoing leader. In these cases, the transition period may actually be undermined by the exiting leader, leaving the new leader adrift when they most need guidance.

We both assumed the mantle of our respective presidencies following men who had each served 10 years or more at the helm. We were both external appointments and neither worked with nor personally knew the exiting leader; neither of us was seen as the heir apparent by the previous president. As the first women to assume the office, we were clearly different, a bit unusual and lacked legitimacy in our respective institutions, largely because we were unknown. While we had carefully studied certain aspects of the university we were joining, we lacked an intimate understanding of the pressing issues and of the competencies of the senior people within the organization. The case for a smooth transition could not have been stronger.

PIPER:

The president whom I followed at UBC was a remarkable leader and an outstanding scholar who, in my mind, put UBC on the map. Thanks to his doggedness and determination over a 12-year period, he propelled UBC into the ranks of the world's top universities. Indeed, I believe David Strangway will go down as one of the most transformative Canadian university presidents of the 20th century. Due to his dedication and tireless efforts, UBC grew from a regional university to a global powerhouse during his tenure.

This type of ambition did not come without its critics, however. He had a reputation for not suffering fools, for forcing his will upon the institution and for single-handedly taking on those who disagreed with his motives. My selection as his successor was viewed as a course change for the university in terms of engaging someone who might have complementary goals for the organization but a different consultative approach to achieving them. Even so, my appointment was not immediately embraced by the community; I was an unknown commodity, coming from physiotherapy, a discipline generally perceived as lacking in academic heft—in addition to being a woman.

It was obvious early in the transition period that my predecessor shared these concerns. In our one and only meeting, he made it very clear he thought it highly unlikely I could handle all the various issues facing the university, that he really did not think I was up to the job. While he was polite, he was neither warm nor welcoming. There were no briefing documents; there were no lengthy discussions regarding the labor, personnel, legal, financial or academic concerns of the university; there was no guidance or advice provided. It was a brief meeting in which he essentially wished me good luck.

I have often wondered whether my gender explained his overall disregard for me and find it difficult to think that he would have treated a male colleague, regardless of his opinion of the individual, in the same dismissive manner. He had spent his entire academic career surrounded by male colleagues and came from the world of geophysics, a male-dominated academic discipline; he might have been unconsciously biased against women academics in general, and a woman physiotherapist in particular.

I also believe his reservations were transferred consciously or unconsciously to the executive team, as I quickly perceived they all had serious misgivings about my ability to take the helm. They were reluctant to discuss in any significant manner their individual portfolios and the challenges they were facing, either with me or among themselves. In fairness, I think they were accustomed to the previous president controlling most of the agenda and action and were not prepared to assume responsibility for their own units. In short, it was a nonexistent transition period. I was on my own.

Over time, I believe I garnered my predecessor's respect, and over time, I occasionally consulted him about difficult issues, knowing that he cared deeply about the institution and would do anything to assist me. For that I will always be grateful. Having said that, during the transition period, I was alone, with almost everyone standing on the sidelines, waiting to see whether I would fail before they would risk jumping on the bandwagon.

Peers, Not Friends

It is a well-known fact that leadership is a lonely affair. Talk with any leader and you will hear something like "I often feel alone" or "Being in charge is very lonely." Individuals who are known for being people persons, who are broadly connected to various constituencies, suddenly find themselves cut off from the associates and friends they used to spend time and relax with. And even though their days are filled with people and interactions, often they find themselves feeling isolated at the end of the day.

The transition from being a member of a group to leading the group is challenging in that it involves crafting a new identity. No longer is she "one of us"; rather, she is alone at the top, resulting in a different relationship with those who previously were her friends and colleagues. She is their boss; she is in charge; she must now make controversial decisions and, in some cases, evaluate the individuals who were her friends.

This change in the relationship between the new leader and her former associates is subtle but real. Can she still join her friends for lunch? How does she react to meeting requests from the people who were her friends and colleagues? Does she seek advice and counsel from the people she used to commiserate with? Can she still confide in the individuals who previously always supported her?

Our experience suggests that new women leaders are often ambivalent about how to manage this dilemma and may struggle more with this issue than their male colleagues, as women tend to rely upon strong personal relationships and networks for support, advice and reassurance. On the one hand, new leaders seek normalcy in their routines and comfort in being with people whom they like; on the other hand, they recognize that their issues and responsibilities have changed, making it difficult to carry on as usual. They quickly discover that there are things they just cannot share with their old friends, that their perspective on issues now differs and may conflict with the thinking of former associates and that they are now being watched, even by their friends, to see how they react, behave and set the tone for the organization.

New women leaders tend to believe that they are collaborative and transparent and, hence, will be able to keep their friends while cultivating new relationships and leading the entire organization. They wrongly find themselves thinking that if they handle this transition appropriately, they will be able to have the best of both worlds. Often in the early days of their leadership, they will look to their old friends for affirmation and honest input. What they fail to recognize is that their old friends may no longer view the relationship as it was, but rather may see the new leader as a resource to be accessed and used. It is not unusual for former friends to seek out the new leader in order to demonstrate their own new status in the organization, thereby trying to influence the leader's agenda or priorities.

How then do new women leaders cope during these early days with managing their past relationships? We believe they first must recognize that things have changed and that their relationships going forward must differ from those of the past. We also believe that the new leader is well-advised to discuss this change openly with her friends, to clear the air and arrive at an agreed upon set of guidelines that will help inform how they relate in the future. Often the easiest path forward is to clarify that the relationship can still be cultivated, but it must be limited to personal matters, such as birthdays, kids, movies, books and travel experiences, for example, rather than talk about business, the organization and specific work-related issues.

Most important, new leaders need to recognize that, more than friends, they need to develop relationships with peers—other leaders with whom they can share their concerns openly and from whom they may seek the guidance and support they need. Some new leaders engage an executive coach or identify a mentor to play this role; others take courses designed for new leaders or use professional organizations with like-minded leaders as their colleagues to assist them with the problems they encounter. The best way to combat the inevitable loneliness that accompanies leadership is to find ways to build outside support networks, people whom you trust and who truly understand what you are facing, rather than relying on your old friends to play a role they are no longer qualified to play.

SAMARASEKERA:

When my appointment as president of the University of Alberta was announced, one of the first to call was a close friend and associate at U of A. In fact, he was an individual with whom I had three decades of shared history. I first met him when I arrived in Canada and enrolled as a graduate student at UBC, sharing an office and graduate supervisor. Our academic interests led us to play active roles in professional societies and to draw on each other for advice on research projects and career goals. Our families became close, attending special events and visiting each other often although we lived in different cities.

My friend was clearly thrilled at my appointment, and he saw himself helping me acclimatize to the new institution. Not long after I arrived on campus, we agreed to have lunch, at which time he proceeded to give me his views of various leaders at the institution. I began to feel distinctly uncomfortable receiving inside information, even though I trusted him. He went further and advised that I should consider replacing one or two of them. At this point, I politely told him that I was new to the job and would take my time to assess the strengths of my team.

After a few months, I agreed to have lunch with him again and, given the earlier commentary, I mustered the nerve to lay down some ground rules for our relationship going forward. After catching up on family and friends, the conversation turned to the university, at which point I said that our friendship was very important to me, but it would not be possible for us to continue to discuss the organization, given my role. I also indicated that I was going to be under enormous time pressure, so our meetings would not be as frequent as we both may have liked. I ended by saying I would be open to seeing him socially when time permitted so that we could catch up on our families and mutual friends and hoped he appreciated my situation. Given the depth of our friendship he understood, and we were able to continue to see each other on these new terms.

I realize this was an important moment in our relationship. I was establishing boundaries on topics we could discuss. Following my retirement, we have returned to the relationship we had before my decade as president. This experience made it clear to me that it is not realistic to have friends who serve as confidantes within the organization you lead. As the leader, you are always juggling competing interests, some of which will conflict with those held by well-meaning friends. So, where do you turn for advice?

Executive coaches are often useful for new leaders, as is seeking out peers whom you can trust for advice and guidance. I was fortunate that the University of Alberta was a member of the Worldwide Universities Network, a group of 18 publicly funded universities from six continents. I met the presidents in the network once a year at an event hosted at one of the member institutions. Whether in Cape Town or Hong Kong, these meetings were stimulating gatherings, both professionally and socially. At one of the dinners, each of us was asked to share a surprising interest with the group. The leaders revealed personal hobbies from wine making to bird watching, accompanied by humorous anecdotes.

My personal revelation was my love of ancient Chinese porcelain. My grandmother had beautiful Chinese vases in her house, a few of which had found their way to my home. I recalled to the group how I scoured markets in Beijing, negotiating with vendors supposedly selling antique porcelain pieces, in a language I did not understand. Armed with catalogs of antiquities, I was hoping to find treasures from ancient Chinese dynasties, but I was never sure whether I had acquired a reproduction!

We were able to let down our hair, knowing that these personal revelations would not find their way back home. To be candid with a colleague, even one from a distant country, was an antidote to an otherwise lonely job. In addition, these colleagues became trusted advisers, individuals I could call upon for guidance when I required an objective, external opinion. They knew me, and I knew them; we were all in the same boat as leaders who felt somewhat lonely and isolated at the top of the institutional food chain. They would return my phone calls immediately, and I came to rely upon them for sound professional advice more times than I can count.

Lessons Learned

The early days of leadership are often cited as being some of the most important and most challenging, in terms of setting not only the tone and style of leadership but also determining the priorities and actions to be taken by the organization. We believe that new women leaders often confront these early days in a different manner than their male colleagues do by focusing on first understanding and listening to the community and its members before taking specific actions and setting key goals.

Women assuming leadership positions are often viewed as a novelty because they frequently are the very first woman chosen to lead the organization. Being first comes with increased attention on unimportant, superficial issues. How the first woman reacts to this enhanced scrutiny, and how well she listens and appreciates the traditions of the organization, often determine how successful she will be in moving forward in terms of strategic planning and taking action.

Leadership can be very lonely. Women who have garnered support from strong friendships over the years may find it especially onerous to manage these relationships as they assume their position of leadership. While maintaining old friendships is possible, it must be done very carefully, with the leader being clear about the new boundaries of the relationship. Although personal experiences, such as birthdays and holidays, can still be celebrated, former friends and colleagues cannot be engaged in business decisions or consulting about organizational issues. New leaders are advised to seek out peers and external networks to assist and guide them in terms of decisions, strategies and actions as they move forward in their first year of leading.

1. Practice patience. Do not be too eager to shape the organization in your image or take the institution in new directions. Time is on your side.

2. Be prepared for increased scrutiny. Everything you do, say or emphasize will be interpreted by members of your community as reflections of your priorities and objectives.

3. If you are the first woman to lead your organization, understand that there will be a heightened fascination in things that should not matter, such as your clothes, partner, children and how you spend your spare time. Try to accept this increased interest in you as being unimportant and not essential to your eventual success.

4. Work at active listening. It is only through listening that you will come to understand the real issues, conflicts, barriers and opportunities that are present in the organization.

5. Become a student of the history, traditions and culture of the organization or unit. Understand that only by first honoring the past will you be able to move the organization into the future.

6. Do not expect the transition period to be smooth or enlightening. Even with the best intentions, transition plans often fail to acknowledge the conscious or unconscious tensions that arise with the transfer of power. Work at developing your own transition plan that identifies your specific needs.

7. Be open with friends and colleagues about how your relationship with them needs to be clearly defined as you assume your leadership role. Be as honest as possible about what the terms of your friendship must be as you move forward. It requires nerve to clarify why it is inappropriate for you to engage with them on issues that directly affect the organization.

8. Cultivate new relationships with people you trust who are external to the organization. Get to know your peers who are leaders of similar organizations, people who understand the issues you are confronting and who are willing to share advice and counsel as you navigate your first year of leading.

9. Consider hiring an executive coach and/or taking a course for new leaders to assist you in becoming a leader. Professional advice and guidance can be extremely useful in the early days of leading.

CHAPTER 7

Assessing talent: it's all about people

*"The secret of my success is that we have gone to exceptional
lengths to hire the best people in the world."*

—STEVE JOBS

How difficult can this be? You would think that recruiting talent
would be easy and quite straightforward. Find the best, hire them
and keep them happy. Unfortunately, talent assessment, recruitment and
retention are harder than they look, and the risks are real. If you get it
right, an organization can soar. If you get it wrong, you may not only
set the organization back, but you may also create additional problems that
are not easily resolved. Fred Terman, who served as provost at Stanford
University during the 1930s and 1940s, and who is largely credited
for elevating Stanford from a comfortable regional college to a world-
renowned university, once said, "The most expensive staff member is the
one who is merely adequate."[14]

Merely adequate. How do leaders avoid the pitfalls of surrounding
themselves with merely adequate individuals—people who can do the
job, but who neither know how to innovate nor have the skill set to
truly make a difference in the organization? Is there a foolproof method

for assessing and recruiting talent? Do women leaders approach talent assessment and management differently than their male colleagues and, if so, how?

In a recent article in *Harvard Business Review*, women who held leadership positions in some of the most successful and progressive organizations in the world scored higher than men on most leadership skills. At every level, more women were rated by their peers, direct reports and associates as better overall leaders than their male counterparts. Contributing to their effectiveness were competencies most often associated with talent management and team building, including developing others, building relationships and inspiring and motivating others. In fact, women were thought to be more effective in 84 percent of the measured traits.[15]

Many studies comparing women leaders with their male peers conclude that women bring a different way of thinking to leading, including, along with many other traits, a "gift for reading people."[16] It remains to be studied whether this difference is significant in terms of overall performance of the organization; however, it can be concluded that their innate intuition may give female leaders an edge over their male counterparts when it comes to assessing and managing talent.

Leading Is a Team Sport

Leading is not a one-person show; it is truly a team sport, requiring the skills of many individuals working together to accomplish the stated goals. While identifying the individuals who possess the specific skills is an important component of leading, how the leader motivates and inspires the team is the more challenging aspect of leadership. There is no clear road map in determining what works and what doesn't. Individual leaders bring their own style to the table, learning from success or failure. Most leaders recognize that regardless of how hard they work, they will not prevail in achieving their goals without a strong team of many individuals working together to accomplish the stated goals. Leadership experts suggest that the new leader should focus their first efforts on assembling the team of people who will report directly to them and are their trusted colleagues. Putting the right executive team in place is key to a leader having the talent and the support required to effectively execute on their vision.

Selecting individuals who possess a certain skill set is essential; but team members must also share the vision and values of the organization and, most importantly, be willing to work collectively with others to achieve the stated strategic goals. There is little if any room for people, regardless of how much talent they display, who are one-person shows and who have no desire to work cooperatively with other team members to move the organization forward.

How team members are selected and hired or appointed is dependent upon the leader. Some will engage executive search firms to assist in the identification of potential candidates; others will go it alone, relying on their own experience, values and gut instincts. Unfortunately, there is no foolproof method in assembling executive teams, as the chemistry between and among members is difficult to assess until the team is actually formed and functioning. And even when a leader has assembled the "perfect" team, it can be short-lived as members move in and out of the team depending upon their own personal issues and career trajectories.

Perhaps more important than the selection of team members is the role the leader must play in managing and developing the team: supporting and advocating for members, providing them with the appropriate resources to succeed and encouraging their career advancement. The real test of leadership lies in motivating and inspiring one's team members, while at the same time assessing each performance in a fair and meaningful manner. What works and what doesn't aren't set in stone. Individual leaders bring their own style to the table, learning from their experience.

Do women leaders do a better job of creating and managing their teams than their male counterparts? Women are generally thought to have well-tuned people skills, but do these skills assist or hinder women when leading their teams? As two women leaders, we believe that our concern for people both gave us a boost and stood in our way as we continuously struggled over time to establish and manage our respective teams.

SAMARASEKERA:

Corporations adopt best practices in talent development, ensuring that a new CEO has a pool of high-performers to draw on when building a team. As a corporate board member serving on the Human Resources

Committees of three public companies, the Bank of Nova Scotia, Magna and TC Energy, I have been closely engaged in the oversight of talent development and team building. I have been impressed with these highly effective practices; they differ significantly from those employed by nonprofit organizations and universities, places that might be well-advised to consider adopting some of these private sector approaches. Building strong teams by developing talent from within and recruiting from outside when needed makes a substantial difference to the performance and future of the enterprise.

When I joined the University of Alberta, I decided to keep an open mind and take some time to assess the senior team, given several members had been recently appointed by my predecessor. After one year, it was clear to me that several of the senior leaders on the team were first rate. They were highly respected by the university community, the board and the government of Alberta. I also found them to be great team players, working well with one another and supportive of my leadership, so I did not replace them.

What I learned from this experience is that teams can be transferable between leaders if the individuals involved are talented and committed to the advancement of the organization, regardless of who is at the helm. In my case, I quickly comprehended that there is no predetermined method of building a team, that each individual must be judged on their own merits and that loyalty to the organization, rather than to the specific leader, is a key factor in being an effective team member.

When I did need to recruit new team members, I recognized that identifying the people you want on your team and persuading them to join you is a contact sport, requiring an enormous amount of time and energy on the part of the leader. With two of my preferred hires, I spent one-on-one time with each candidate, trying not only to assess fit, strengths and weaknesses, and future potential but also to convince them to accept the position.

One of my best recruits was a young man who came from a leading private university in Boston. As I flew to meet him, I remember reflecting on the genius of U of A's first president, Henry Marshall Tory, who believed that a great university could be built right on the banks of the North Saskatchewan River if he attracted the best talent. He recruited his first four faculty members from outstanding universities, including

E.K. Broadus from Harvard. In recalling his first meeting with Tory, Broadus stated, "On a day in June, 1908, the president of a university not yet in being, in a province which I had never heard of, in a country which I had never visited, came to Harvard and offered me the professorship of English. The offer sounded like midsummer madness. I think that what I accepted was, not the position or the salary, but the man."[17]

Drawing on this lesson of being uncompromising in recruiting the best talent, I sat across the table from a young man at Legal Sea Foods in Boston, telling him about the opportunity at the University of Alberta, while trying to convince him to move from Boston to Edmonton, a place he had barely heard of and never visited. I had studied his accomplishments in detail and was impressed by his creativity and transformative initiatives. Fortunately, he accepted my offer and exceeded my expectations on all counts.

The other person I recruited was an accomplished research scientist who had never served in a senior administrative position such as dean or department chair. I had known him for many years, having served on national committees with him, and his reputation was stellar. Uninterested in becoming a senior administrator, he was committed to his research career and was determined to stay where he was. I believed fervently he was exactly what the university needed, and I devoted enormous effort to convincing him to come to U of A. I was not wrong. He was hired and ended up being a superb appointment.

I often wonder whether a male leader would have spent as much time convincing someone to join his team or been prepared to take a risk on an individual who at first was truly disinterested in the position and had limited experience as an administrator. Why did I do so? I believe my people skills were kicking in; there was something about these individuals I admired and respected, and I was confident they could not only do the job but also would be a great fit with the team and the culture of U of A.

Let me be clear. External appointments are not risk free, but they often result in a transformative impact. All of the individuals I recruited from the outside had to overcome the inertia inherent in the organization, where resistance to change was endemic. They also had to adjust to the new culture and gain credibility, notwithstanding their credentials, before they could be the change agents I had hoped they would be. They encountered considerable pushback, which I countered with constant assurance that I had their back.

PIPER:

Once my team was established, I was aware of how hard everyone was working as we were being pushed in every direction; the team was rising to the task every day, seven days a week. Harry Potter was a sensation at the time, and I, like him, believed in luck and magic—because so much of what happens is beyond our control, it helps to be lucky. Symbolically, I presented each of my team members with a magic wand—recognizing that we would, as a team, need a bit of luck and magic to prevail.

I told them I expected them to carry the wands at all times, and that we would need them especially when we met as a team to call upon our magical powers to accomplish the more difficult tasks. Can you imagine their reactions? Most of the team members were male, and I think they thought I had gone mad. But they did as they were told, bringing their wands to our meetings. And I, of course, summoned them to wave them from time to time to call upon the magic we needed to confront whatever challenge we were facing.

Did it work? Were we always lucky and able to avoid crises? No, of course not. Would a male leader have engaged in such an endeavor? I doubt it. But of one thing I am certain: the wands built trust, support for one another, goodwill and moral fortitude. I also believe that the magic we created was largely our commitment to work together to accomplish our collective goals.

Behind the Scenes

Leaders go to great lengths to create their executive teams, identifying key individuals who possess the required skill sets and experience, and who will work diligently to advance the organization's agenda. The emphasis on team building at senior levels of the organization is well recognized and completely justified; however, what sometimes goes unnoticed or ignored by the incoming leader is the importance of bringing the same level of scrutiny and personal attention to assembling the team of individuals who work behind the scenes—the back office, so to speak.

Without the support of exceptional administrative services, technological know-how and key individuals to assist the leader in everything they do, from communications to meeting preparation to scheduling of appointments, leaders will most likely fail not only at using their time effectively but also in meeting the daily responsibilities of the office. A well-run office seamlessly fosters a well-prepared and efficient leader. And, like we tend to ignore our bodies during times of good health, the administrative support systems frequently are ignored by the leader until something dreadful happens.

We both inherited administrative offices from our male predecessors that were largely structured for an era that preceded electronic communication and computer programming. Everything from donor and alumni records to financial spreadsheets and large data sets were still in hard copy, with few if any computer programs or systems in place. As we assumed our leadership positions, the digital age was expanding rapidly into all areas of administrative support; whereas our predecessors relied on typed memos, traditional mail, telephones and handwritten responses, both of us were adept at using email and other forms of electronic communication and computerized data sets. Unfortunately, the offices we inherited were neither structured to handle the shift to rapid communication nor had staff who were proficient in computer technology.

Creating new and efficient systems and hiring competent staff who were well versed in the digital era caused great heartburn as we worked to establish the back offices and infrastructure that could advance our aims and the objectives of the university. As a result, settling in was not easy; we quickly learned that little can be accomplished without the behind-the-scenes support of extremely skilled individuals who remain largely out of sight of the larger community.

This experience taught us several things. We learned the hard way that leaders need to give as much attention to setting up their offices and the administrative systems as they do to building their executive teams. And, if one were to prioritize these tasks, we both agree that first developing an efficient and effective behind-the-scenes operation is key to getting anything—including the identification of a strong executive team—done, and done well. In short, ignore the importance of administrative support systems at your peril—without them, you can be certain that you will stumble and most likely fail to execute effectively on meeting your own personal goals and reaching the aims of your institution.

Cut Your Losses

As one embarks on building a cohesive team, one of the most difficult things any leader has to do is letting someone go. The individual may have been a member of the team of the previous leader or a new recruit who just did not work out. No one likes to inform a colleague that they are no longer needed, that they are either redundant, incompetent or non-performing. While there are protocols in place for how to best terminate an employee, it is never easy to deliver the bad news. As a result, leaders tend to avoid making these tough decisions, erring on the side of ignoring poor performance and wishfully thinking that the situation will resolve itself. Underperforming employees are not always incompetent, lazy or emotionally unstable; they can be caring, nice, intelligent people whom you enjoy being with, making the task of letting them go even more complicated. As a result, the default position for many leaders is delay, delay, delay.

Are women leaders more likely to be guilty of this form of procrastination? Our collective experience is not stellar. We both encountered situations where it was necessary to terminate associates. At best, we failed to do so in an expedient fashion; at worst, we looked the other way and failed to act, living with the inappropriate person in the position.

Hindsight suggests there is nothing to be gained by delaying the decision. Why then our reluctance to move quickly to replace underperforming individuals? Our view is that the easiest cases are those where the individual has either done something totally unacceptable or is blatantly incompetent. Unfortunately, in the majority of cases we have dealt with, the individual in question was neither; rather, they were either very capable of only a subset of the job requirements or just mediocre, thereby resulting in the hope that with constructive feedback they might improve.

We have both subsequently observed male leaders in the corporate world who have encountered some of the same conundrums. The employees in question are almost always good people, hard-working and deeply committed to the organization; but, and this is the issue, they for whatever reason are not excelling and should be removed and replaced with someone who is a better fit or possesses a stronger skill set. And yet, there is almost always a reluctance to do so. These are friends, colleagues and people you socialize with. You know them well and trust and respect them as individuals, making any decision to terminate them even more difficult. Nevertheless, the well-being of the organization depends on the leader making tough decisions to move on, to advance the organization's goals in an expeditious manner by having the best talent in place. That is always the conflict.

SAMARASEKERA:

My efforts at replacing members of the team by recruiting from outside were met with mixed outcomes. Did I do an inadequate job of due diligence in assessing their track record? Was I blinded by an interview? In some cases, the answer to these two questions is, unfortunately, yes. Even though I secured the services of the best executive search firms, reading between the lines of reference letters or asking the right questions of referees in phone calls did not always result in an accurate picture of past performance or personal weaknesses.

I recruited a professional who was superbly creative but with time exhibited management deficiencies that could not be overlooked. HR advised me to terminate the individual without cause and to unceremoniously escort the employee out of the building, as is common practice. I balked at the suggestion and spent sleepless nights agonizing over what to do, especially since I liked the person very much. I ultimately drew upon my nerve and decided to offer the individual another position that played to their strengths. This was one of the most painful talent management decisions I have had to make, and I continue to wonder what I could have done differently. I learned an important lesson: I needed to do as much due diligence as possible without relying entirely on search firms.

Developing and Promoting Top Performers

"Before you are a leader, success is all about growing yourself. When you become a leader, success is all about growing others."

—JACK WELCH, *WINNING*

Great leaders are always cultivating talent, working assiduously to identify those individuals who are capable of moving up in the organization and then consciously providing them with guidance and direction to prepare them to take on more and more responsibility. This effort may include the identification of possible successors, people who in the mind of the leader have both the talent and experience to replace the leader when they exit the organization. Working to promote talented individuals is a key component of strong leadership.

As mentioned earlier, in the corporate sector enormous attention is paid to identifying and developing a strong roster of successors for the top positions in the corporation, especially that of CEO. This does not mean that companies never bring in top talent from outside the organization, but it is usually the exception rather than the rule. Universities, on the other hand, generally recruit from outside the organization and rarely engage in succession planning or ensure there are high-performing individuals within the organization who can step into senior roles. The reasons are historic and cultural, including the archaic search processes universities employ where faculty and staff members serve on the committee that selects the leader. Internal candidates who have either offended someone or made difficult decisions that a member of the search committee disagrees with are often passed over. As a result, universities tend to look to external candidates who have none of these "warts," nor a track record to criticize, but who in the end may not possess either the required skill set or experience. And qualified internal candidates often find that they have to move from their home university to another institution in order to obtain a suitable leadership position—resulting in an unnecessary talent drain in the home university.

No matter what kind of enterprise you are leading, identifying and promoting top performers at all levels of the organization are key to leveraging the talent available and to keeping high-performing individuals engaged, fulfilled and motivated to remain with the organization.

PIPER:

One of the most significant, and unusual, appointments I ever made as a leader occurred in the 1980s when I was a dean at U of A. I was in desperate need of an associate dean, someone who could represent me and the faculty on campus, serve in my absence, chair committees and be my adviser and confidante. We were a small unit with a relatively limited number of players to choose from. For about a month, I would repeatedly review the list of faculty carefully, considering each person and then eliminating them for various reasons.

One night, I awoke with a start; it had come to me as I slept. The obvious candidate was staring me in the face, and I had overlooked him for the wrong reason. He was an outstanding scholar, an award-winning teacher, an able administrator, admired and respected by all, and he understood the culture and standards of the faculty and the university. Most of all, I liked him and knew I could work with him. Why had I rejected him for promotion before? Why had I consistently jumped over him and moved on to the next person?

His name was Jim Vargo, and he was a quadriplegic, and I had made the classic error of thinking he could not or would not be able to do the job physically; therefore, I had not previously given him serious consideration.

How wrong was that? I shook my head in disbelief that I had reached a conclusion for someone else based on my presumptions and inherent bias, rather than offering him the position after assessing him on his merit, as I would do with anyone else, and letting him make his own decision. The next morning I approached him and offered him the job. He accepted my invitation and was magnificent in this position, working with me throughout my entire deanship. That experience taught me to never second-guess what a candidate might do when given the opportunity to serve and to recognize the talent that is sometimes overlooked despite being right in front of me.

Too often, leaders assume an individual will not be able to do something—they are too old or too young, they will not relocate, their partner is not supportive, their kids are too young, they have parents who need looking after and so on—and they make the decision for them without providing them the freedom to determine their own fate. Is this a woman thing, or are male leaders just as likely to conclude, based on personal assumptions, that certain people either cannot or will not accept a position? I do not know. But I do know one thing. I continue to hear leaders and search consultants raise perceived issues and objections that in my mind should not even be considered, let alone discussed, when assessing candidates. In the end, the only standards for consideration of a candidate should be merit and qualifications; and the only person who should raise issues or objections over any opportunity is the candidate, not the person making the hire or appointment.

———

Women leaders are believed to have an additional responsibility in terms of assisting other women to advance, cultivating female colleagues who, for various reasons, might have been overlooked by male leaders. There are numerous anecdotal accounts of women leaders being resistant, or even standing in the way, when it comes to promoting women. Our experience suggests that the relationships between women leaders and aspiring women leaders can be complicated. Indeed, our own relationship and how it was fostered speak volumes not only about the important role women leaders can play in terms of encouraging talented women to seek leadership opportunities but also how personal feelings and emotions might come into play and even interfere with potential leadership opportunities.

PIPER:

When I arrived at UBC I had not met Indira in person, but I had already been introduced to her. Before leaving U of A, I attended a guest lecture delivered by one of UBC's most outstanding scholars, an international leader in the area of metallurgical engineering. Afterwards, I introduced myself and told him how much I was looking forward to joining UBC and working with him and his colleagues. Without missing a beat, he told me there was someone I should meet and keep my eye on—Indira Samarasekera. In his mind, Indira was a rising star, someone who not only was a remarkable scholar but also possessed all of the qualities of an outstanding leader. In short, he was her sponsor, and he was promoting her as a potential leader.

It was a conversation I did not forget. So, when I was recruiting for a new Vice-President, Research, and Indira applied, I perked up. Despite her lack of administrative experience, I saw something in her—a spark of genius, a commitment to excellence, a wide-ranging curiosity and a team player. I believed inherently I could work with her. She was clearly remarkable in every way and, on top of everything else, a woman; I felt she was someone who needed to be encouraged and supported to lead. While I knew I was taking a risk, her sponsor's advice and counsel rang in my ears.

I was not disappointed. Indira was the most amazing Vice-President, Research, UBC had had in decades—doubling our research funding, setting extremely high academic standards, establishing policies and procedures, advancing the humanities as well as the natural sciences and acting as a terrific advocate for research in the broader community. I knew I had picked a winner, and I saw "president" written all over her. I had clearly identified my successor, and I began to quietly work with her on her development, providing her with all the experiences she would require to assume the mantle of president at UBC.

But as life often demonstrates, best-laid plans go astray. Prior to my stepping down at UBC, the presidency at U of A became available and, not surprising, the U of A presidential search committee had their eyes on Indira. She was their obvious choice, for all the reasons I knew that she should be a university president. The only problem for me, and it was a major one, was that it was the wrong university.

I did everything in my power to dissuade her from leaving as I so wanted her to be the next UBC president. I was blinded to the fact that she had to go where there was an opening rather than waiting for an opportunity that was uncertain. I was hurt when Indira decided, rightfully, to leave UBC for U of A, and I experienced a major sense of personal rejection. How could she defy me when I had worked so hard to mentor her and prepare her for the UBC presidency? As a result of my selfish reaction, our relationship became tense and difficult. It was hard for me to celebrate her appointment, knowing deep down it was UBC's loss.

I now know that I was thinking only of myself and my own feelings of repudiation and disappointment. Instead of believing in her and celebrating her decision, I was wallowing in self-pity. Her decision to move to U of A was the right one, and I should have done everything in my power to support and assist her in that decision. Of course, she became a spectacular president, and over time I came to understand how unreasonable I had been. I began to watch her with pride, respect and admiration, cheering her on from the sidelines, knowing that U of A was so very fortunate to have her as their leader. In fact, when people would ask me what my legacy was after serving UBC, I would respond without hesitation, "Indira Samarasekera," claiming credit, as well as giving her her due, for her outstanding performance as U of A's president.

We began to reconnect; whenever she would visit Vancouver, we would meet to reestablish the friendship that had been put on hold during the early years of her presidency. Fortunately, Indira is generous of spirit and forgave my selfishness and despicable behavior, permitting me back into her life. As we explored our shared experiences, we acknowledged that all relationships go through difficult times, but enduring relationships prevail—as did ours.

SAMARASEKERA:

Being selected to take on the Vice-President, Research, role during Martha's presidency was an exhilarating career move that I never anticipated. I could not believe my good fortune when I was offered the position despite my lack of administrative experience. I will never forget my first day on the job when on my desk was a manila envelope from the president's office. When I opened it, I discovered a Harry Potter wand and a note in Martha's unmistakably elegant handwriting, which read, "Welcome to the team! Let's make magic."

My time as vice president was the best preparation for a presidency I could ever have had. Martha was an exceptional role model and a skillful mentor as she encouraged me continuously to raise our research performance, while offering advice when I needed it. She set the bar very high and was outcome-oriented, with an eye on excellence as measured by the standards of the leading universities in the world. As a leader, she did not believe in micromanaging, nor did she engage in hand-holding. She grew impatient if you came ill prepared for meetings or if the agenda item you had requested did not merit being discussed. And yet, she remained supportive and led by example, holding herself to the highest standards. Her warmth and keen mind made it a stimulating and enjoyable professional experience, requiring hard work and discipline.

My decision to apply for the presidency at the University of Alberta was one of the most difficult decisions of my life. I was torn, because I knew Martha very much wanted me to succeed her when she stepped down. However, I was becoming restless and found the possibility of moving and advancing a new institution tempting, especially since I had been at UBC for almost 30 years. Furthermore, there were no guarantees that I would be selected president of UBC when the job became available, and I even wondered whether a search committee would prefer an external candidate.

When I told Martha that I was going for the U of A interview, she tried to dissuade me from leaving and to convince me that I could make a great contribution to UBC if I stayed and became president. I felt sad that I was going against her wishes, especially since I was indebted to her for preparing me so well for a presidency. After my selection was announced, we had a tense few months planning for my exit. I knew she was very hurt by my decision, but I knew it was because she believed in me and wanted the very best for UBC. She provided a stellar reference to the U of A search committee and hosted several events to celebrate my departure. I was touched by her public support and magnanimity.

It took a few years to bridge the gulf that had grown between us. Looking back, I learned that close professional relationships, especially between leaders and their protégés, are never easy—particularly when the plans of the mentor are not realized because the mentee takes a different direction. However, our relationship was founded on a strong bond of mutual respect and genuine fondness that in time overcame that bump in the road on my leadership journey.

Recognition Is the Best Reward

Leaders spend a great deal of their time trying to motivate their employees to meet the strategic objectives of the organization. Consultants are hired to determine the appropriate pay grades, compensation packages and bonuses. Salary negotiations and terms of employment, including specific advancement policies focused on career progression, consume hours of the CEO's attention and focus. Employment contracts are revised to include as many non-salary benefits as possible, such as club memberships, car leases, supplementary pensions and insurance policies.

All of these components of compensation are clearly important in recognizing talent, rewarding outstanding performance and retaining top performers. They provide financial benefits but also validate an individual's standing in the organization and offer a perceived sense of fairness when they compare their compensation with that of their colleagues. No one would suggest that leaders should ignore compensation when assessing and retaining talent. But is compensation enough to acknowledge employees and motivate them to go the extra mile? Are there other critical components of a reward system that are as or more effective in encouraging innovation and a strong commitment to the organization?

In a 2015 study, Zarina Abdul Munir and colleagues suggest two forms of leadership, transactional and transformational, and propose that transactional leaders generally are associated with masculine characteristics such as power, competitiveness, authority and control. These leaders reward their followers when they perform specific tasks well and withhold rewards when the tasks are either not performed or performed poorly. Transformational leaders, on the other hand, are associated with more feminine characteristics, such as cooperation, collaboration, consultation and collective problem solving. These leaders tend to build relationships and generate results based upon these relationships. They inspire others to creatively invest in the culture and climate of an organization, thereby leading to a shared vision.

Whether women leaders truly are more transformational and male leaders more transactional, the real question is, "What motivates people to perform at their highest level?" This further raises questions around what reward systems are best aligned to today's work environment and culture, and how a particular leadership style might translate into a reward system that motivates specific actions and results.

PIPER:

I have spent countless hours negotiating contracts with new employees and determining the appropriate compensation packages for my direct reports, but I quickly learned that people who work with you want more than money. They want to be valued. They want to know that you, as their leader, think they are doing a good job. They want your attention and your recognition when they succeed. And they want to know that you care about them as individuals.

UBC is a large institution with over ten thousand employees, so it was not easy to know everyone or know what everyone was doing. But when I did learn about someone's achievements or efforts, I tried to take the time to recognize them. Every evening, I would take about 30 minutes to write to individuals who had distinguished themselves, acknowledging them, congratulating and thanking them. These were short notes— no more than three or four sentences—but they were handwritten. No emails, no form letters, no missives that my assistant had typed up. They represented me and were the closest thing to interacting personally with the individual.

To this day, no one has ever thanked me for their compensation package; but people still tell me they saved the note I wrote to them years ago. Who would have predicted the effect these notes had? So easy, so fundamental, so effective. In my mind, leaders often underestimate how important the personal touch is. I can tell you that of all the things I was known for, the handwritten notes became legendary. In my mind, they were instrumental in motivating people throughout the university not only to be committed to the institution but also to strive to be the best they could be.

Lessons Learned

In the end, the success of an organization is all about people. Leaders are largely responsible for assembling and promoting the people who can best work together to advance a common agenda. The tasks of talent recruitment and retention require the abilities to assess and evaluate performance and to motivate and inspire. These two aspects of talent development entail different skill sets and are critical to optimizing the performance of your people and of the organization.

Are women leaders better at talent management than their male counterparts? Current research suggests that women leaders do things differently and excel in areas such as building relationships, supporting others and motivating desired behaviors when compared with men at the same level. It is still unclear whether these differences significantly affect performance outcomes. Nevertheless, outstanding leaders understand that they cannot alone achieve their goals. They rightfully acknowledge that leaders lead by encouraging others to be the best they can be and, hence, are dependent upon others to move their organizations forward.

1. When assessing talent, recognize that past performance is the best predictor of future performance. Evaluate carefully each applicant's record of performance and attempt to identify the specific accomplishments the applicant has achieved over the course of their career.

2. Keep an open mind. Do not reach judgment too soon when evaluating candidates. Falling in love with the candidate before all the information is available can result in blind spots and lead you to the wrong conclusions.

3. When hiring from outside the organization, recognize that newcomers will require additional support in orienting to the culture and initiating change. The leader's assistance during the first year or so is critical in the eventual success of the new hire.

4. If you are certain that a candidate is the person you want, go the extra mile to recruit them. Making it clear that they are your choice can go a long way in convincing them to accept the position and join the organization.

5. If a person is no longer performing at the level you expect, find the nerve to cut your losses. Identify clearly the reasons for your decision and communicate them directly and honestly to the employee. The sooner you move on, the better.

6. Do not make assumptions about how employees will react to a career opportunity. How they view it in light of their personal circumstances should be their decision, not that of the person making the offer.

7. Recognize that building your team includes ensuring that the appropriate administrative support systems are in place, as well as identifying your executive team members. Be aware that team building is a continuous activity, as people are always coming and going.

8. The easy aspect of team building is identifying and recruiting the people. Motivating the team and keeping them focused on being the best they can be is more difficult. Think

about events, opportunities, occasions and circumstances that will facilitate the commitment of your team to one another and the achievement of mutual goals.

9. The best reward for outstanding performance involves personal recognition by the leader. Do not underestimate the power of a simple thank-you and the importance of including a personal touch in recognizing individuals. This applies to acknowledging people at all levels of the organization, not just the higher levels of management.

CHAPTER 8

Grit and grace: making things happen

"Grit and grace, together, can be formidable for women in the leadership game. They provide women with their own road map to success that allows for bold leadership combined with warmth. If you think of the combination of grit and grace as a recipe, grit would be the cake. Grace would be the icing."

—CARI HAUGHT COATS, *FORBES*

"If you want anything said, ask a man; if you want anything done, ask a woman."

—MARGARET THATCHER

Grit is what you do. Grace is how you do it. A simple yet exquisite way to capture the difference between female and male leaders. Women seem to have a knack for combining "firmness of mind or spirit: unyielding courage in the face of hardship or danger" (*grit*) with the "disposition to or an act or instance of kindness, courtesy, or clemency" (*grace*),[18] and it is the unique synthesis of these two qualities that often propels women to be in charge and to excel as leaders.[19]

Leaders are always challenged to act, to do. As a result of this expectation, they generally focus on the *what*, that is, what they should do as leaders. What are their priorities and strategy for the organization? What actions should be identified and accomplished? Hundreds of books have been written and consultancy groups have flourished to assist leaders in creating a strategic plan for the organization, with timetables for completion and accountability measures in place. This emphasis on action requires all the components of grit, including nerve, tenacity, focus, determination and discipline. It also requires hard work, keeping track of issues and goals and endless hours of *doing*.

Leaders, generally, are good at *grit*. Focused on results and high standards of performance, they have worked hard all of their lives, achieved milestone after milestone, climbed the ladder as required and impressed people with their ability to get things done. Grit is organizationally recognized and reinforced, and a fundamental prerequisite for career progression. Male and female leaders almost always have grit.

The attention to *how* one leads is less well emphasized and understood. Some call it style; others categorize it under the umbrella term of *management*; and certain folks describe it as "having the royal jelly," or a leader's executive presence—whatever that might mean to the beholders. Regardless, most would agree that how a leader leads is based on a personal quality that is often hard to accurately define or identify. Unlike *what* a leader does, which is measurable, *how* a leader leads remains largely an enigma.

As Cari Haught Coats so brilliantly notes in her *Forbes* article "Grit and Grace," the combination of grit, the *what* of leadership, with grace, the *how* of leadership, may be the secret weapon women bring to their leadership positions. Together, grit and grace provide the basis for strong, capable leadership combined with warmth, kindness and empathy—a powerful combination that may indeed explain and define women leaders who have distinguished themselves and led successfully.

We believe that grit or sheer determination has played a significant role in our efforts to make things happen at our respective institutions. We worked hard, sometimes perhaps too hard, to ensure that our strategic agendas moved forward. But we are also aware that our style of leadership differed from that of many of our male colleagues. Some might label it as consultative; others might find it to be collaborative; still others might define it as a "personal touch" or instilling a respectful environment. At the time, we were not acutely aware that we were leading in a manner that might be called graceful, but upon reflection we do think the term *grace* captures the essence of the unique style many women bring to their leadership. Is it effective? Can you accomplish more when you combine both grit and grace? These are two of the important questions we pondered when we reviewed our own leadership journeys. Where do we sit on this grit and grace continuum, where did we acquire the grit or nerve to lead and to persevere and what led us to discover our own sense of grace?

True Grit

Anyone who has watched the award-winning movie *True Grit* recognizes that the old, hardened, over-the-hill U.S. Marshal Rooster Cogburn has grit; indeed, he epitomizes the word and it defines his character—grizzled, tough and fearless. But it is wrong to assume that he is the person the movie title refers to. It is the 14-year-old girl, Mattie Ross, who truly exhibits the meaning of grit. Determined to find her father's murderer, she hires Cogburn and accompanies him on the journey, displaying cunning, nerve, strength, stubbornness and determination, to track down the killer and bring him to justice. True grit.

While this action-packed film is somewhat unbelievable, you can't help but wonder how did that young girl become so formidable? Were there certain circumstances in her childhood that prepared her for the fight of her life? In the end, she exhibited more grit than the men around her while retaining her own identity and sense of womanhood. What has built our grit over the years? What journeys have we taken or what events have we experienced that developed our own personal sense of grit—building our strength, will and nerve to face adversity, make controversial decisions and speak truth to power? While our stories do not hold a candle to Mattie Ross's, they do provide a glimpse into how life takes twists and turns that force us to decide whether we can dig deep and face our fears. Did these experiences prepare us for leadership? We believe so.

PIPER:

In 1973, we moved to Montreal from the United States when my husband accepted an academic appointment at McGill University. It was a time of political turbulence with the Parti Québécois in power and the introduction of significant French language legislation. I wanted to work as a physiotherapist, and as a pediatric specialist I first applied to Montreal Children's Hospital, an English institution, but there were no openings at the time. Desperate to work, I decided to apply to the French children's hospital, Hôpital Sainte-Justine. My French was limited, but I had worked diligently at learning the language and thought I could manage. I was wrong. In the end it was one of the hardest things I have ever done.

Every morning I would get on a bus in Westmount, the English-speaking part of the city, and settle in for the ride to the hospital. As the bus traversed the city, it moved through the predominantly anglophone neighborhoods and entered the French-speaking area of Montreal. Passengers would embark and disembark along the way until, by the time I reached the hospital, I was the sole English-speaking passenger. I came to dread the bus trip, as it foretold what the day would hold.

Working in French was doable, largely because I was treating infants and young children who required little if any verbal interaction. That is not to say it was easy. I spent hours every night writing my progress notes in French with a dictionary at my side. I avoided speaking with physicians over the phone, meeting them instead in person. I worked at communicating with parents and others by writing down in French all the points I wanted to make before conversing with them.

More difficult, in fact almost impossible, was the language barrier I faced when relating socially to my colleagues and coworkers. At the time, the separatist movement was alive and well, and the animosity of the francophone community towards anglophones was palpable. English was *not* to be spoken in the hospital, even with other anglophones; those who uttered even one word of English were shunned. I found myself isolated at lunch and during coffee breaks. I could not keep up with the conversations or the humor or anecdotes that were being discussed in the staff room. It were as if I did not exist. For the first time in my life I felt alone in a crowd of people. My ability to relate to others was cut off.

I dreaded every morning when I had to leave for work. Waiting for the bus, I was tempted to bolt, to go back home, to call in sick, to find any excuse to avoid going in. I constantly considered quitting, leaving the position, moving on; but I did not. Somehow, I dug deep and found the grit to stay, to fulfill my obligations and to see my work commitment through.

Did this experience prepare me to lead with grit? I am not sure, but early in my tenure at UBC I was similarly forced to find the nerve to stay in my job when there were calls for my resignation. Within the first months of my presidency, UBC played host to the international APEC meeting, a controversial decision agreed to by my predecessor and which I had inherited. The attendance of certain world leaders known to have committed human rights violations incited student protests, culminating in the infamous incident in which students who were lying in the road to prevent the leaders from leaving the campus were pepper sprayed by members of the RCMP. Thankfully, no one was injured, but the community was outraged at the treatment of the students, and I, as the president, was asked to account for how this could have happened. Worse, after only three months as president, the students were demanding that I resign over the incident.

Did I want to quit? At times, yes. I had been denied a honeymoon period and was being tested in a manner for which I was unprepared. I knew few if any people at the university and had little personal support as the leader. I felt alone dealing with, and being held accountable for, an issue not of my own making. How I reacted to this difficult situation would clearly set the tone of my presidency. I knew I had to stay, that I had to respond to the critics, that I had to demonstrate leadership, but it was not easy. Grit? Maybe. Clearly, my early experience working in that Montreal hospital gave me confidence that I had the strength to continue as long as I stood firm, did the best I could and stayed on the bus!

SAMARASEKERA:

Today, close to five hundred million tons of steel are produced worldwide using continuous casting, in which molten steel—at a temperature of 1,600 degrees Celsius—is poured into a copper mold. If the mold changed shape, it could cause cracking in the steel, and my doctoral thesis was aimed at addressing whether this was the case (notwithstanding the machine builders' assertion that the mold was rigid). Although the question was simple enough, it took me two and a half years to develop a computer program to demonstrate that continuous casting molds do indeed change shape during operation. I was exhilarated and thought all I had to do was to write up my thesis to obtain my doctorate.

"Not so fast," responded my supervisor when I approached him with my conclusive findings. He wanted experimental proof and asked me to go to a steel plant and make measurements. I was aghast, as this sounded like an impossible task. When I asked him whether I could take a technician along, he said that it was my doctorate and I should go alone, and he arranged for me to visit Stelco in Edmonton, Alberta, to conduct my experiment.

It is not an exaggeration when I say that I was petrified. I had spent years tinkering with a mainframe computer, conducting simulations but never doing any experimental work. My doctorate degree hung in the balance. After losing a few nights of sleep worrying, I had to get down to work and slaved away with the help of a technician to prepare for the trip and develop a sound experimental approach.

The flight to Edmonton and my time at the steel plant are seared in my memory. The fear and uncertainty were terrifying. What if the equipment I had chosen failed during measurement? What if the measurements revealed that the mold did not change shape after all, that the machine builders were right, and I was wrong? The trial was to be conducted over three days to enable me to collect enough information on a data recorder.

When I started the test, water began to leak out of the mold. I was in a panic and feared I would be asked to stop the test because if liquid steel and water come into contact there could be an explosion. With the help of one of the operators, I hastily managed to contain the leak. I could not work through the night, so I left my equipment gathering data. While I was gone, the operators on the night shift disconnected it, and I remember having to hunt it down in the morning. It was stressful being alone, and I was weary, the noise and dust exacerbating my exhaustion. An added inconvenience was that there were no women's washrooms anywhere close to where I was working as all the operators were men; I had to climb down three stories and head to the administration building just to use the bathroom. The thought of quitting was ever present, but what were my options? Give up my doctorate? Go back and try to convince my supervisor these measurements were not necessary? Or dig deep and persist? I carried on, sustained by grit that I did not know I had.

I am now convinced that grit develops when you are faced with a seemingly insurmountable challenge: a challenge that calls on all of your creative, emotional and intellectual resources; a challenge where the consequences of failure are very high; a challenge that serves as a prerequisite for growth and accomplishment. I discovered that molds change shape during casting, as my models had shown, which had a profound impact on steel quality and transformed how molds were operated worldwide.

Did my early experience prepare me to draw on grit to survive and lead in complex situations? I believe it did; it taught me to rely on creativity and determination when faced with the unknown and the chance of failure, as was the case early in my tenure as Vice-President, Research, at UBC. Tasked with significantly improving UBC's competitiveness in a new program to fund research infrastructure, I had to devise an entirely new process tailored to meeting the criteria and increasing our success rate. It was a major, daunting undertaking, and it took grit to meet with researchers to convince them to participate in a review process they had never experienced. It took grit to convince the academic leaders and the hospital research institutes that multidisciplinary collaboration and a 20-year vision for the research project were essential. It took grit to prepare the financial case, find matching funding and demonstrate the benefits to Canada. The consequences of failure were high. Not only was UBC's reputation at risk, but also in the balance was access to large financial resources to modernize and enhance our research infrastructure—equipment, laboratories and buildings. When the results were announced, UBC ranked number one in the country in attracting the most funding. The team effort had succeeded beyond my wildest expectations because we had collectively mustered the grit and creativity necessary to raise our game.

Amazing Grace

It's hard to think about "Amazing Grace" without conjuring up the image of President Obama breaking out in song during the eulogy at the funeral of Reverend Clementa Pinckney. The lyrics are well known and are often sung at funerals or memorials, emphasizing how grace can guide us and provide solace in times of sorrow and disappointment.

Grace can also guide leaders when they are confronted with adversity, controversy or conflict. Graceful leaders draw upon their empathy for others, their ability to consider divergent views and their willingness to compromise, as well as their compassion and personal vulnerability, when dealing with issues that tend to divide and distract.

Women leaders are said to be more likely than their male peers to exhibit grace under pressure. That is not to say there are not male leaders who are graceful—again, think of President Obama and his singing so openly at a funeral. But, by and large, women are more comfortable with showing concern for others, putting grudges aside to work cooperatively with their foes and acting in a caring, compassionate manner in circumstances that call for understanding and personal empathy. Perhaps more difficult to describe than grit, grace is something you feel rather than see, experience rather than do, respond to rather than react to. It is intangible, hard to clearly define and impossible to measure; but when you feel it you know it, and when you receive it you are moved.

Brené Brown in her famous TED Talk, "The Power of Vulnerability," underlines the importance of authenticity and truth as the key components of courage. She believes that being vulnerable, being open and honest with others about your failures and disappointments, is essential for leaders to garner support and trust. In many ways, what she labels as the power of vulnerability describes what others might define as grace or authentic leadership.

How did we as women leaders demonstrate grace or vulnerability in our leadership? How did we best combine it with grit to avoid letting it dominate and keep us from making difficult decisions? Can you be both strong and graceful? And does grace or vulnerability strengthen or weaken your leadership?

As women leaders, we have been told over and over again, stay firm, hide your emotions, keep a stiff upper lip and, whatever you do, don't disclose personal information or cry in public. We have been coached to be tough, to stifle all of the softness we might feel, to be more "male-like" as we lead. Are the rules now changing? Are people beginning to recognize that some of the tendencies women possess are now viewed as assets rather than liabilities? How do we interpret what we are currently hearing, and how do we manage our true grit with our amazing grace?

PIPER:

UBC is a unionized environment, making labor negotiations always challenging and stressful. To make matters even more contentious, the provincial government has wage controls in place and becomes the third party at the negotiating table, thereby reducing management's flexibility to meet labor's demands.

During a particularly difficult series of labor negotiations, there was a strike over what we viewed as an unreasonable demand from the unions— one of the first times UBC had experienced a work stoppage. Opinions on how we should resolve the conflict were numerous, and tempers were running high, with students, faculty and staff all taking sides. It was a difficult time for the university; my family even experienced veiled death threats and had to leave our home on campus and move into a hotel downtown.

I had little prior experience negotiating with unions and believed that the university was ineffective in the messaging of our point of view; how the administration was trying to balance the government's restrictions with its ability to meet the union demands was being lost in the background noise. Against the advice of our legal counsel, my chancellor and male colleagues, I decided to hold a campus-wide forum where I could answer the community's questions, communicate directly with employees, express my understanding of their concerns and outline the provincial constraints we were faced with. In short, I believed in the *grace* factor.

The union membership filled the hall with bullhorns, noisemakers and expletives; the atmosphere was tense and electric. At first, the questions were extremely hostile, focusing on my salary, the president's house and how unreasonable the university was being. However, as the discussion progressed, and I was able to stand firm but also express sympathy for the issues, as well as lay out the government constraints, I sensed the mood changing. Instead of being confrontational, I tried to listen carefully, to demonstrate empathy for the workforce and to express my gratitude for the important role all of the staff played in the university's mission. While it was clear to me that I would never change the mind of some of the employees, I could clearly see that a large portion of the crowd heard me, understood the dilemma we were facing in meeting their demands and, perhaps most important, respected me for speaking with them directly and addressing their concerns with honesty and compassion.

SAMARASEKERA:

When I became president of the University of Alberta, I decided to focus on building relationships in a few priority countries, India being one of them. My team and I chose to aim high, and we sought a meeting with the head of the Indian Institute of Technology (IIT) Bombay, one of India's preeminent institutions. I received a lukewarm reply indicating that the head of the university was not available, but if I so desired I could meet the director of international affairs. Clearly, U of A was not of interest to them. I have often wondered whether I would have taken this as a rebuff and declined the meeting if I had been a man. Instead, I accepted their offer.

The meeting started badly. They had rounded up a few disinterested academics to speak to me, and the director of international affairs kept leaving the meeting intermittently, claiming that he had important telephone calls. He returned at the end of the allocated hour and said that IIT Bombay had signed memorandums of understanding (MOUs) with many universities, which then gathered dust. As a result, they had decided that they would not enter into any new MOUs. If ever there were a door being slammed in my face, this was it. My instincts were to thank him as politely as I could and leave. However, I risked further rejection by offering an alternative. Was this a demonstration of nerve or vulnerability? I believe it was both. I said that I had identified India and IIT Bombay as a priority for U of A and was willing to partner with him to bring resources to the table that would benefit both our institutions. His demeanor changed; he suddenly became interested and suggested that we should meet with the head of the institution if I could stay a little longer.

As I reflect on that important moment, I realize that because I was prepared to listen and be rejected, I was able to turn the meeting around. Over the next several years, our joint efforts resulted in us attracting significant funding from the Canadian government for a Canada-India research center, IC-IMPACTS, bringing in as partners IIT Delhi, IIT Kharagpur, University of Toronto and UBC. Pradipta Banerji, the director of international affairs at IIT Bombay, with whom I forged the partnership, became a good friend. We visited one another over the years, spending many delightful evenings in Mumbai or Edmonton. We often recalled our first meeting and would laugh at the tenor of that encounter. Overcoming initial impressions of people you encounter and rising above obstacles requires grace. Grace to be vulnerable, grace to understand another's point of view and grace to engage with authenticity and courage.

The Vision Thing

Leaders are expected to develop and support a vision for the organization or department they are leading, such that all stakeholders are cognizant of the long-term goals and ambitions of the enterprise or unit. According to the *Global Executive Leadership Inventory*, developing a vision entails doing three things well: sensing opportunities and threats in the environment, setting strategic direction and inspiring constituents.[20] Visionary leaders do not just chart the course of the organization, they also bring along and motivate their respective communities.

How the vision is developed varies from leader to leader: some prefer to use consultants to assist in its crafting; others pronounce their own version of where the unit should be heading; some work with their governing board; others engage the entire community to assist in determining how the future should unfold. Regardless of the approach, grit is required to develop an ambitious vision, and grace is needed to listen to others and incorporate their input.

Do women leaders approach the vision thing differently than male leaders? In a study of 360-degree assessments collected by INSEAD over a five-year period, it was discovered that women surpassed men in most of the leadership dimensions measured, with one exception: women scored lower on "envisioning" or "the ability to recognize new opportunities and trends in the environment and develop a new strategic direction for the enterprise."[21]

A more in-depth analysis of why this difference might exist revealed one possible explanation: women may be equally visionary, but may approach visioning in a different manner. Women leaders tend to be collaborative and work extensively with others in forming their vision, thereby taking into account the input of various stakeholders and formulating a vision that is not viewed as the leader's alone, but rather is perceived as being the group's vision. As a result, women leaders may not always get the credit they deserve for being visionary.

A clear exception to that perception is Indra Nooyi, former CEO of PepsiCo, who is not only recognized as being visionary but also is viewed as a consultative and inclusive leader. Known for the vision she promoted at PepsiCo, "Performance with Purpose," she stands out as a clear model of a woman who went about the vision thing in her own way—working with others to formulate what she saw as the path to the future while putting her own stamp on what she wanted to see happen, developing a comprehensive, transformational vision that valued sustainability and contributed to a positive imprint on society and the environment. Her vision encompassed everything from reducing sugars, fat and salt in PepsiCo's products to respecting the environment and working to advance human rights.

Unlike many of her male colleagues, she not only engaged her community to help craft the vision but also served as a role model by pushing everyone in her organization, including even herself, to be better: ethically, productively and personally. The vision belonged to everyone, but she led the way through her actions and the decisions she made every day. While clearly Nooyi is seen as a visionary leader, she is also recognized for bringing a different approach to setting and directing a large organization's vision.[22]

What was our experience when crafting the vision for our respective institutions? Did we bring our own style to the task, and if so, was it different than that of our male peers? Was the vision widely adopted by the academic community and seen as a collective vision or was it perceived to be the leader's alone?

PIPER:

Before assuming the UBC presidency, I had thought a great deal about what the future of the university should look like and had outlined some of my aspirations in my installation address. However, I quickly realized that the vision for a large diverse organization, such as a university, must reflect the views of the community in question rather than solely those of the leader. As such, I established an extensive consultative process which included listening sessions, workshops, visits to corporate leaders, board retreats and surveys of faculty, students and alumni. In addition, I held a major town hall meeting where all the stakeholders were invited to discuss what the future goals for the university should be.

In that town hall meeting, one of our leading scholars stood up and angrily addressed me: "You think we need a vision? We do not need a vision, we need money. Don't you understand—we don't even have chalk for our blackboards! Why are you spending time crafting a vision when you should be demanding the government provide us with more financial support?"

It was as if I had been hit by a truck. I had made the classic error of assuming that the community understood the need for a vision, that they realized our future depended upon us being clear about where we were going and how we would get there. How wrong I had been. I had moved too quickly and had erred by not laying the groundwork by first explaining the rationale for a vision—without that, all my efforts to bring the community along would be unsuccessful.

I listened intently to the scholar's complaints and concerns, trying to comprehend his sense of frustration and despair. The university had suffered severe financial cuts and was reeling with low morale and a sense of being devalued. I slowly caught my breath and said something like this: "I understand what you have been experiencing and how difficult things have been. But if you think we can succeed in convincing the government or the taxpaying public to provide us with more support without a vision of where we are headed, you are wrong. The only way we will succeed in garnering that support is to clearly and convincingly outline why they need to provide us with additional resources and what they will get in return for their increased investment."

Was I convincing in my argument for the need for a vision? I have never been certain whether that specific scholar eventually agreed with me, but that interaction allowed me to slow the process down; I concentrated first on laying out the rationale for a vision and then gradually proceeded to listen carefully to what others had to say—their disappointments, their frustrations and their desires. Only after people had been able to vent a bit, to tell me all that was wrong and what they wanted to achieve, were we able to move ahead with the visioning exercise.

By engaging in a lengthy consultative process and incorporating many of the community's suggestions, I learned a great deal about the culture, the people, the strengths and weaknesses and the provincial constraints and demands. The strategic ideas and initiatives for the final vision came not only from the academic core, but from every corner of the university, including support staff and administrators. One of the best examples of a key contribution came from my Vice-President, Finance and Administration, the only VP at the time who was not an academic. In one meeting of the executive team where we were struggling with the wording of the vision, he said something like this: "Every time I look at the vision statement, I think there is something missing. Nowhere in it is the word *students*. How can we have a vision statement without including *students*?" Thanks to the only non-academic member of my team speaking up, we recrafted the vision statement to include the most important word. I was forever grateful to him for reminding us what we were about and for helping us to craft the statement in a manner that reflected our fundamental values.

Because of the collaborative approach I took, I might not have been viewed as a visionary leader; however, I firmly believe that in the end, what we crafted was clearly not only different than the vision I had originally contemplated when joining UBC but also stronger for having been created together.

Partners

All leaders need help accomplishing their goals. Such aid comes in many forms, including their executive teams, their associates and senior advisers. But in addition to these formal reporting relationships and strategic appointments, leaders almost always identify and nurture special relationships with key partners: individuals who at first may not be known to the leader, but who over time appear on the external landscape and play a unique role in advancing the leader's agenda— corporate CEOs, government officials, alumni and thought leaders, to name a few.

While numerous books have been written about the key components of team building and recruiting senior people into the organization, few references cite the importance of those individuals who often go unnoticed in assisting a leader to achieve their objectives. These partners are unofficial, rarely receive the attention or credit they deserve, are often unknown in or unseen by the community and have no accountability within the organization. They play their roles behind the scenes and often are instrumental in opening doors to other opportunities or people whom the leader could not typically access.

How then do leaders identify these partners? What do they need to do to cultivate their assistance, and how do they continue to build the support and trust of these key individuals? It is clear to both of us that partners were essential in moving our organizations forward, in allowing us to access strategic events and people, and in ensuring our voice was raised where it needed to be heard. Key partners are critical in helping leaders do their job and accomplishing those things that without their assistance would be unattainable. These partnerships are nothing more than special relationships, built upon trust and respect and, perhaps in some cases, friendship. As with any special relationship, they require personal time to develop and sustain, giving as well as getting. For these reasons, women, who are known for relationship building, may, indeed, be better than their male peers at building and maintaining key partnerships over time that pay off in the long run.

SAMARASEKERA:

One of the most difficult aspects of being a university president is fundraising, or advancement as it is now called. Although I had no experience in asking people for money, my board was expecting me to deliver some quick wins while I was putting in place an effective organization for building alumni relations and fundraising.

Around the time I became president, a wealthy Hong Kong businessman, Mr. Li Ka-shing, had made a large gift from the Li Ka Shing Foundation (Canada) to a hospital research institute in Toronto. Because Mr. Li owned a significant percentage of an oil company in Alberta, I was hoping that he could also be persuaded to make a sizable gift to U of A. But how could I get to him without any direct connections?

I got nowhere when I met with the CEO of the Canadian bank where the funding for the Li Ka Shing Foundation was being held, other than learning that Mr. Li's priorities were health and education. Then a door to Mr. Li opened. Through one of our leading researchers and his contact in Hong Kong, I learned that the individual who oversaw Mr. Li's philanthropic ventures was Ms. Solina Chau. Although securing a meeting with Ms. Chau was generally very difficult, we gathered intelligence and then made the overture. I was delighted when she agreed to meet me in Hong Kong over lunch. It was an enjoyable meeting, and I sensed a rapport quickly developing between us. While I had reams of material on U of A's health research strengths, rather than present these, I decided to listen to her intently and gain as much insight as I could about the priorities of the foundation. The meeting was fruitful, and I was elated when she agreed to visit U of A on her next trip to North America. Needless to say, we prepared assiduously for her visit, based on all the insights I had gathered during lunch.

Our efforts paid off, and following her visit she invited us to submit a proposal; after several rounds of discussion the gift was secured. The Li Ka Shing Institute of Virology was born, and a building on the U of A campus was to be named in Mr. Li's honor. I flew to Hong Kong a few months later to meet Mr. Li and thank him for the gift, one of the high points of my presidency.

This gift from Mr. Li, along with a contribution from the government of Alberta and a Canada Excellence Research Chair, enabled us to recruit Dr. Michael Houghton to the University of Alberta in 2010. Dr. Houghton had discovered the hepatitis C virus, and Dr. Lorne Tyrell, an internationally renowned fellow virologist at U of A, advised me that Dr. Houghton could win the Nobel Prize. A decade later, on the morning of October 5, 2020, I learned that Dr. Houghton had done just that—won the Nobel Prize in Physiology or Medicine. While a U of A alumnus, Dr. Richard Taylor, a professor at Stanford, had previously been awarded a Nobel Prize in physics, this was the first time a U of A faculty member had been so honored. I was over the moon. The Li Ka Shing gift to the University of Alberta was a result of the partnership I forged with Ms. Chau, an alignment between the goals of the foundation, the research strengths of the university and our common interest in women in leadership. The right partners can move mountains.

I spent a great deal of my time lobbying the federal government, the primary funder of university research. Because UBC was a major research university, the level of federal government support was key to our overall performance, and I spent endless hours in Ottawa meeting with key officials and ministers trying to make the case for this or that idea or research project. Progress was slow and sporadic with few tangible examples where I could state clearly that my efforts had paid off.

Then one day, it was suggested that I meet with Eddie Goldenberg, senior policy advisor to the prime minister. It was to be a perfunctory get-to-know-you meeting, but in fact it turned out to be one of the most important meetings I would ever have in Ottawa. From the start, it became apparent that Mr. Goldenberg was the key person who advised the PM—the person the PM listened to, the person who was responsible for many of the government's major decisions. It was then that things began to happen.

Upon reflection, I think there were three factors that made this partnership so very significant. First, I had determined who the key person was in terms of decision-making, clearly focusing my efforts. Second, I cultivated the relationship, traveling across the country to meet personally with him as often as I could, calling upon him for advice and counsel, relying on him to assist me in framing my requests in a way that would meet the government's agenda. And third, and probably most important, there was a real chemistry in the relationship. We enjoyed each other's company, had the same sense of humor, saw the world in the same way and shared a passionate desire to make a difference in terms of the role universities played in the country's future. In short, we were like-minded and enjoyed our time together—a key feature in identifying partners who can assist you in making things happen.

Who's the Boss?

Every leader has a boss. Leaders are hired by, report to and can be let go by the boss, whether it be a governing board, a superior, an owner or even a family member. Knowing who the boss is, what they value and how they govern are essential components of the success of any leader. The underlying cause of many failed leaders is the inability to acknowledge the boss's key role and not spending enough time to earn their ongoing confidence and support.

Complicating this relationship can be the leader's view that she is "right" even when the boss believes differently. Regardless of the facts that may or may not support the leader's position, leaders are well-advised to accept the sometimes-unfair conclusion that the boss is always right; when the chips are down, the boss will always win. However unjust this may seem, rarely do leaders prevail when the boss is determined to undermine their leadership.

How then do gender differences affect this leader/boss relationship? Is there a different standard of performance that a boss requires of a female versus a male leader? Are women more likely to be dismissed from their leadership positions than men who have committed the same transgressions? Or are women more likely to understand and negotiate the leader/boss dynamic because they tend to be more intuitive and relationship-oriented? Little research is available to adequately answer these questions, but anecdotal evidence suggests there may be gender differences. For example, the boss of an organization is more likely to be male than female, given the history of power and male dominance in leadership positions; hence, women leaders will often have male bosses. Governing boards have traditionally had more male members than female; similarly, the chair of the board is more likely to be a man than a woman. As well, male leaders are more likely to belong to the same networks as their bosses. It is not uncommon for the male board chair to play golf and socialize with the male CEO of the company, providing the leader more opportunities to discuss issues informally with the boss and establish personal relationships. The male leader likely has a greater chance of succeeding in the role as a result of this social access and informal counsel; and even if there are performance issues, the termination of the leader is less likely when the chair of the board has social ties with the leader. According to a recent study, when things do go wrong with a woman in charge, it's been demonstrated that women are actually less likely than men to get a second chance when they fail.[23]

What then can we conclude from these observations? Women leaders, especially those who do not have the benefit of extensive networks with their bosses, need to focus early in their tenure on developing strong relationships with the person or people they answer to, seeking out opportunities to informally consult on and inform them of the issues at hand. No boss likes surprises; hence, effective and ongoing communication is essential in developing a positive relationship between the leader and her boss. Understanding that the boss has the final say goes a long way in informing the ongoing interactions between the two individuals. In all, it is not unreasonable to presume that women leaders, especially those who inherit a male governing culture, are well-advised to seriously attend to who their boss is and aim to work effectively with them to obtain their support even during difficult times.

SAMARASEKERA:

One of the first things I learned as president was that my "boss" was the Board of Governors of the university. I knew from others' past experiences that if a president loses the support of their board, they most likely will not survive. Unlike many corporate boards that are made up of "independent" directors, a university's board comprises government appointees, faculty members, staff, students and alumni, all of whom have agendas specific to the constituency they represent. As a result, it becomes a difficult balancing act for any president to enact the strategic goals of the university, while maintaining the support of the various members of the board. Such was my challenge in 2013.

After being assured of stable government funding over a three-year period, including a 2 percent cost of living increase, we received a bombshell. With no prior warning, we were informed that the Alberta government was reducing all of the universities' operating budgets by 7 percent, resulting in a cut of $43 million for U of A. It was catastrophic news. Because the university is not permitted to run deficits, we would have to achieve significant budget reductions within weeks. There was dismay and outrage across the campus, as it was evident that we would have to lay off up to seven hundred people in order to balance our budget.

I was determined that we were not going to act precipitously. With support from the Board of Governors, especially the chair, I made an appeal to the government to allow us to take the reductions over three years, balancing our budget in 2015. I was also convinced that I could reverse some of the reductions if I had time, and so we began asking the deans to plan for a range of budget reductions. To communicate our efforts to the campus community, we launched a blog entitled "Change at U Alberta," so that everyone could keep track of the progress we were making to grapple with the budget reduction.

While we were hard at work, blogs were sprouting up across campus, criticizing me and the administration for not having done enough to prevent the budget reduction. The final straw was when a university-appointed male member of the Board of Governors, in essence one of my "bosses," submitted a public report to the board, stating that morale had never been lower in the university, thus intimating that my leadership was inept. I wondered at the time whether gender was an issue; that is, would he have been so bold to openly criticize a male president for "low morale" on the campus? Nevertheless, it was clear; he was publicly communicating a lack of confidence in my leadership.

Knowing how important it was to have the confidence of the board in order to continue to lead and being keenly aware that the boss always prevails, I knew that I had to determine once and for all if I had the full support of the board in order to move ahead with the plans for budget reductions. I was frustrated but aware that I had no alternative. Gathering all the nerve I had, I approached the chair before the board meeting and told him that I would lay out the strategy for dealing with the budget reductions and then would leave the meeting so that he could ascertain whether or not there was unanimous board approval for the strategy. While I do not like to deliver ultimatums, I had no choice, and continued by informing him that if I did not have the unanimous support of the board, I would resign effective immediately so that they could appoint an interim president. The board was my boss and as such I needed their full support. Failing that, it would be better for the institution if I resigned, so they could select a leader they had confidence in.

I suspect the meeting was tense. The board chair came to see me after what seemed like an eternity to assure me of the unanimous support of the board for my leadership. It was a pivotal moment for me as a leader. As difficult as it was for me to put my presidency on the line, I understood inherently that without the support of your boss you cannot legitimately lead. Once the support of the board was secured, we moved forward with our budget strategy without the constant threat of mutiny.

This difficult experience taught me that any leader must be assured of the support of their boss, especially when times are tough and when difficult decisions must be made. It was not an easy lesson to learn, and I had to dig deep to find the nerve to ask the boss the question, "Do I have your support?" Without a clear answer to that question, I knew that I would no longer have the mandate to lead and, hence, would not be able to move the institution forward during the turbulent times we were facing.

Lessons Learned

Women leaders are increasingly being acknowledged as having two important traits—grit and grace—that complement each other in terms of making things happen in their organizations. For that reason, women are well-advised to review how they have developed, or can further develop, both of these skills and how well they are able to combine them effectively in making difficult decisions and executing controversial actions. Within this framework of "making things happen," taking decisive action is, of course, necessary; but leaders also need to recognize the importance of charting the course of their organization by crafting a vision that is inclusive and inspiring. As well, developing strategic relationships with partners outside of the organization is often critical in terms of opening doors to individuals you might otherwise be unable to access and in promoting your goals and objectives. Acknowledging that you have a boss to whom you are accountable and cultivating their ongoing support are key to strengthening your leadership position and to moving your organization forward.

1. Review the tough decisions you have had to make in the past and the difficult situations you have encountered along your career path, where you have had to dig deep and call upon your grit to see you through. By recollecting these experiences, you will gain confidence that you have the nerve to lead.

2. Do you have grace when confronted with conflict and difficult situations? Are you able to listen to the contrary side of an argument without getting angry and defensive? Are you empathetic to others' situations? Are you prepared to be

vulnerable and expose your human side to your constituents? By exhibiting grace in the face of adversity, you will earn support for your leadership.

3. When facing adverse situations or making difficult decisions, attempt to combine your grit with your grace. While calling upon your strength and determination to do the difficult things, also draw upon your empathy and compassion to ensure that others are acknowledged, that their issues are recognized and that they are treated fairly.

4. When crafting a vision for your organization, listen carefully to the members of your community in terms of their values, their concerns and their vision for the future. By coupling your own ideas of where you want the organization to be with those of the broader community you serve, you are more likely to develop an inspirational and achievable vision.

5. Be aware that you will need help from people outside of the organization to advance your goals. Strategic partners will appear when you least expect them; by recognizing the significant role these partners may play in assisting you, and by cultivating an ongoing relationship with them, you will be more likely to make things happen.

6. Acknowledge you have a boss—the person or persons you report to and to whom you are accountable. This boss should never be taken for granted or ignored. You are more likely to retain the support of the boss by communicating regularly with them, ensuring they are well briefed on all of the key issues you are facing and seeking their advice and counsel. Even when you are right, and the boss is wrong, recognize that the boss will almost always prevail.

CHAPTER 9

What could possibly go wrong?

"A woman is like a tea bag—you never know how strong she is until she gets in hot water."

—ELEANOR ROOSEVELT

At some point in their tenure, all leaders will encounter rough waters. How a leader responds to a crisis often represents a defining moment in their leadership, highlighting both their strengths and weaknesses, while also determining the fate of their organization, at least in the short-term. Crisis management, as it is known, is an inexact science requiring leaders to make choices between imperfect solutions, many times with limited data and constrained resources. Every leader will face the inevitable challenge of having to take charge of a situation that is difficult and unpredictable, with potentially devastating consequences. What could possibly go wrong?

How well do women leaders handle crises? Do they manage a crisis differently than their male colleagues? And, what contributes to successful crisis management? Despite the often-held perception that women negotiate poorly, lack confidence and are too risk-averse, research from 2020 by Grounds and Haffert suggests just the opposite. They believe that women possess three significant leadership attributes that position them to excel at crisis management: being risk aware, prioritizing safety and looking at the whole picture. They emphasize brain research that suggests women process information differently than men by using both the logical and intuitive parts of their brains to formulate interconnected decisions. Men, on the other hand, tend to be more targeted and single-minded in resolving issues. Women are more open to taking in all the factors associated with the issue at hand, resulting in solutions that address the range of complexities accompanying the crisis.

As university presidents, we both dealt with our share of major disruptions—everything from labor strikes, to student protests, controversial academic issues and personnel decisions—most of which were not of our making but, like any crisis, appeared without notice and required 150 percent of our attention. We learned quickly that no leader is immune to crises, that leaders often do not initially give the crisis the attention it deserves, hoping that it will just go away, and that leading at the time of a crisis is a lonely affair.

Did we manage our respective crises differently than a male leader would have? One will never know for sure, as each crisis has its own characteristics and presents itself in a different time in the organization's trajectory. We do, however, believe that we brought to our decision-making certain leadership traits that distinguished our presidencies from those of our male colleagues and had us approaching the problem in a different way. If we were to summarize these competencies, they would include such things as listening to various inputs, having the nerve to make principled decisions and maintaining open communication. How those approaches affected the long-term impact of the crisis is unknown. And while we observe that some male leaders also demonstrate these abilities, we maintain that women leaders are more than capable of managing crises in a thoughtful, deliberate, effective and purposeful manner.

Detecting Ripples, Riding Waves

When a crisis first appears, the initial reaction of many leaders is to either ignore it completely or underestimate the scope of the problem. Because most crises are unexpected, their appearance is neither welcomed nor believed. How could this have happened? Why now? What is the basis of the problem? Leaders who are not solely or directly responsible for the specific predicament are also prone to sticking their heads in the sand and hoping that somehow the issue will magically disappear.

But you can only be in denial so long before the ripples become waves, and the crisis can no longer be ignored or dismissed. By ignoring the dilemma or by delaying your response to it, the situation is given room to grow, making the eventual management of the problem—of potentially greater magnitude—much more difficult. When a leader refuses to acknowledge a crisis, they risk giving up control and compromise their ability to effectively resolve the issue.

As perpetual optimists, we both admit that we were prone to dismiss the ripples. We were often slow in confronting the problem, in acknowledging that it existed and accepting that it was serious. Why was this? Were we unwilling to believe that something awful was happening—that bad things do happen to otherwise good institutions? Or were we prone to taking the crisis personally, thinking that we were at fault in some way and that the situation could have been prevented? Or were we just scared and frightened to confront reality? Who knows ... but one thing is certain: crises do not magically disappear. They do happen and, generally, no one is at fault. Most important, the sooner one recognizes the ripples for what they are, the better they will be able to ride the waves.

PIPER:

Early one morning in October 2001, I arrived in my office and found my chief legal counsel and head of public affairs waiting for me. Not a good sign. One of UBC's scholars had just delivered a speech addressing the September 11 attacks. This speech—which essentially rejected the commonly held assumptions surrounding the attack as an act of terrorism and instead linked the attack to American foreign policy—was unleashing a firestorm of controversy. The phones were ringing off the hook. How could such an "anti-American view" be tolerated by UBC? What were we going to do to discipline the scholar for such an outrageous speech? Why wasn't UBC firing this professor?

At first, I was calm. What was the fuss about? While the speech might have been untimely, didn't she have the right to express her opinion? Since when did universities silence or discipline their professors for making controversial speeches? Was not informed debate a necessary component of academic freedom? I was certain that this was a clear case of free speech, and that any reasonable person would also view it through that lens. While my advisers tended to agree with me, I sensed they thought I was underestimating the seriousness of the crisis we were facing. And yet, I still resisted reacting to these early ripples.

On counsel's advice, we agreed to get a copy of the speech and have it reviewed by several independent lawyers to determine if it was deemed to be hate speech. All of them concluded that it was not, and, in my opinion, the issue was closed. She had the right to say what she had.

While I might have been *legally* correct in my assessment, I was completely flawed in my perception that this was not a major issue. It was in fact a full-blown crisis—one of the most difficult I would face as president. I had underestimated the sensitivities that such a speech would arouse, how raw people's nerves were following 9/11 and how few people would understand that academic freedom permits controversial opinions to be openly expressed by professors without retribution. Over the course of several days, I received calls for the professor's dismissal from the highest levels of government, my own board members and, most astonishing, members of my senior team and respected faculty members. And then there were the alumni and donors who threatened to withdraw their donations if I did not act swiftly to terminate the professor. The media were unrelenting—opinion pieces decrying and misquoting the speech, publishing misleading facts about the professor and calling me to speak out for the university and reject her point of view. In addition, my email server crashed with thousands of messages from all around the world, requesting that she be fired as well as targeting veiled death threats against her and me.

As with many leaders in the midst of a crisis, I found myself alone. I was feeling not only isolated but also discouraged and confused. I began to realize that I had underestimated the scope of the issue, and by downplaying it I had lost valuable time in responding and controlling the message. But what proved to be the most difficult issue for me was my fervent belief that this crisis should not be a crisis at all; that regardless of what I or others thought of the professor's opinion, she had the right to express it and, hence, my role was to defend that right. Full stop.

What I failed to see was that most people did not agree with my view—and that difference in perception precipitated the crisis. The crisis was not the speech itself; rather, the crisis was my inability to convince people of my principled decision to defend the professor's right to deliver the speech, regardless of what I personally thought of its content. That what I thought of the speech itself was, in fact, irrelevant.

In the end, I stuck to my guns and worked tirelessly to try to garner support for my position. I do not believe for a moment that I was effective in changing people's minds during the heat of the debate. But I do know two things. Over time the uproar subsided, and the only way I managed to navigate my way through this very stressful period was in having the nerve to base my actions on the principles I held. It would have been easy to have been swayed to make the wrong decision if I had not been so grounded by the core university tenet of academic freedom. But I also know that I was naive in believing that such a principle would be clearly understood and accepted by the public when an idea they vehemently disagreed with was being debated; a perfect example of me not acknowledging the early ripples that quickly became major waves.

In the Arena

"It is not the critic who counts; not the man who points out how the strong man stumbles, or where the doer of deeds could have done them better. The credit belongs to the man who is actually in the arena, whose face is marred by dust and sweat and blood; who strives valiantly; who errs, who comes short again and again [. . .] who spends himself in a worthy cause; who at the best knows in the end the triumph of high achievement, and who at the worst, if he fails, at least fails while daring greatly, so that his place shall never be with those cold and timid souls who neither know victory nor defeat."

—THEODORE ROOSEVELT, "CITIZENSHIP IN A REPUBLIC"

Leadership is all about being in the arena. Day after day, getting out of bed, putting your shoes on and stepping into the fray. And leadership is all about hearing from and receiving critiques from people who have never been nor ever will be in the role. It is always easy to be in the opposition, to opine on every issue, to criticize every action, while never having to be accountable for the impact of your decisions or actions. Monday-morning, armchair quarterbacks. Individuals who always have an opinion about what a leader has done or said, but who have never led anyone or anything themselves nor been responsible for acting on their judgment.

Brené Brown, in her book *Daring Greatly: How the Courage to Be Vulnerable Transforms the Way We Live, Love, Parent, and Lead*, states that being in the arena is why leaders find being vulnerable such a hard thing to do. Exposing yourself to criticism requires courage and honesty, thereby invoking vulnerability. It is not easy. As she notes, "When we spend our lives waiting until we're perfect or bulletproof before we walk into the arena, we ultimately sacrifice relationships and opportunities that may not be recoverable." In her view, leadership requires the nerve to discount the criticism that comes freely from individuals who have never stepped into the arena, and to embrace instead the support, advice and encouragement from those who have been there and experienced leadership first hand. She continues by noting, "I carry a small sheet of paper in my wallet that has written on it the names of people whose opinions matter to me."

As women leaders who have been in the arena, we find Brown's advice not only accurate but also surprisingly simple. As a leader, your actions and decisions will always be fair game for the people sitting in the wings, who readily suggest that they would do it differently, but never, ever accept the responsibility of a leadership role. That is a given. The simple part of her advice is the recommendation that as a leader you need to identify those individuals who have been in the arena, whose opinions you respect and who inherently understand the complexity of the issues you are facing. Seek out people who are either in or have been in the arena; listen to their advice and counsel; respect their points of view; at the same time, realize that all the other critics are white noise, only blurring the landscape rather than serving as legitimate judges. By so doing, you will inevitably find the support you need to withstand the criticism of those who at no time have ventured into the arena.

Never is this more important than when a leader is confronting a crisis. Crisis management, by definition, involves conflict, controversy and difficult decisions that almost always require the full engagement of the leader. Often people close to the leader, such as members of the executive team, quietly disappear and run for cover, ensuring they are nowhere to be found. Associates and friends who have traditionally supported the leader when things were going well take to the hills, afraid of becoming embroiled in controversy. Exacerbating the situation, people to whom the leader is accountable are quick to demand a solution, reserving their judgment until the crisis is resolved. In short, the leader is in the hot seat—alone, with only their own resources, values and experience to rely upon.

How then does a woman leader manage when a crisis strikes? Who do they turn to for assistance when managing crises, recognizing that people close to the problem may be the least able to extricate themselves from the issue to offer clear, insightful and helpful advice? We believe crisis management both tests a leader and represents one of the loneliest times that they will experience. Never is it more important for a leader to identify those individuals who have weathered similar experiences, who have been in the arena themselves, to help guide and advise them when they are dealing with big issues. By doing so they will not only be better informed as to how to manage the crisis but also understand that others who have gone before them have faced similar situations.

SAMARASEKERA:

Universities grant honorary degrees to distinguished leaders, thinkers and scholars from all fields and all walks of life in recognition of extraordinary contributions. The degree is awarded at a convocation ceremony at which the recipient delivers an inspiring address. The University of Alberta, like all universities, has a well-established process for selecting individuals from a pool of nominees.

One rarely expects intense criticism when awarding honorary degrees, but it is not uncommon for groups of academics, students, members of the community or alumni to object to particular individuals. I was faced with such a situation and remember it well because of how it escalated into a full-blown crisis with the potential to embarrass the individual and cause reputational harm to the university.

The degree recipient was a retired CEO and board chair of a major international firm in the food and beverage business. He was also an active member of the World Economic Forum board, where he was coordinating a global effort to raise awareness on water scarcity and the need to develop sound policy on water resource management. Once news of the decision to award him an honorary degree was made public, several academics in the university began a campaign to revoke the decision because they objected to business practices of the company he had led. The faculty members pointed out that the company had been reprimanded in the early 1970s for selling baby formula in third world countries, making it easier for mothers to abandon breastfeeding. The second complaint was that the company sold bottled water, which they claimed exacerbated water scarcity in parts of the world while the company profited.

I knew that I was between a rock and a hard place. My initial reaction was to defend the decision by pointing to the robust process undertaken by the university to ensure that high standards were maintained in the selection and the individual was being recognized for his efforts in water conservation. But the efforts to discredit the individual grew and soon the media, NGOs and others began to take up the cause. I received numerous emails and phone calls demanding that I do something.

While I did not have the authority to reverse the decision, I could have requested that the chancellor reconvene the committee. I was also hearing from board members who were not happy with the media coverage. I heard only from those who opposed the decision, not the silent majority who either did not object or supported the choice. I felt alone in the arena.

What was I to do? I agonized over the approach. Would a male president have struggled as I did? I asked myself, "Should we allow the opinion of several academics to dissuade us from awarding an honorary degree to an individual whose leadership and accomplishments were worthy of recognition? What about the NGOs and other public groups who opposed the practices of certain corporations? Should we as a public university be responsive to these concerns? How much responsibility does the CEO of a major corporation bear for past actions of the company?" All legitimate concerns, but there was an important principle at stake. The candidate had been considered fairly and squarely on the merits of the nomination, and revoking the degree would compromise our commitment to due process. It would tarnish the university's integrity and reputation. As lonely as I was, I found the nerve to stand firm and take the heat despite feeling very vulnerable. *Being in the arena* took on very real meaning.

The intensity of the opposition grew, and it was clear to me that several academics were planning to storm the convocation in protest. In the middle of a crisis, it is essential that one seek support and counsel from individuals in the arena. There were several university presidents who had faced similar situations, and I drew from their experience. I also sought the counsel of those in the arena with me—my chief of staff, the provost and the Vice-President, University Relations. The chief of staff stepped up to help me manage the crisis, responding to every single email and listening to irate callers who were important stakeholders. The provost also rose to the occasion, calming the deans and the numerous heads of departments. The Vice-President, University Relations, and her team monitored all the media channels, ensuring I met with the media to counter the negative publicity.

To the chancellor's credit, she offered her full support and assured me that she would manage the protests should they occur during convocation. Several academics who opposed the awarding of the degree attended the ceremony and in the middle of the event, stood up, turned their backs to the honorees on stage and chanted "shame, shame, shame," at which point the chancellor politely reminded them that convocation was an important tradition that required respect and decorum and requested that they leave. I was very grateful to her for taking the heat with me in the end.

Being in the arena tests one's nerve to the core. There is no easy path, as there is a price to be paid irrespective of the decision. Even when the leader thinks she is defending a fundamental principle, not everyone agrees and many don't think it is worth the cost. Others want the leader to act expeditiously and don't always understand the complexity of the issues, as they have never been in the arena themselves. And yet, a leader is expected to exercise judgment, considering all sides of the issue, and make the best decision.

Me Too

While the Me Too movement is a relatively new phenomenon, the issues it addresses have always existed. This new focus, however, has highlighted how things can go horribly wrong for women who are sexually harassed and assaulted and has encouraged women to come forward to openly discuss and acknowledge the pain they have experienced.

Women leaders are no different. Many of them have encountered sexual harassment of varying degrees as they have advanced their careers, competed with male colleagues for leadership positions and confronted power imbalances. Despite all of the measures that have been put in place over the past several decades—including ombudsmen, sexual harassment officers and diversity and inclusion policies—women still face unwelcome situations in work environments. In addition, women continue to be accused of using their sexuality to advance their careers—that is, sleeping their way to the top—with the unspoken suggestion being that the only way a woman can be promoted in a male-dominated environment is to promote or succumb to sexual overtures from male colleagues and bosses.

We unfortunately experienced these kinds of tensions and situations early in our careers, and we recognize that the Me Too movement has driven the problem out of the shadows, shining a spotlight on the issue. Although we acknowledge that men are not always guilty as charged, and that some cases are blown out of proportion, recent studies indicate that the number of false allegations of sexual violence is extremely small; only 4 percent of cases of sexual violence reported in the U.K. are found or suspected to be false, with the rates in Europe and the U.S. being around 2 percent and 6 percent, respectively.[24]

The Me Too movement has legitimized women's concerns and in some cases identified predatory behavior that has taken place as a result of historical power imbalances. While these stories need to be heard and carefully assessed for their truth and authenticity, the importance of women relating their experiences must not be underestimated. It is only through the recounting of these stories that the next generation of women leaders will have a better sense of how to deal with certain situations, both as the potential injured party and final arbiters, and that men will understand that certain behaviors are no longer acceptable, regardless of the power structure.

PIPER:

In one of my academic leadership positions, I reported administratively to a senior male colleague, an individual who was extremely well regarded by his academic peers. As such, I was not only dependent on this person for all of my budget requests as well as any personnel or program changes I wanted to make, but I was also in awe of his reputation as a leading academic and scholar. Clearly, he held the power.

When I went to meet with this individual for the first time, there was nowhere to sit except a sofa situated on one wall of his office—no armchairs, just a sofa. Once I was seated, he closed the door and then sat down next to me. Immediately, I felt uncomfortable; he was invading my space and was much too close to me physically—closer than I would have expected for a professional meeting. Before I could blink or think, he moved to put his arm around me and aggressively lunged at me, groping and trying to kiss me. I froze, then quickly extricated myself as I jumped up, asked him what he was doing and moved to exit the room.

I was scared. What was I to do? What could I do? I had neither the power nor the experience to assist me in facing this dilemma. As well, his reputation was well established and garnered him the respect and trust of his colleagues. Who would believe me? At first I was naive and simply tried to avoid him at all costs. I relied on the phone as much as I could, and I did my best to only see him in meetings with others around. I kept my secret to myself.

One day as I was entering the underground parking garage to collect my car, I saw him following me, gradually picking up his pace. I was petrified. Running to my car, locking the doors, I exited the garage as quickly as I could. That event proved to be the tipping point, causing me to act. Because these were the days before equity offices or policies on sexual harassment and respectful work environments, I confided in the senior administrative officer of the unit, a woman I liked and respected, believing she would direct my concern to the appropriate person within the organization.

At a time when sexual harassment charges were rarely acknowledged and largely ignored, why did I speak out? Why did I think something would be done to remedy the intolerable situation I found myself in? I now know that I was able to summon the nerve to lodge my complaints because I trusted the people in charge, the values they espoused and the climate of academic excellence they supported. And why was this? Where did this level of trust emanate from at a time where women's concerns were not front and center and were not necessarily being heard?

In looking back, I think it was related to the fact that as a new administrator I had received the support of my male superiors on several very contentious issues, such as my efforts to introduce new faculty performance standards. It would have been extremely easy for these male leaders to have looked the other way and left me flailing in the wind; instead, they stood up for me and supported me in the face of serious repercussions. They trusted me implicitly to make the decisions that I thought were appropriate for the academic unit I was leading. In my mind, it was simple. When individuals are trusted by others, they are more likely to return that trust. This experience emphasized to me how important the presence of a culture of trust and respect is in terms of permitting women to come forward and have confidence that their voice will be heard.

A careful, quiet internal investigation was conducted, and it was discovered that I was not alone in terms of his advances—numerous women surfaced, reporting the same predatory behavior. In the end, the alleged abuser resigned his position after receiving an ultimatum from his superiors that if he did not leave, he would be fired. This event occurred decades ago, long before it was acceptable for women to speak out and light years before the Me Too movement. There was no public inquiry or formal complaint proceedings and even if there had been, it is hard to believe that the women involved would have been willing to come forward publicly or, if they had, that they would have prevailed. It is remarkable to me, given the times, that my complaint was heard and that instead of being ignored or excused or not believed, this man's behavior was deemed unacceptable by his male superiors and action was taken.

Am I alone in having experienced this form of sexual assault? Certainly not. Unfortunately, my incident only demonstrates what numerous women aspiring to lead in male-dominated fields have experienced over the course of time. But surely times have changed since that awful episode occurred? I am not so sure. What I have seen in my role as a university president suggests they haven't.

During my first term as UBC president from 1997 to 2006, I never dealt with a single case of sexual assault. Does that mean it was nonexistent at that time on campus? Of course not; but unfortunately, even with all of the sexual harassment policies, equity offices and diversity efforts that had been introduced, victims of assault were still often either unwilling or unable to come forward with their complaints. As illustrated in Jon Krakauer's devastating book *Missoula*, the track record of universities dealing with alleged cases of sexual misconduct has not been stellar; this lack of accountability within the university community may account to some extent for the reluctance of women to come forward with their complaints in the past.

In 2015 when I returned as interim president, I had to manage a number of sexual misconduct cases over a 10-month period. What had changed? In my mind, it was Me Too. As a result of this burgeoning movement, women were no longer willing to be silent and were more confident that their voices would be heard. Many of the cases I had to make a ruling on were complicated, and, while I cannot comment on the specifics of any individual case, it was discouraging to recognize that sexual harassment and assault were still occurring despite all of the "progress" we had made over the past several decades.

Unfortunately, women leaders and those aspiring to the role are still sometimes in situations where men hold the balance of power, and as such, they may be in a compromised position when responding to unwanted advances. While the real remedy may only occur when women leaders hold the balance of power, I believe that in the interim the Me Too movement will continue to play a significant role. By providing permission to speak out, to condemn unacceptable behavior and to share their stories with others, the movement has given women from all walks of life the strength and courage to confront sexual advances with honesty, integrity and confidence.

What did I learn from my experience? Several things. First, know that sexual assault does happen even in the most unlikely circumstances; be aware of the situation and your surroundings. Second, if you are uncomfortable when in the presence of a male colleague and think he may either be coming on to you or acting inappropriately for a professional relationship, you most likely have reason to be concerned. Third, if you are the target of unwanted sexual advances, draw upon your nerve, speak up and confront the person directly, making it clear that his behavior is unacceptable. And finally, use all of the resources available to you, whether it be the company's policies on sexual harassment and a respectful environment, an ombudsman or the equity and diversity office, to follow up on your concerns, as there are likely to be other individuals who require protection. Be confident in knowing that others have gone before you, that you are not alone in what you have experienced and that you are neither responsible for nor the cause of the unwanted behaviors.

This Too Will Pass

No matter what kind of crisis you may be facing as a leader, no matter how awful things may seem in the moment, there is great value in remembering the phrase "This too will pass." Understanding this sentiment places any crisis you might face in the long arc of time, a reminder that nothing lasts forever. The phrase originated in the writings of medieval Sufi poets and became known in the Western world in 1852, when English poet Edward FitzGerald retold the fable and named it "Solomon's Seal." In the fable, a sultan asks King Solomon for a sentence that would always be true in good or bad times, and Solomon responds with, "This too shall pass away."

This perspective is invaluable, particularly for inexperienced leaders who, when encountering their first crisis, can become overwhelmed and imagine that the crisis will pull the organization into a downward spiral from which it will never recover. Rarely is this the case. Women leaders may be more apt to become emotionally engaged and take the conflict and controversy personally, placing themselves under undue stress. Instead of recognizing that all leaders experience crises from time to time, women may panic and be more vulnerable to feeling out of control; their response is often a knee-jerk attempt to manage every aspect of the situation down to the smallest details, reacting to the storm in the moment with little appreciation for the long term.

How leaders respond to a crisis sets the tone for everyone around them. If a leader appears stressed, their associates will become stressed, often making the situation more difficult than it need be. On the other hand, if the leader remains calm, keeping a broader perspective, reassuring others that they will be able to manage the crisis and lead by principle, the whole organization is more likely to face the dilemma in a more thoughtful manner. As someone once said, the trick is to "Always behave like a duck: keep calm and unruffled on the surface, but paddle like the devil underneath." Easier said than done. But in the end, the role of the leader is to retain the bigger perspective and assist others in weathering the crisis by understanding that it won't last forever.

It has often been said that great leaders must never let a good crisis go to waste. By understanding that the challenging situation will never be as large as it appears in the moment, leaders may also seek opportunities for change, reflection or transformation in these difficult times. Strong organizations do this well and use these moments to strengthen the enterprise, using a crisis as an opportunity to improve culture or communications, restructure or acquire other businesses, develop new products or attract talent. Maintaining perspective on the long-term needs of the organization when it is in the midst of a short-term dilemma is challenging indeed, but regardless of the circumstances, leaders are well-advised to lead with calm fortitude at all times—not only in the good times but also in the bad, as both are transitory—taking the long view and keeping their vision and principles top of mind. As King Solomon so wisely noted, it really does not matter, good times or bad . . . both are short-lived and both will pass.

PIPER:

When I stepped down as president of UBC, I had the good fortune of being asked to join the board of directors of the Bank of Montreal. I was honored to do so and began my directorship in late 2007, just before the financial crisis of 2008. The timing could not have been worse. I was an inexperienced director, beginning my term exactly at the moment of one of the largest financial crises the world has faced since the Great Depression. I was overwhelmed not only by the steep learning curve but also terrified by the enormous responsibility of serving on the board at such a critical moment in the bank's history.

While I tried to find my way as a new director, I was exposed to the remarkable leadership of the bank's CEO at the time, Bill Downe. He had recently taken the reins of the organization after having served as a senior administrator of the bank for most of his career. As the bank began its treacherous journey navigating the turbulent waters of the crisis, I was in awe of Bill. He was not only experienced and competent but also calm. His hand was steady, his determination steadfast and his demeanor always spoke confidence. He was clear in his messaging: whatever the bank would encounter in these uncertain times, it would prevail. I marveled at his composure and admired his resolve under pressure.

In the end he was right. The bank did prevail, as did all Canadian banks. In the middle of the turmoil, that outcome did not always feel certain from day to day. But I do know this: Bill's leadership, his ability to remain calm under pressure, his reassuring composure provided not only the board but also management and shareholders the ability to stay the course and work resolutely to bridge the crisis. It was an amazing lesson for me; no matter how dire the situation, leaders do not have the liberty to panic. They set the tone and by so doing determine how others react to the situation. A steady leader who takes the long view ensures that everyone pulls in the same direction and works together to manage whatever obstacles are on the horizon.

When I was recalled to UBC in 2015 and encountered a major crisis associated with the previous president's resignation, I was fortunate to be able to call upon Bill's example. I recognized quite early in my tenure that the university would survive the crisis; that this too would pass. My job was to smooth the waters, to reassure all of the constituents that we could manage this crisis and would survive and to ensure that the university would retain its reputation and its academic excellence. We did not need to panic. My view was shaped by Bill Downe's exemplary leadership—realizing that above all else I needed to stay composed, help others to remain focused and move slowly but determinedly forward without being sidetracked by panicking or worrying excessively. I needed to be the Calmer in Chief.

Lessons Learned

Despite the belief that a leader will be remembered and acknowledged for their visionary leadership, they are often most associated with nasty surprises known as crises and how they manage them. One thing leaders can rely upon: bad things happen. No matter how well prepared they are, they can be assured that at some time during their tenure they will encounter a crisis, totally unexpected and possibly not of their making. Women leaders in particular are left feeling alone and ill-equipped to face the music, and they are prone to blaming themselves when things go badly wrong.

How a leader reacts to challenging situations, how they manage both the organization and themselves during these turbulent times, often defines their leadership in intangible ways. It has been said that it is easy to be strong in good times; the real test of character occurs in bad times. Where does a leader find the strength to deal with controversy when others have removed themselves from the situation? How does a leader face the test of character when she is alone in the arena and in the hot seat? Where does she find the nerve to confront issues, such as sexual harassment and assault, that have been ignored and overlooked for decades? And how does she recognize when in the midst of the hurricane that "this too will pass"?

Each crisis has its own unique set of circumstances and demands, but there are some universal tenets that can assist a leader when managing a crisis.

1.   It is important to acknowledge that all leaders at some point will face a crisis, even if it was not of their making. By recognizing that this is an inherent aspect of leadership, you will be able to avoid personalizing the issue.

2.   Do not expect others to rally around you when dealing with a crisis. No one likes controversy, and most people will run for cover, leaving you alone to manage the issue. It is at this point that you must rely upon the principles that have always guided your leadership. Have confidence that if you stick with those principles, you will prevail.

3.   Identify the key individuals whom you trust and who can assist you in dealing with the crisis. Consider engaging consultants on crisis management if you do not have the expertise in house to advise you with communications, dealing with the media and managing various constituencies.

4.   If ever you find yourself in a compromised position, even when there is a power imbalance, know that you have the nerve and determination to deal with any unacceptable behavior. Use all of the resources available to you to assist you in your response.

5.   Recognize that a leader must always remain calm during the storm, setting the tone for others in the organization. Try to

avoid panicking and worrying excessively; instead, work at projecting a composed and confident demeanor.

6. When you are in the midst of managing a crisis, take comfort in knowing that they are generally short-lived. As difficult as it is in the eye of the storm to imagine that the sun will eventually come out, it is important to remember that "this too will pass."

CHAPTER 10

Public personae: living in the public eye

"For people to see you, you have to rise above the crowds. In doing so, it makes it easier for them to throw rocks."

—PACIFIC WAVE JIU-JITSU

All leaders are in the public eye, some more than others, and all are scrutinized by their staff, professional communities and, to some extent, the broader public. Putting yourself in the public eye, regardless of whether you are a prime minister, senior executive, chair of a committee or director of a unit, requires both competence and courage. It is not for the weak of heart. Assuming a leadership position automatically means opening yourself to being exposed, thereby becoming more vulnerable to both praise and criticism. Everything you say, acknowledge or do will be interpreted by others as a representation of who you are and what you stand for. There is no hiding place for leaders.

Women leaders are both blessed and cursed by being in the public eye. People will notice and remember them just because they are a woman. Often, they represent the first woman in a particular leadership position, which in itself brings more recognition and possible praise. They will have an impact by just showing up, let alone speaking up. But sometimes by being more visible, they attract more scrutiny.

Women leaders are often held to a double standard when compared with their male counterparts. Anecdotes abound about female leaders who report that their interventions, actions and messages were discounted or ignored, while male colleagues who voiced exactly the same opinions were credited for their wisdom and insight. Women leaders often report that in addition to being evaluated on their leadership skills and actions, they are also judged on their personal attributes. What are they wearing? How old are they? Are they gaining or losing weight? Do they look tired and haggard? What about their partner or kids . . . are they being neglected? Very rarely are male leaders assessed in the same manner, thereby making life in the public arena more challenging for women.

While not everyone handles being a public figure in the same manner, we believe our experiences may help other women leaders manage and deal with the associated risks and opportunities. Although neither of us became totally comfortable with the ongoing public scrutiny that accompanied our leadership roles, we did develop coping mechanisms over time. In our minds, Shakespeare's immortal words "to thine own self be true" underline what is truly important when taking on the responsibilities of the public experience. It is not what others say or believe about the leader, but rather what the leader believes about herself and how she stays true to her personal values that will guide and sustain her while being in the public eye.

Mirror, Mirror on the Wall

"Sure he was great, but don't forget that Ginger Rogers did everything he did, backwards . . . and in high heels."

—BOB THAVES, REFERRING TO FRED ASTAIRE
IN A *FRANK AND ERNEST* COMIC STRIP

What is it about women's clothing and appearance that attract so much attention? Is it because women do not have a work uniform—that is, a tailored dark suit, dress shirt and understated tie—that they all don before showing up every morning? Or is it because women make a statement about who they are by the clothes they wear? Whatever the reason, the sartorial style of women leaders is constantly being scrutinized, criticized and commented upon. Remember all the fuss about Hillary Clinton's pantsuits? What was that all about?

And it does not stop with a woman's fashion choices. What is she doing with her hair? Is she coloring it or letting it go natural? Are her nails too flashy? Is she too fat or too skinny? Does she look tired? Why is she wearing pearls instead of a beautiful scarf? Whatever she chooses, she should be doing something else. Everything from shoes to hair, nails to jewelry are fair game when it comes to women leaders. Male leaders simply do not have this experience.

There are those who argue that it is inappropriate to worry about how you appear and what you wear. Shouldn't people just accept you for who you are and what you do, not how you dress and what you look like? While there is some truth to this view, we are of the opinion that how women look and choose to present themselves does speak volumes about who they are and what they stand for. It is never a matter of how much you spend, or how much time you devote to choosing your wardrobe. Rather, it is about how your appearance reflects the respect you have for the office you hold and how seriously you want people to take you.

We have both struggled with this seemingly superficial issue in our leadership journeys. As women who lacked self-confidence early on and had few if any role models to assist us in our choices, we both floundered when it came to creating a look that was appropriate for our positions and reflected our personal styles. Our stories underline the dilemma women leaders face in defining their image—from makeup to accessories—without it dominating their own agenda or becoming the focus of others' attention.

PIPER:

As a young child I never thought I was pretty. I never remember anyone telling me I was pretty—smart, maybe; but pretty, no. My mother was unhappy with my hair; it was too fine and poker straight. She insisted on giving me smelly home permanents so that I would have curls. They were dreadful, the solution stinging my eyes as it dripped off the curlers and down my face. And if that wasn't enough, my grandmother thought I was too skinny, telling me that if I closed one eye I could pass as a needle.

Did these experiences mar me for life? Absolutely not. But did they make me feel self-conscious about my appearance? Maybe. I entered adulthood questioning my ability to look "right." I lacked interest in clothing and makeup. I spent all my time studying and working hard to excel, expending very little effort on putting together outfits or experimenting with lipstick or mascara. I grew up wearing the hand-me-downs of my sister and cousin, and hence, lacked the confidence or desire to choose my own wardrobe. In short, I was neither interested in nor focused upon my appearance.

As I began to assume leadership positions, I was forced to consider what I wore and how I appeared. I hated shopping, but started purchasing outfits that were in my price range and were off the rack from the local department stores. Nothing fancy, nothing expensive. Just simple ensembles that could be worn with black or navy shoes and interchanged with other tops and jackets. A major breakthrough occurred when I went to a stylist in Montreal to have my hair done; prior to that, my hair had been cut by either my mother or my husband.

Things changed considerably when I was put on the short list for the presidency of UBC. Knowing that I was to be interviewed and fêted over a two-day period, my husband and I decided that I needed to up my game. One Saturday before the interview, we went to a high-end women's store in Edmonton to select a new outfit for the occasion. It was our first visit to this store, and we were overwhelmed with the choices and prices. A fashion consultant steered us to a beautiful jacket that was absolutely perfect. As she slipped the garment on me and I looked in the mirror, I was surprised by how it made me feel—calm, confident and pretty. Yet, as my husband and I contemplated the cost, we agreed it was beyond our means. As we left the store without the jacket, we decided that one of my other outfits at home would do.

But the story does not end there. As my husband was dropping me off at the Edmonton airport to fly to Vancouver for the UBC interview, he opened the trunk of the car and gathered a suit bag in his arms—the very jacket we'd had our eye on. Unbeknownst to me, he had returned to the store and purchased it. I was shocked and totally overwhelmed. I couldn't believe he had done that for me.

Fast forward to the Vancouver hotel lobby, where I was met by a member of the selection committee before the UBC interview. He greeted me warmly and, turning to accompany me to the elevator, said clearly and concisely, "Nice jacket." I almost lost it. It was like he was speaking to me in code, saying, "You look nice; you are appropriately presenting yourself." Those two words, "Nice jacket," affirmed who I was at that moment and propelled me forward to confront the interview with confidence and a sense of self-worth.

I learned several lessons from that experience. First, how you appear is not only about how others see you, but how you see yourself. Second, by feeling good about how you appear, you can focus on the tasks at hand, rather than worrying about how others are assessing you. And third, if you lack confidence in your own ability to figure out what to wear and how to dress, seek assistance. Such assistance may come in many forms: a friend or relative who knows fashion, a clerk you trust or a nonprofit organization that works to assist women to "dress for success." My jacket story started with my lack of confidence in how to present myself in the best possible manner and ended with my having the self-assurance to meet the interview head-on. That single item of clothing became so much more than just a nice jacket.

SAMARASEKERA:

When I moved to Canada from Sri Lanka at age 24, I thought I was well prepared to integrate into this new country, as I had received a superb education and spoke fluent English. What I had not anticipated was how difficult it would be for me to figure out how to dress appropriately. Most women in Sri Lanka wore a sari to work and for special occasions, rarely pants or dresses.

When I first arrived, my primary goal was finding inexpensive clothes that looked appropriate and attractive. I remember trying clothes off the rack at department stores and recall that nothing ever fitted me properly and the colors did not suit my dark skin. I realized that the clothes were manufactured for people of European ancestry, who are lighter skinned and with physiques different from their South-Asian sisters. I also noticed women changed their wardrobes for every season. It was always summer in Sri Lanka, and we wore bright colors year-round. Finally, I discovered that North American women use cosmetics to enhance their appearance. My mother wore red lipstick, the same color no matter what sari she had on, and that was it. When I tried to add makeup to my repertoire, I observed that drugstores only stocked items that suited lighter skin tones. I looked terrible when I put on foundation, as my face turned a pasty beige, so I abandoned that plan and have not used it since.

When I became an academic, I was relieved; being the only woman in the department, I did not have to conform to some dress code, nor did I feel any pressure to look attractive. Most of my male engineer colleagues wore corduroy pants and tweed jackets with leather patches on the elbows. This suited me perfectly, or so I thought, and it was my attire for 20 years. Becoming a senior executive, first vice president and then president, presented me with the same conundrum I had encountered 25 years earlier. What to wear? I started looking at magazines my teenage daughter was poring over, so I could step up my shopping game armed with fashion tips. While there was more choice for women of color by this time, it was still not easy to find clothes that I felt comfortable in.

By the time I became president, I had finally learned how to dress to appeal to my own sense of style. Shopping for the occasion of my installation as president was even enjoyable, and I splurged on a few outfits that I felt special in for the once-in-a-lifetime moment. Through it all I learned that when you rise through the ranks of leadership, what you wear is a mark of respect for the office you occupy. It also endows you with quiet confidence that comes from knowing you look poised and elegant.

Myth: If I Do It Right, I Will Be Liked

We all like to be liked. It is human nature to believe that if we do the right things, behave properly, are kind and compassionate, we will be liked. Many of our behaviors are driven by the desire to be accepted and appreciated. Don't be mean or vindictive; be polite and respectful; be generous and thoughtful of others' feelings; don't gossip or disparage another person's reputation; don't talk back or pick an argument. These rules are the foundation for many of our responses and reactions to daily events, based on the belief that if we follow them we will be not only respected but also liked. This desire for approval and affirmation is normal.

But it's important to distinguish between *wanting* to be liked and *needing* to be liked. The two are distinctly different: "While the desire to be liked is normal, feeling that it's necessary that everyone likes you and experiencing anxiety and stress when they don't isn't."[25] This distinction, while subtle, is crucial for any leader to keep in mind; when you are in the fishbowl and constantly under scrutiny, there will always be people who will not like you, regardless of how you act or behave. It's okay to want to be liked; you may feel bad or upset when someone doesn't like you, but eventually you accept it and move on. It's not okay to need to be liked; to think that if someone does not like you there is something wrong with you, that you need to do things differently in order to win them over or compromise your principles to gain their approval.

Some people believe that women naturally tend to want or need to be nice and worry about what others think more than their male counterparts, thereby jeopardizing their effectiveness as leaders. We believe that while there may be some truth to this view, it is far too simplistic. Sheryl Sandberg in her book *Lean In: Women, Work, and the Will to Lead* profiles a body of scientific research that clearly demonstrates that success and likeability differ for male and female leaders. While female and male leaders may be similarly competent, they can receive different likeability scores—especially when an aggressive or controversial decision is required. In short, when acting with strength and in an authoritative manner, women leaders are disliked much more than men. Sandberg notes that it is not the case that women are more disliked than men when they are successful; rather, they are penalized only when they behave in ways that violate gender expectations.

Our experience suggests this may indeed be the case. As women we were not only expected to be nice, warm, friendly and nurturing, but were also expected to exhibit those qualities when leading. These traits clearly served us well throughout most of our leadership journey, resulting in consultative decisions and consensus on many issues. However, when we were forced to act assertively and decisively, we not only deviated from those feminine traits, but also we were not as popular and were perceived to have failed as leaders. The fact that we sometimes were disliked for our decisions made us ponder what we had done wrong, rather than understand that gender stereotypes may have undermined how we were being viewed as leaders.

Trying to be liked when in the public eye almost always runs counter to making the right decisions, especially in universities where everyone feels they have a say. A course of action may seem obvious but surprisingly does not guarantee that you will be liked unless everyone fully approves, a lesson I learned the hard way when attempting to honor the legacy of Peter Lougheed, a remarkable Canadian and one of Alberta's greatest premiers. Premier Lougheed had been a catalyst for the development of the oil and gas industry in Alberta and created the Alberta Heritage Savings Trust Fund to ensure that revenue from exploitation of non-renewable resources would be of long-term benefit to the province. Alberta underwent a significant transformation on his watch. I felt fortunate to have spent some time with him to fully appreciate his impact and legacy.

After Mr. Lougheed's death, a prominent business leader and alumnus approached me with the consent of the Lougheed family to explore what the university could do to honor the late premier, who had earned two degrees from U of A. These discussions gave birth to the idea to build a Peter Lougheed Leadership College on campus, attracting $75 million from the Government of Alberta. As the plans to develop the program progressed, opposition sprouted across campus. The animosity increased further after I appointed The Right Honourable Kim Campbell, former prime minister, to lead the establishment of the college.

How could I attract so much antipathy for a project that had so much merit? How many universities had the privilege of attracting a former prime minister to build a leadership college in honor of another great Canadian? Was it because she was a female leader that it aroused pushback stemming from an unconscious bias? How often does a provincial government provide $75 million of funding to create a leadership college, without strings attached? Surely, this was a dream project, and yet I was disliked for taking the initiative to advance a project outside the realm of a normal academic program.

First, even though all undergraduate students were eligible to benefit from Peter Lougheed Leadership College programs, some of them opposed the fact that the residential component was being designed for just two hundred or so students. As far as they were concerned, this was elitist; they already had several leadership initiatives, and I was stepping on their turf. A number of students mounted a campaign to protest the initiative, writing in the student newspaper, stoking animosity towards me and the program. Then there was the university's academic senate that had several outspoken members who voiced their opposition when the program was brought to them for consultation. They were not interested in offering suggestions on how it could be improved, instead they tried to scuttle it. Many of the academics also did not think former Prime Minister Kim Campbell should have been appointed, since she had not been an academic and scholar, although she had taught political science at UBC before she entered politics and taught at Harvard's Kennedy School in the Center for Public Leadership after her term as prime minister ended. If she were a male leader, would there have been such objections? I will never know. What I do know is that I was disliked for spearheading an honorific initiative outside the traditional academic purview and for appointing a former prime minister to lead it. Had I been a male leader, would I have had such sustained opposition? I remember feeling weary and frustrated by all the negativity the project was attracting.

Fortunately, former prime minister Campbell is an experienced and dynamic leader, whose passion for the project and determination to bring it to fruition prevailed. Along with another academic leader, they brought the initiative to life and the college was built on the north end of campus overlooking the Alberta Legislature across the North Saskatchewan River. The students who enrolled in the inaugural program provided testimonials about the value of being mentored by leaders. Though I retired before Peter Lougheed Hall was officially opened, I note with pleasure that the college is thriving today. Had I yearned to be liked, by the students, the academics and the deans, I may have relented to the pressure. Had the need to be liked overpowered my intent to do the right thing in the face of animosity, and had I not had the nerve to prevail, I could have forgone the opportunity to build a legacy for Premier Lougheed to benefit generations of students. I believe a tolerance for not needing to be liked is a prerequisite for strong leadership.

Using Your Voice

"It took me quite a long time to develop a voice, and now that I have it, I am not going to be silent."

—MADELEINE ALBRIGHT, *HUFFPOST*

Words matter. Whether we like it or not, what we say and how we say it are often perceived to be the best representation of ourselves. People are often remembered for what they say, and their words reflect their feelings, beliefs, views, emotions and frustrations on everything from the weather to issues of substance. We use words to talk, share, joke or gossip with one another; to have a good time or tell a secret; to say "I love you" or lash out in anger. Words matter, for better or for worse.

Effective leaders understand they need to use their voice. Whether giving directions or feedback, making a speech or outlining a vision or simply in casual conversation with a colleague or employee, the words leaders use to express themselves speak volumes about what they value and how they see the world. Leaders are continually being asked to speak, at dinners, at receptions, at conferences, at meetings and at celebrations. How they use these opportunities to express their opinions and views, raising their voice in a timely fashion, will have a significant impact on how they and their organizations are perceived by their respective communities. If you ever doubt the power of a leader's voice, think of Lincoln and the "Gettysburg Address," Kennedy and his inaugural address when he challenged the public to "ask not what your country can do for you, ask what you can do for your country," or Martin Luther King's "I Have a Dream" speech. As for women leaders who have used their voices to make significant statements, you need only consider Margaret Thatcher, Malala Yousafzai or Gloria Steinem, to name a few. These women leaders, and hundreds of others, have put to bed the anachronistic adage that women should be seen and not heard.

Public speaking is not easy; it requires enormous effort to figure out what to say, how to say it and when. The message must be crafted to the audience you are addressing and also be relevant for the occasion. Writing a good speech involves intent, determination and just plain hard work. Rarely are you able to just speak off the cuff; rather, when you are asked to use your voice through speech-making, you must determine how to turn your ideas into words, making the points you need and want to, without boring the audience. It is an art that is not easily learned but when conquered can be one of the most powerful tools a leader has to bring people along, to make things happen, to change behaviors and to demonstrate leadership.

People remember what a leader says, recounting and interpreting the message long after they have heard it. Every year, we both had the occasion to speak to thousands of people at our respective graduation ceremonies. Recognizing that we had a unique platform to address not only the graduates but also their family and friends, we both expended a great deal of time and energy in preparing these speeches. Years later, people would approach us at the airport or in a grocery line and say something like this: "I remember the speech you delivered when I graduated or when my son graduated . . ." It was clear that these speeches, which many people would discount as being ceremonial and inconsequential, were more than that—they were memorable because they were personal and crafted for the specific occasion, they represented us, our values and the role our institutions played in society.

By raising our voices as leaders in meetings, conferences, around the boardroom table or delivering after-dinner speeches, we could affect people's opinions, promote strategic ideas and move our organizations forward. Repeating important themes, keeping messages clear and consistent, and speaking openly about key issues proved effective means of making things happen and influencing the broader community. In short, a leader needs to use her voice, at every possible opportunity, to express directly and forcefully the themes and messages that will define who she is, what she believes and the strategic initiatives of her organization. How a leader communicates may be one of the most powerful components of her leadership journey.

SAMARASEKERA:

Very early in my tenure as U of A president, I was invited to give an after-dinner speech at the Gairdner Awards Gala. The Gairdner Foundation selects the best medical science researchers from around the world and honors them at an annual dinner. These awards are generally viewed as precursors to the Nobel Prize, since nearly a third of the Canada Gairdner International Award winners have subsequently won a Nobel Prize. Not a medical science researcher myself, what could I possibly say to them in eight minutes? I was terrified at the prospect of giving a speech to such an august audience; it was going to require a lot of nerve.

I fretted about this for weeks until suddenly an idea popped into my head. I would talk about "Extraordinary Minds." Howard Gardner, a renowned psychologist from Harvard, had written about the characteristics of extraordinary minds, and I would link these attributes to two Gairdner Prize winners I knew, Michael Smith from UBC, who had also won a Nobel Prize, and Raymond Lemieux from U of A.

I went to the dinner confident that I had a good speech, which allayed my jitters. I was seated next to a recent Nobel Laureate who asked me who I was. When I introduced myself, confessing that I was not a medical science researcher, but had been invited as the after-dinner speaker, he looked incredulous and said, "I don't know why they invite people like you to speak at these dinners!" I smiled politely and said something like, "I wondered about that, too." I also wondered whether I was eliciting disdain because I am a woman of color.

My speech was a hit; I could tell from the audience response and the feedback I received afterwards that the remarks resonated. Even the Nobel Laureate I was seated next to, who thought I should not have been invited to speak, was complimentary.

Of the many speeches I gave during my tenure, this speech stands out since so much was at stake. One of my goals for the evening was to elevate the reputation of the University of Alberta in a gathering of influential international medical scientists. A bad speech would have set the university back. I was gratified that I rose to the occasion.

Taking a Stand

Leaders, as a result of their unique roles in the community, have an opportunity to take positions on issues of general concern, lead the public debate, support causes and offer ideas and informed opinions on events and trends of great public interest—in short, to take a stand. And yet, they are often reluctant to either express their personal views or take actions to support a position they hold, as they often fear the repercussions that may follow from weighing in on controversial topics.

The responsibility of today's women leaders to contribute to the public discourse, to initiate dialogue and conversations on difficult issues, to act in support of positions they believe in has never been greater. For decades male leaders have controlled much of the discourse that has underpinned our policies, our approaches and our priorities as a society. Clearly, it is time for women to make their positions known and advance the causes they believe in. Whether it be fair employment practices, the need for social justice reform, women's humanitarian rights or financial support for women entrepreneurs, women need to stand up and be counted. It is not easy, but if our women leaders fail to weigh in, to take action, lead the debate and discuss controversial issues, who will? Who better to begin these important conversations, to take up certain causes that promote a more just society than women leaders at every level, in every area of pursuit?

The few times when we did take a stand on a controversial issue, we opened ourselves up to criticism at best and vitriol at worst. Nevertheless, we continue to believe that it is in the public interest for leaders in all areas to summon the nerve to take a stand and contribute to the public debate about significant issues. Whether it be supporting others who need defending, protesting unjust decisions or initiatives, writing position papers, lobbying governments, lending a hand to the oppressed and forgotten or giving of your time and energy to causes you believe in, women leaders have an obligation to stand up for the positions they support.

SAMARASEKERA:

In October 2009 I was interviewed by the *Edmonton Journal* for an article comparing male and female enrollment in undergraduate programs across the country. Statistics showed that females comprised about 58 percent of the undergraduate population at most Canadian universities at the time, a number that has held fairly consistent over a decade. While young men outnumbered women in fields like engineering and computer science, there were more women than men in professional disciplines like medicine and law. In Alberta, many young men preferred to go to the oil fields where there were high-paying jobs rather than attend university and incur debt. Research also showed that, on average, boys in high school were getting lower grades, and girls appeared to be more competitive for university admission, leading to the gender disparity in enrollment overall. While I did not suggest that we should go out on a special recruitment drive to attract more young men, I asserted that educational leaders should examine how curriculum is delivered in high schools and questioned whether change was needed to raise the academic success of young men.

I noted that the situation was no different than when women were underrepresented. I believed that if the situation with boys was left unquestioned, it could over the course of 20 years lead to a loss of gender diversity in all positions in society. I went on to say that as a woman and a visible minority, I had chosen to speak out on the issue stating, "I'm going to be an advocate for young white men, because I can be. No one is going to question me when I say we have a problem."

The thought that any woman leader would advocate for young white men was unfathomable to many people. The outcry in response to my comments was immediate and extremely negative. A group of female students launched a satirical poster campaign with one poster featuring the words, "Only White Men Can Save Our University." Another shouted, "Women: Stop! Drop! Men: Enroll." One of the women who led the campaign asserted that white men do not need advocates, and that it was still a white man's world. They pointed to the low number of women in C-level jobs and other leadership positions and said that the situation was still unfairly tilted against women, which is still unfortunately correct today.

To address the legitimate concerns my remarks had caused, I organized a series of roundtables on campus, while also outlining the risks of ignoring a problem that warranted attention. I pointed out that if enrollment trends continued, we could have a growing number of under-employed young men, leading to similar social unrest as at various times in history. I also assured the participants that I would continue to advocate for the resolution of ongoing issues faced by women in the workplace, notably discrimination, wage gaps and sexual harassment.

In time the controversy died down, but I was never sure whether taking a stand convinced a significant number of people that this was an issue worthy of attention. Should I have ducked the reporter's question and offered a more conventional answer? Or had I done the right thing in expressing not only my personal opinion but also initiating a public debate on an inconvenient truth? With the passage of time, I have no regrets about saying what I said and creating such an outcry. I believe more than ever that leaders must use their position of authority and privilege to call out inequities wherever they may exist. As women, we have endured a long history of disadvantages in the workplace, and although we have made progress there is a still a long way to go. Nevertheless, that should not deter women leaders from looking out for others, whether they be Indigenous peoples, LGBTQ, visible minorities, individuals with disabilities, recent immigrants or, yes, even white men.

Lessons from the Queen

People in the public eye are often prisoners to protocol. Invariably, they are placed in situations where certain behaviors are either anticipated or required. Leaders are no exception, as they are often expected to obey unwritten codes of comportment or conduct. Who do you recognize or thank first in your community address? What is the dress code for the specific occasion you are attending? What is appropriate when interacting with heads of government, including foreign heads of state? Who do you send Christmas cards to or invite to your open houses? Do you greet someone by their first name or their more formal title?

As we have noted, women leaders are particularly prone to being under the microscope when it comes to their public conduct, and never is this more apparent than in international dealings. North American women often face very different cultural norms and expectations than in their home country and need to be especially sensitive to matters of protocol when on business overseas or receiving international visitors. Do you remove your shoes when entering a room? Should a woman go first or follow their male peers? Should you greet your male associates with a kiss on the cheek or just a handshake? Are pants or sleeveless blouses acceptable in certain situations? Is a woman expected to wear a head covering in specific countries and cultures? An innocent gaffe or misstep in the public domain can sour a relationship or even jeopardize a potential contract or agreement. Knowing what to do, how to do it and when to do it become critical components of a woman's success as a leader.

Unfortunately, many of these rules remain unwritten and are learned only through careful study or by being tutored by knowledgeable protocol officers, individuals whose job it is to know what to do or not to do and when to do it. It's tough, if not impossible, for female leaders to learn the appropriate rules of engagement from their male peers and mentors because the rules are often different for women. Things such as dress codes, greetings, the playing of golf and giving a toast to the host have long been decoded and explained for the male leader, leaving the lone woman in the group adrift. Furthermore, because a female leader is often the first woman to lead her organization, she must pave her own way when it comes to protocol.

How then do women manage this confusing terrain of "acceptable" behaviors? The best tutors for women leaders when it comes to protocol may be other women in the public eye. By watching and observing other well-known and respected women, women leaders are well-advised as to what they should and can do when confronted with similar situations. And what better model of conduct is there than Queen Elizabeth II? Her life has been defined by rules of comportment, with tradition and history guiding her every move. No woman leader is more in the public eye than the Queen. Because of her extraordinary profile, she might be viewed as the final word of what is acceptable for women leaders to do, when to do it and in what forum it is to be done.

PIPER:

One of the privileges of leadership is being able to meet and interact with powerful, inspirational and sometimes famous individuals. Such was my encounter with Queen Elizabeth II. Several years ago when she was celebrating her Royal Jubilee of 50 years on the throne, she visited Canada and spent time in Vancouver, including a royal visit to UBC. Our protocol officers worked tirelessly with hers to ensure the visit was flawless. What activities were acceptable for the Queen to engage in when she was on campus? Should we name a building in her honor? How would we involve the students and guarantee her safety? Who could meet and greet the Queen? Did we need to curtsy when introduced to her? Should I wear a hat and, if so, where would I buy it?

Could I greet her with a handshake? On and on and on. My brain was swimming with rules. Panic set in, and I began to dread her visit. What if I did something wrong and offended her?

To make matters even worse, before her visit to the campus I was invited to attend a luncheon where I would be seated next to the Queen. I was a mess. What would I say? What would I do? How could I possibly even eat one thing without breaking protocol?

My fears were unfounded. The Queen was lovely, engaging, warm and welcoming. Conversation flowed easily, and amazingly I got through the lunch without any obvious missteps.

As protocol dictated, the Queen was scheduled to speak between the main course and dessert. Now every woman leader can identify with the age-old dilemma that no male leader has when speaking after a meal— lipstick! How do you graciously apply lipstick before standing to speak? One thing is certain, one rule is never to be broken: you do *not* put your lipstick on at the table. And so it was with interest and curiosity that I watched as the Queen opened her purse, retrieved her lipstick and put it on without reservation in full sight of everyone. Two quick swipes and she was done; ready to stand and speak.

My life changed that day! For the first time, I was liberated to do the most convenient thing, to be myself, to have the nerve to do things that are unconventional when it makes sense. In reality, this lesson was about much more than when and where I could apply my lipstick; it extended to bigger things, such as being able to say no to gifts that did not advance the university's mission, to decline invitations to travel when my time was better spent on campus. The Queen, through her gracious example, had shown me that being comfortable in your own skin is, in the end, more important than honoring lifelong rules that really are absurd. What is wrong with following your own principles? What is wrong with putting your lipstick on at the table? No one is hurt or made fun of; no one is offended or maligned by the action; and in the end, no one really cares. Important lessons from the Queen.

Lessons Learned

Inherent in the role of leadership is living in the public domain; leaders inevitably attract both praise and criticism for what they say and how they perform. How leaders manage and deal with both their public image and the input they receive is an important aspect of their leadership journey. Women leaders are especially open to review, given their unique status in the community and the fascination the public often has with the fact that a woman is in charge.

We believe that women leaders receive more public scrutiny than their male colleagues. As a result, they may find it more difficult to express their vulnerability, while at the same time demonstrating strength and courage when interpreting public input. In the end, women leaders are well-advised to recognize that they must be true to themselves and do what they believe is right, rather than being overly concerned about what others, who often do not have the complete picture, think and say.

1. Recognize that your physical appearance is more a statement of how you respect your leadership position than the value you place on clothing and fashion. Attempt to develop a style that reflects who you are and makes you feel confident and comfortable.

2. If necessary, seek professional help in crafting a look that suits your needs. Remember that if a woman feels good about herself and how she appears, she will be more confident in doing her job.

3. Wanting to be liked is natural; needing to be liked is problematic. Acknowledge that as a woman leader you may be viewed through a different lens than a male when making controversial decisions, and that success and being liked do not always go hand in hand.

4. Recognize the importance of raising your voice and the power of your words. By embracing every opportunity to speak and making certain you have crafted the messages you want to impart, you will communicate not only your personal values but also those of your organization.

5. Seize every occasion you have to take a stand and use your nerve to advance positions on issues and causes you care about. By so doing you will assist in making our communities better places to live and work.

6. Remember that protocols, or accepted rules of comportment, sometimes make things more difficult than necessary, particularly for women. Do what makes sense to you and allows you to be true to yourself. When in doubt, remember the Queen.

CHAPTER 11

Balance: Is there such a thing?

"A career is wonderful, but you can't curl up with it on a cold night."

—MARILYN MONROE

Balance. The new standard for living a full and meaningful life. In addition to being competent, accomplished and compassionate, leaders are now being asked to couple hard work with more attention to their personal life; to carve out time for exercise, healthy eating, blissful sleep and meaningful engagement with family and friends. Leaders are encouraged to seek peace and harmony, attain physical wellness and manage their emotional and mental health—all while doing their day job with energy, expertise and excellence.

And what if you fail to find or achieve this important but elusive aspect of life? Beware. According to the experts you will, somehow, pay dearly for the lack of balance in your life; your leadership will be in jeopardy, and you will most likely end up with a chronic disease, living alone with no family or friends or becoming depressed—or maybe all three. The pressure on leaders to achieve balance is such that coaches have been hired, courses have been developed and endless lectures and blogs have been written to guide clueless leaders as they navigate this new terrain.

Women leaders, we believe, are under even more pressure than their male counterparts to seek balance in their lives. We are not certain why this is the case, and some of this pressure is self-imposed; but perhaps it is explained to some degree by the value they have consistently placed on health, recreation, food, family and friends. Women have traditionally been the primary caregivers and keepers of the home; in many ways, they have long been the "Balancers in Chief" within their families and their social circles—the individual who has been largely responsible for the health and well-being of not only themselves but also of the people close to them. As they have entered the workforce in growing numbers over the past several decades, and more so as they assume leadership positions, women often struggle to rediscover the balance they once enjoyed before leading. Others, too, put increased emphasis and attention on women leaders to achieve balance, thereby unwittingly stressing them even more.

If we had a dollar for every time someone commented on our need to achieve balance in our lives while we were leading, we would be extremely wealthy. People have had no reservations whatsoever about commenting on our appearance, our weight or our fatigue levels, nor about questioning whether we were exercising, eating well, working too hard or taking enough time away. It were as if they thought they were helping us manage our priorities, when in many cases their comments only made us feel more pressured and anxious.

Is it a myth to assume that you can have it all—good health, eight hours of sleep, fulfilling relationships, well-behaved children, emotional stability and private personal time—while at the same time leading your institution, organization or department? The demands on women leaders are endless, while the hours of the day are limited. How realistic is it for women leaders to be successful while also achieving life balance? Although our personal experiences in attempting to look after ourselves while leading are mixed, we believe there are some aspects of this juggling act that are worth discussing and reflecting upon.

Something's Gotta Give

Because of the weighty responsibilities leaders assume, and the sheer number of them, there are never enough hours in the day to deal with everything that is on your plate. Do you attend the meeting or write the memo? Do you travel to Asia for work or stay at home to deal with a crisis in the making? And, when you mix in the personal issues, such as dinners with kids, celebration of birthdays and anniversaries and taking time away just to have a break, the famous words of the Johnny Mercer song take on new meaning.

How then do leaders cope with the endless tasks and responsibilities, personal and professional, they face day to day? Many begin by trying to add an hour or so to the day, waking up earlier or going to bed later in order to get to the gym or answer one more email before hitting the hay. Others attempt to block off certain days and times that are sacred, hours that are kept free to meet a personal commitment or simply provide time to think and reflect. Still others give their assistants strict instructions to follow in making up their schedules: no breakfast meetings, no telephone calls to a different time zone before 6:30 a.m. local time and no dinners unless attending as the invited speaker. Numerous strategies abound to assist leaders in making the best use of their time and ensuring that they have some balance in their lives.

Nevertheless, managing it all almost always comes down to delegating, giving up some of the things you think you ought to do, but that can be done by someone else. Delegation is never easy; it signals a loss of control and suggests that you do not value the task since you have assigned it to someone else. Yet, delegation is an essential skill for leaders—even a survival skill of sorts. Whether it be personal responsibilities, such as keeping the house clean or making dinner, or professional duties, such as speaking, attending receptions or travel, delegation is the key to keeping your life balanced.

We believe that women leaders of our generation are faced with a particular conundrum when it comes to delegation, and that is the role mothers played in Western society. They, by and large, did not delegate; they did it all, with the major exception being they did not work outside the home. They kept the house clean and the beds made, collected the kids from school and scheduled play dates, made dinners and cookies, gardened and shoveled snow, kept the cars running, organized medical and dental appointments and volunteered at the local hospice. They were extremely busy and productive and set the example of what activities were to be done by women; no wonder we think we have to do it all—on top of our day job!

Women leaders in today's world tend to be unrealistic when it comes to what they feel they should be doing. Yes, they want to be great leaders and are prepared for the responsibilities and complexities of the role; but they also think they have to cover everything that's required on the home front. In assuming the mantle of leadership, they remain reluctant to shed the duties and demands of their personal life, and they feel incredibly guilty about it if they do. Male leaders, on the other hand, rarely think, let alone believe, that they need to be doing anything other than performing their leadership role. Hence, the double standard. Now, while today's men are assuming more and more of these "extra" duties at home, we still believe that women, for whatever reason, think they should be doing the bulk of them. Female leaders need to figure out how they can best meet the demands of their leadership roles, while still fulfilling important personal responsibilities and learning how to delegate the rest . . . something's *gotta* give.

PIPER:

I am not a good delegator. I am too much of a control freak. For years I prided myself on being able to do it all—have kids, a marriage, a clean house, family dinners, reasonable health and fitness and a career. This worked for a while—thanks largely to the partnership I had with my husband, who did more than his share of child rearing and house duties, while also being in a demanding profession. The well-oiled system started to creak and groan, however, when I began to assume leadership positions that made more professional demands on my time, and it came to a screeching halt when I became president of UBC.

There just were not enough hours in the day, pure and simple. I could not continue to do everything I thought I needed to do. I was slow in realizing something's gotta give. Some things were easier to delegate than others; house cleaning, baking cookies and gardening were the easy tasks to relinquish. Others took longer to forgo, but slowly I realized the wisdom of what someone had once told me: "Spend all your disposable income on help." Delegation often comes with a cost, and your ability to pay varies according to your circumstances, but you can, in theory, buy almost any service you need, once you accept that you don't have to do everything yourself. You can find people who will shop for you, take your clothes to the dry cleaner, cook and organize birthday parties for the kids. There are companies now that prepare your meals in advance, deliver almost anything you need to your door and organize everything, from your taxes to financial planning and paying your bills. Although financial resources are often limited, I still would recommend the wisdom I was given: spend whatever disposable income you have on help.

Having said that, there is one thing that cannot be delegated, and that is exercise and personal fitness. My story is classic. During my presidency, my husband and I tried to keep fit by walking frequently, biking occasionally and hiking on holidays. Every time I had my annual checkup, my physician would ask me, "Are you exercising?" And I would reply, "Yes, of course." I actually believed I was. My weight was fine, I was reasonably healthy, and I thought I was exercising regularly.

Move the clock forward. After I left the presidency, I became serious about my fitness and exercise. I took up yoga and set a goal of walking ten thousand steps a day. At my next annual checkup, when my physician asked me the routine question, "Are you exercising?" I responded with something like this: "I lied. I was *not* exercising when I was president, even though I thought I was; I now know how much time and energy need to be devoted to fitness." While we both chuckled, it was a real eye-opener for me. It's easy to underestimate what is required for your own personal well-being, and although you can contract out other aspects of your life, you cannot have others exercise for you. Without a set routine and firm commitment to fitness, this aspect of your life will most likely fall off the table, which is fine . . . if you understand and are prepared to live with the consequences.

Teeter-Totter

All of us have played on a teeter-totter at some point in our lives, trying to either lift our side into the air by pushing both feet firmly against the ground without flying off the end of the board or to gracefully exit the board without causing one's partner to descend too rapidly and be injured. So it is with life: constantly maneuvering the ups and downs of your daily existence without either flying off in a spin or crashing to the ground. Balancing the seesaw of life is a critical component of coping with the unknown without ending up in a heap.

Leadership is all about riding the teeter-totter: learning how not to be thrown off course by the jolts and bumps of unplanned life events. Things do happen in our personal lives, regardless of our day job, that are out of our control: kids get in trouble, partners file for divorce, basements flood, loved ones get sick and die. These occurrences are almost always surprises, unanticipated happenings that come out of nowhere, hitting you in the stomach when least expected. The phone rings, and your life changes. You have little if any control over these situations and they almost always deserve your attention, taking your focus away from leading and forcing you to drop everything and respond. How you react to these occurrences may not only define your leadership journey but may also impact your personal life with far-reaching effects.

No one goes through life unscathed, not even successful leaders; and almost always these "teeter-totter" events take precedence over your leadership responsibilities. How then do you manage to continue to lead while dealing with a major life event? Do you take a leave of absence, or do you carry on in absentia? Do you name an acting leader to replace you while you focus on the problem at hand, or do you continue to lead? While each situation differs according to its seriousness and intensity, they all share a heart-stopping quality—forcing the leader to either continue to glide upward on the seesaw or bump forcefully to the ground. A personal crisis can be a pivotal moment in your career as well as your life.

SAMARASEKERA:

It was early October 2006 when I received the unexpected punch-in-the-gut phone call from my sister in the U.K. She told me that our 82-year-old father had suffered a stroke, resulting in paralysis and loss of speech. "How bad is it?" I asked, followed by, "Is he going to survive?" She said she was flying to Sri Lanka in a few hours to assess the situation, and she would call me. I was utterly distressed and could not believe the bad news.

I phoned my mother, and she was in denial. When I inquired whether I should come, she said he would recover soon, and there was no need for me to make the 24-hour journey. I was torn, because on the one hand my agenda was full with presidential duties and on the other I wanted to see my dad, who had been such an important influence in my life. I was thrown off balance and could not concentrate on the tasks at hand. My sister, a physician, called to tell me that contrary to our mother's hopefulness, our father did not have long to live. He passed away a week later. Within hours I was on my way.

Nothing prepares you for the death of a parent and the emotions that engulf you. My father's funeral was a whirlwind. We held a wake, attended by family, friends and colleagues, and a service of burial. My mother was devastated to lose him quite suddenly after 56 years of marriage. I was mostly numb and very sad, and I had to process all my emotions within a week because I had to return to Edmonton.

Should I have simply taken time off to be with my father until the end? Should I have stayed longer after the funeral to mourn his passing with my mother? When one is immersed in leading, it is very difficult to make decisions that are best for your personal life if they have the potential to distract from your leadership responsibilities.

To this day, I feel sad that I was not able to see him alive one last time. I feel I never had time to properly mourn my father's passing, nor time to comfort my mother or reminisce with my siblings about the wonderful qualities of our father. This was a teeter-totter experience, where my personal life collided with my professional obligations as a leader, pushing and pulling me in both directions and leaving me with unresolved regret. I have often wondered whether a male leader would have considered taking time off or accepted without question that with responsibility comes personal sacrifice.

Another unwanted intrusion into my leadership journey was a health scare. Following a checkup and biopsy, my family doctor informed me in late April 2012 that I had early-stage uterine cancer. I was stunned and shocked, as there was no history of cancer in my family. She referred me to a surgeon who recommended a total hysterectomy within a couple of weeks. I tried suggesting to the surgeon that perhaps we postpone the surgery to the summer when I would have more time. She looked perplexed and repeated the diagnosis, emphasizing the seriousness of it as if I had not heard her properly the first time. It was another teeter-totter moment, throwing me off-kilter, causing my emotions to seesaw and rendering me unable to process what I was facing.

It took me several sleepless nights to acknowledge the diagnosis and to set aside all that I had to do over the next three months and recognize that my health required my full attention. Luckily, my team rallied so I could take a leave of absence. My children visited for a few days prior to the operation, and my sister took two weeks of leave to be with me post-surgery. The emotional support of family was extremely important to me. I was struck by how quickly a life-changing diagnosis shattered my sense of invincibility as a leader and permanently altered my priorities in life. I am fortunate that I remain healthy with no recurrence, but I am fully aware that not everyone is so lucky, and remission never equals cure.

Teeter-totter moments happen to every leader and are a reminder that body, mind and soul need care.

Lessons Learned

Leading is all-consuming. It takes every hour in the day and every ounce of energy you can bring to it. It will eat you alive unless you are determined to balance the demands of the job with time for yourself. Time to reflect, time to refuel, time to exercise and eat properly, time to be with others. The dilemma today's women leaders face is not understanding how important balance is to their personal and professional lives, but rather to be disciplined enough to achieve it in their day-to-day living.

How then do you balance the demands of being a leader with the desire to be a healthy person with strong, meaningful relationships? How do you reconcile your own needs with those of the organization? As two leaders who have attempted, sometimes successfully and sometimes unsuccessfully, to juggle the responsibilities of leadership with the joy and hardships of living, we recognize this is not an easy task. We also believe, however, that by being aware of the natural tendency of leaders, especially women, to downplay their personal needs, you will be better able to counter the all-consuming nature of leadership, thereby permitting you to achieve some level of balance in your lives.

1. Acknowledge both the importance of looking after yourself while leading and the difficulties associated in actually doing so, especially as a woman who expects and is expected

to manage a happy home life with a demanding professional career.

2. Be aware that others will feel free to express their views on your personal appearance and family life. Try to keep these observations in perspective by recognizing that the same individuals would never comment in the same fashion on a male leader's appearance or home duties.

3. Identify the key personal priorities in your life and then develop a system to address them to your satisfaction. Use all the resources available to you, including your delegation skills and financial means, to assist you in meeting these priorities.

4. Unexpected life events will occur that will require your undivided attention, taking your focus away from leading. Understand that in these moments, personal issues take precedence, and your role as a leader must either be assumed by others or put on hold for a period of time.

5. Learn to delegate. Only through effective delegation will you be able to carve out the time required to do all the things you need to do to stay physically, mentally and emotionally healthy.

PART 3

Life after leading:
the nerve to redefine yourself

CHAPTER 12

Best-before date

"You know, it is just one small step from legacy to lame duck."

—BILL CLINTON

Leadership does eventually end. Whether it is a voluntary decision or one that is triggered by term limits, age, a performance review, merger or board action, leaders must inevitably face having to forgo their leadership positions. Occasionally, the exit is well planned with the date being established several years in advance. Some leadership positions, such as political appointments or committee chairs, come with term limits, and the end dates are anticipated and set in stone. More common, however, is that the end of a leadership cycle comes unexpectedly, initiated by a specific event or undertaking that precipitates a decision by the leader or the governing board.

While most leaders understand that their tenure must cease, the timing of their departure is rarely known or well planned. Even if leaders acknowledge that the end is inevitable, many have difficulty accepting it and are unable to predict when or how it will occur. Many leaders, who tend to be type A, are reluctant to even think about an exit strategy and often put off contemplating, planning and worrying about the end of their leadership, unconsciously assuming that their leadership will be ongoing.

Furthermore, everyone has a best-before date. After a certain period of time, regardless of the leader's performance, their effectiveness is compromised. Recruiting new leadership periodically is now viewed as best practice. And while leaders themselves may underestimate the value to the organization of such a change, the rank and file are often excited by the idea of fresh beginnings.

Knowing when and how to exit is probably one of the most important decisions leaders will make. It is also one of the hardest—especially if the leader believes either 1) they are at the top of their game, or 2) there is more work to be done to advance their agenda. Even though the timing and circumstances of a leader's exit will often determine how they are viewed by the organization, what the impact of their legacy is and how smooth the transition to a new leader will be, leaders are often reluctant to deal with the reality that they will be replaced, that their effectiveness is time-limited and that others, if necessary, will take control of the decision.

Nevertheless, it is commonly understood that leaders are wise to exit on their own terms, rather than waiting until others believe it is time for them to leave. Most experts suggest that great leaders exit when they are winning—when they are well respected and recognized for the contributions they have made to date.[27] In addition, if leaders exit before they are forced to, they are much better positioned to negotiate the terms of their exit and control the transition of leadership. Why then do so few leaders quit while they are ahead?

The reasons are never absolutely clear, but in most cases, a timely exit requires both a push and a pull. The push comes from the sense of boredom, fatigue or frustration that the leader harbors when they recognize that their enjoyment of the job is waning, or that the same problems keep recurring with little if any resolution. The pull comes from the belief that there are other things they would like to do—that life on the other side is more attractive—or that there is something else beckoning to them that they must attend to, whether it be personal issues or professional opportunities.

While little is known about whether women leaders differ from their male colleagues in knowing when to exit, recent studies confirm that women in general retire at an earlier age than men. Reasons for this difference include women are more likely to 1) be downsized or laid off, 2) become full-time caregivers to aging parents, 3) marry men who are a few years older and retire at the same time as their husbands, and 4) suffer poor health.[27] Whether these findings are transferable to women leaders is unknown, but anecdotal experience suggests that women leaders more actively plan for their retirement, are more likely to anticipate stepping down and are more confident that their lives will be full with other pursuits, professional and personal.

Lame Duck

The interval between the announcement of a leader's decision to leave and the date the leader actually exits is commonly referred to as the *lame duck period*. Lame duck: a creature that is injured, no longer operating at full capacity and dismissed as defective. Is this a fair descriptor of an outgoing leader, regardless of their performance to date? Probably not. But leaders are wise to recognize that regardless of who they are or how well they have performed, they will be perceived differently by the organization starting immediately from the moment they announce their departure or retirement.

How often have you heard a leader strongly proclaim they will not be a lame duck, that they intend to work as hard as ever to accomplish the goals they have established and keep the organization focused and on track? No leader accepts the fact that their job is finished from the moment they declare their intention to leave. However, despite all the leader's bravado, once she has made it clear that she is exiting, her status and influence in the organization change. Typically this lame-duck period has two components: 1) the time between the announcement of the current leader's intention to step down and the naming of a successor, and 2) the period of time between the announcement of a successor and the departure of the current leader.

In some situations the announcement of the CEO's retirement or departure is accompanied by the immediate announcement of the individual's successor. While this is the tradition in the corporate world, it is rarely the case in the public sector or NGOs. A premier resigns, and a leadership convention is held. A CEO of a community foundation or a hospital declares their intention to leave, and the board creates a selection committee to identify the successor.

Regardless of the sector or situation, whether the successor is named immediately or there is a period of time when a search is conducted to identify the new leader, the attention of the organization focuses at once on the next cycle of leadership. Efforts to learn about the new leader abound; it's easy and natural in this transitional time to feel sidelined, like yesterday's news, like that poor lame duck.

SAMARASEKERA:

A few months before the end of my term at U of A, my successor had been named, and the university had swiftly begun to focus on his arrival. The president's residence, where I had been living for a decade, had last been updated in the mid-1990s and was in need of renovations, something an incumbent would be unwise to attempt during their tenure. It seemed appropriate for me to move out of the house, so the improvements could be completed before the new president's start date. Where would I live in the interim? After weighing the options and relative costs, it was decided that I should stay for the next three months in Campus Towers, a hotel on the university grounds, where I soon found myself living out of a suitcase in a small suite.

When I had first arrived as the new president, I was accommodated for six weeks at the Fairmont Hotel in downtown Edmonton; my needs and comfort were a high priority for the board. Now that I was departing, cost was the only serious consideration. The shift in institutional priorities during my lame-duck period was clear, and I reflected on the contrast between my arrival as the incoming president and my departure as I ate dinner by myself at the Earl's restaurant in Campus Towers. It was a lonely and deflating time.

Who's Next?

The role the exiting leader plays in selecting her successor varies according to the traditions, culture and policies of the organization. In some cases, the current leader has significant input into the selection process; in others, the role is minimal if it exists at all. While the current leader may have very strong views on who should succeed them and may be asked to comment on a candidate's suitability, the final decision very often reflects the board's choice rather than the exiting leader's preference.

Accustomed to handpicking members of their team and evaluating the experience and background of candidates, the exiting leader believes, consciously or unconsciously, that they are in the best position to identify the needs of the organization and match them with the ideal candidate. Nevertheless, the board may hold a different perspective on what the organization requires and is often looking for someone entirely different from the person identified by the previous leader. This inability to control the selection process and single-handedly anoint your own successor is often the first indicator of exactly how lame the exiting duck is.

PIPER:

When I resigned from my first term as UBC president, I was invited to present to the selection committee my evaluation of the obstacles and opportunities the university would be facing in the next several years, along with the most important personal qualities a candidate should possess to be an influential university president. I worked diligently on the presentation, thinking strategically about UBC and where it was headed, and what type of person should be selected to lead the institution. Although I did not offer any names of possible candidates, I was clear on the type of person and the skill sets that I thought would best suit UBC.

As I made my presentation, I glanced at the members of the committee. It was clear to me that although they were listening politely and nodding at appropriate times, they had very little, if any, interest in hearing from me on the subject. No note-taking, no questions, no real engagement with what I was saying. They had moved on and had already conducted their own assessment of the needs of the institution and really did not need or value my input. Clearly, I was yesterday's person.

Staying Focused

With all the background noise associated with an incumbent's departure and the selection of a new leader, how does the current leader remain focused? How do they continue to show up day after day, retaining their personal commitment to lead and keeping the organization on track? What should their priorities be and how do they best spend their remaining days in the leadership role? How can they stay relevant and continue to make an impact when they are perceived as a lame-duck leader?

Leaders, in general, are extremely focused. The issue is not whether the leader can stay personally engaged during a transition to new leadership, but rather how she can ensure that her team is not sidelined by all of the buzz associated with her reasons for leaving, what is next for her, the appointment of a new leader or the inertia that may accompany the wait to see who the next leader will be. Given all of the possible distractions inherent in any lame-duck period, it is the exiting leader's responsibility to continue to guide and direct the team and set the agenda for the organization. At the very least, there are three critical priorities an exiting leader needs to tackle during this time: identify specific tasks and goals that realistically may be accomplished; develop an appropriate transition plan to ensure a smooth passing of the leadership baton; and plan for a graceful exit.

In deciding what to tackle during the lame-duck period, the leader needs to assess the environment and prioritize the objectives that can be realistically achieved. One thing is for certain: colleagues will lobby hard for their pet projects—things they want to see accomplished before there is a new leader with different priorities. Some of these projects may indeed have value, but it is important for the leader to assess all initiatives with the aim of taking on only those one or two things that absolutely must be done before a new leader takes over. What achievements will help a new leader succeed? What are the items and issues that need to be resolved so that the new leader is not confronted with difficult decisions within their first few months? Despite being viewed as a lame duck by some, an outgoing leader can continue to forge ahead and make a difference by staying focused and motivated, even in their final days in the role.

PIPER:

I remember thinking there are two issues that no new leader needs to face in the first year of their tenure: office renovation and labor negotiations.

As a result, we decided to tackle both in the time remaining before the new leader took the helm. Everyone agreed it was time to move the president's office from the ground floor of an old building to the fourth floor of a newly renovated building, but because of the anticipated cost it had not yet been done. The ground-floor location allowed easy access and was appropriate 50 years ago, but it posed a major security problem in today's world. With board approval, we moved ahead to put this change into motion before the new president arrived. Similarly, as we began labor negotiations with our local unions, our goal was to obtain a long-term contract, thereby ensuring labor peace for at least the first three to four years of the new leader's term. There was nothing lame in tackling some of the hard stuff before I left, to help shield the new president from controversy early in his tenure.

Swan Song

Leaving a leadership position gracefully and positively is an art form in itself. It is not done easily; nor does it happen naturally. Given all the tensions and worries, obligations and responsibilities, exiting leaders can easily become overwhelmed and jaded about the time that is left in their term. The requests and invitations in the last several months are excessive. People want to meet with the leader to lobby for their project; friends and associates want to go to lunch or dinner to say goodbye; boards are anxious to resolve outstanding issues and leave a clean slate for the new leader; colleagues are nervous and jumpy about the future of their positions and seek wage increases and guarantees that they will be protected in the new administration.

As a result of these increasing demands, many exiting leaders become exhausted by and negative about their last few months on the job. And yet, these can and should be some of the best days of their career. Great leaders understand that these concerns are short-lived and that they are much better served if they are able to experience the end of their leadership on a more positive note.

During this time, the exiting leader can and should have interaction with the new leader. This relationship is unique in many ways and may be fraught with tension and ambivalence; the new leader is anxious to become involved with the organization; the exiting leader is often uncertain how their own legacy will be perceived and how the new leader will be received. Occasionally the two leaders are strikingly different—they often have different skill sets and come from diverse backgrounds. They may or may not view the organization similarly and may or may not identify the same strategic thrusts. In short, this may appear to be a forced relationship, but it should be one that is positively embraced by both parties.

The typical scenario is for the exiting leader to focus on the major issues, spending endless time preparing briefing documents and background information to share with the new leader. While well intended, this information is overvalued and often either goes unread or at best is only scanned by the incoming leader. Much more useful is introducing the new leader to colleagues, singing their praises to the community and genuinely welcoming them to the organization. Not only will this generosity ease the new leader in, but it will also allow you to make a gracious exit. Whether through a community reception for the new leader sponsored by the exiting leader, holding small group luncheons to introduce the incoming leader to staff or external stakeholders or permitting them to reconfigure and organize their office space before taking over, outgoing leaders need to be as generous as they can possibly be in making the new leader feel at home. Based on our experience and observations, we believe that women leaders who are stepping down are more likely to take this approach—openly expressing their support and genuinely accepting them as partners in the transition period—than are exiting male leaders. It serves everyone well to remember that how an incumbent treats their replacement says volumes about the character of the exiting leader. Nothing is to be gained from being small minded or resentful during the changing of the guard. Instead, being positive about the new leader will set the tone for a warm and welcoming response from the entire organization.

PIPER:

Twice I greeted a new male leader to the presidency of UBC; twice I worked tirelessly to document the major issues upon which I thought the new leader should be briefed; twice I was discouraged and disappointed by the new leader's reaction. I guess I am a slow learner, but eventually I understood that a new leader does not really want to be instructed by the exiting leader. Incoming leaders have their own ideas about how best to proceed and do not really want to be a student of the former leader. They are anxious to make their mark and have studied the organization on their own in anticipation of taking the reins and moving ahead.

I did observe, however, that new leaders need to be reassured, stroked and praised. They want to be congratulated for their accomplishments and hear how well their appointment is being received. Instead of informing and briefing the new leader, former leaders can be most effective by emphasizing how good a fit the new leader is for the organization and how lucky it is to have this person as the next leader.

Lessons Learned

All leaders risk becoming lame ducks. As soon as a leader makes clear they are leaving, their status within the organization changes. The demands associated with the period between announcing the intention to exit and the actual date of the leader's departure are numerous, including how they manage the transition period, the ways in which they welcome and advise their replacement and their ability to sustain their own key priorities and resolve critical issues before handing over the mantle of leadership.

Every situation is different, and the specific circumstances surrounding the decision to step down vary from leader to leader. There are, however, some general guidelines to permit the leader to exit graciously and honorably. Most important is for the leader to recognize that her turn to lead is coming to an end and to acknowledge that stepping down is a normal aspect of leading. Good leaders lead with expertise and confidence. Great leaders exit with grace, dignity and humility.

1. Leaders are best served if they control the timing of their exit. Planning ahead for the best date to step down is preferable to being asked to go.
2. Leaders should attempt to leave when they are still respected and trusted. Leaving at the top of one's game is always better than leaving on a low or when the organization is in a crisis.
3. Leaders should realize that regardless of their track record or the level of respect they garner from their associates, once

their departure has been made public, they will likely be seen as a lame duck—powerless and yesterday's news. Being perceived as a lame-duck leader at the end is not the exception, but rather the norm; it is a natural aspect of leadership that accompanies the transition from one leader to the next.

4. While it seems to make good sense for the exiting leader to play a significant role in the selection of the next leader, in reality it is rare for this to occur. Exiting leaders need to accept the fact that their input into the selection process will most likely be limited; that boards are often seeking a leader who possesses different strengths than the current leader; and that it is commonly viewed as inappropriate for the exiting leader to name her successor.

5. When identifying the institutional goals to be completed during the lame-duck period, the exiting leader needs to have the nerve to tackle some of the more difficult issues that no new leader should be encumbered with. By addressing some of these controversial issues before the new leader takes over, the exiting leader will assist in ensuring a smooth transition.

6. New leaders rarely if ever want to be tutored by their predecessor. Rather, the exiting leader needs to focus on introducing the new leader to the community, emphasizing to others the strengths of the individual and celebrating their appointment. Incoming leaders are anxious to place their own stamp on the organization and may even want to distance themselves from some of the priorities of the previous leader.

7. Recognizing that all things in life must come to an end, including your time to lead, will enable you to exit with the same dignity and grace with which you led.

CHAPTER 13

————

Loss

*"It's so much darker when a light goes out than it would
have been if it had never shone."*

—JOHN STEINBECK,
THE WINTER OF OUR DISCONTENT

Leadership positions come with enormous privileges and personal
fulfillment. They present unequalled opportunities to make a
significant difference to the organization and are often accompanied by
admiration and respect. Leaders feel a sense of purpose and develop a
degree of self-confidence. Work associates want to see and be seen with
them; colleagues covet their attention, answer their phone calls and
emails and work hard to know and influence their views and opinions.
At dinners and receptions, people are eager to sit next to the leader,
introduce their colleagues and friends and capture the leader's attention. In short, leaders are different than their colleagues in that they are
perceived as having power and influence and are often viewed as being
instrumental in the advancement of others' careers.

Leadership positions also may be accompanied by significant personal
perks. Of course, there is the salary, which is often the highest an individual

will ever earn, along with other forms of compensation, including pensions, life insurance and bonuses. But these positions may also come with other benefits, including the use of a car or a residence, financial counseling, expense accounts and club memberships. Leaders have their own assistants, who manage everything from daily schedules to organizing travel and luncheon reservations. Technology issues are immediately resolved, and access to the latest, most up-to-date phones and computers is granted. The concerns and needs of the leader top everyone's priority list.

But no one is a leader forever. When a leader steps down, is let go or retires, they are left with a huge vacuum. Gone are the busy days and event-filled nights; gone are the trusted colleagues and support staff; gone are the responsibilities and benefits of the role. Life can feel strangely empty without thousands of emails and pings to your phone; without having to run from one meeting to the next all day long; without clear goals and objectives to strive for; without the social world of work; without the strong sense of purpose that drove you for all those years. Whether a leader is pushed out or leaves voluntarily, the end of their leadership feels like a huge loss and signals a major change in their life.

How then do leaders deal with the major changes they will face upon stepping down, including a profound sense of loss and lack of purpose? And do women leaders cope differently with these feelings and life changes than their male counterparts? As two women leaders who chose to step down and worked to redefine our sense of purpose, we can only speak to our own experiences and have to rely on anecdotal evidence to compare our journeys with those of our male colleagues. Research findings, to date, largely address the gender disparities in financial status, with women falling significantly behind men in terms of pensions, accumulated investments and net worth. While these differences are extremely important, especially given that women are expected to live longer than men, we are more interested in how women leaders cope emotionally, psychologically and behaviorally with their change of status and loss of title, position, purpose and perceived influence.

Initial Response

All former leaders share a common experience. They will no longer be defined by their titles or the status of their position; they will no longer derive the sense of purpose and meaning they found primarily in their jobs or be viewed as the key spokesperson and strategic leader of their organization; they will no longer have access to key individuals, networks and associations that were available to them as leaders; they will no longer receive all of the benefits associated with their leadership position, making time management, travel and use of technology more stressful; they will no longer be able to depend on the skills and work experiences that got them to the top of their career to bring personal fulfillment; and they will no longer experience the seasonality and rhythms of the year, such as quarterly reporting, AGMs and the rituals associated with their positions.

Although leaders generally experience a sense of relief when they relinquish their demanding role, they are often unprepared for the emotional responses that accompany leaving life as a leader behind: yearning for what they no longer have, sadness in knowing they are no longer leading, frustration in recognizing their influence is diminished, loneliness in being separated from colleagues and associates. In short, former leaders often suffer several losses when stepping down from their position.

While some may find the term *loss* rather negative in this situation, and perhaps somewhat hyperbolic, it is an accurate characterization. Giving up a leadership position truly represents a loss in terms of identity, standing in the community, purpose, compensation and other benefits, along with the accompanying demands on one's schedule and personal time. Former leaders often experience the loss of confidantes and key supporters, including significant networks of colleagues. The intellectual stimulation of decision-making and problem solving is replaced with unscheduled time and potential boredom.

Although male and female leaders have much the same initial experience when they leave their leadership role behind, research has shown that men and women face different issues in dealing with their reactions.[28] While both genders have to deal with the loss of their primary identity and sense of purpose, a female leader must also confront the reappearance of a second identity, that is, her traditional role as the primary caregiver and domestic worker in the home. When leading, women often forgo the second shift at home, hiring help for everything from childcare to folding the laundry.[29] However, upon leaving their leadership positions, women are more likely than their male colleagues to believe that they are now expected to assume many of the domestic tasks they had relinquished when leading. Because they no longer have any "acceptable" excuse for not doing these tasks themselves, women may think they are expected to perform this domestic work. How should former women leaders deal with this expectation? Is it okay to continue to seek help when confronted with many of the tasks that are part of daily living, now that they have the time to assume these responsibilities? Is this really the new identity they want for themselves after leading for so many years?

We believe, for most women leaders, the significant losses they feel are balanced by the sense of relief and freedom that accompanies the forfeiture of responsibility and stress. While men may yearn to retain the power and obligations that accompany leading, most of the former women leaders we have observed were happy to know that they no longer must shoulder the 24/7 duties of running the organization, department or program. They relish the control they now have over their personal lives; many have looked forward to this time when they do not need to prove themselves to their peers and colleagues. And yet, even if women leaders anticipate a reduction in the stress in their lives, they, too, will most likely experience a sense of being adrift, a feeling of becoming unmoored in the early days of their newfound freedom.

SAMARASEKERA:

About 10 days after I stepped down from the presidency of the University of Alberta, I was sitting with my feet in warm water at a spa in Pasadena, California. I had flown down to visit my friend, Cherine, and she had arranged for a trip to the spa. Cherine and I had met in school when we were 12 years old and had a bond that had survived long periods of little or no contact. In the midst of a relaxing pedicure, I found myself glancing at my phone from time to time, expecting it to ring or beep, alerting me to a message. It was silent. I had no idea why I was checking, other than the practice had become so deeply ingrained in my routine.

As the hours passed, the realization that I was not in charge of anything started to sink in. I remember the feeling of freedom that I experienced that day. Freedom from a crowded schedule and a scripted agenda. Freedom to enjoy lunch in the California sunshine without constantly checking my watch. Freedom to browse in antique shops for sheer pleasure. I had looked forward to my visit to California, but I could not have anticipated how much I would enjoy this special time, which marked the passage to freedom—freedom from the unrelenting responsibilities of a leader.

And then it hit me hard. The first September after stepping down as president, as the leaves began to rustle and the back-to-school ads were appearing, I felt lost. With Labor Day approaching, I was grieving the absence of the general excitement surrounding the start of the school year. I was not gearing up for the first day of classes; I was not writing my welcome speeches; nor was I preparing the agendas for upcoming executive and board meetings. It was different, and I was not sure I liked it. I knew I no longer had the responsibility associated with running the place, but I also was aware of the loss in purpose I was experiencing. There was a sadness associated with the knowledge that this chapter of my career was over.

No Longer in Charge

One of the more difficult losses experienced by former leaders is the realization that they are no longer in charge of anything. Accustomed to leading on every front—determining strategic directions, chairing meetings, motivating the workforce, cultivating key partnerships and relationships—exiting leaders slowly and painfully come to the recognition that they no longer are running things and their impact is severely diminished.

Departing leaders often struggle to find their voice, to determine how they can contribute and the manner in which they can be heard. As one of many, they no longer command the attention they previously had as the leader and are often surprised at how little influence they have over anything of substance in a life after leadership. This can be even more of an issue for women than for men. Men are more likely to be moving on to either new leadership positions or corporate board appointments; whereas women are expected to be more relieved by their newfound freedom, more satisfied with finally having more time to spend with family and friends after feeling guilty for all the time spent away from home in their working years. And yet, although women who have stepped down undoubtedly relish the slower pace, they often experience a void so large it borders on discomfort or despair. Even if they do go on to new and different leadership roles, women who are no longer in charge of an organization can feel their identity as a leader shaken to the core.

PIPER:

Upon joining several corporate boards after being president of UBC, I was disillusioned and confused about the role I was to play. I no longer was in command of the organization's agenda or the priorities for discussion; I no longer had a bully pulpit from which to express my views; my suggestions and ideas were often ignored or rejected. As a result, I began to question my competence and self-worth; I was constantly worried that I was not adding any value to the overall strategic discussions. My response was to prepare even harder, to read even more, to study everything diligently. What I failed to understand was that my role had changed. I was no longer the leader of the organization with ultimate responsibility for its success or failure. Rather, I was one of many contributors—a cog in a much bigger wheel and, hence, played a different role in the overall direction of the organization.

Lost Associates

No leader exists in a vacuum. Every leader has relied upon people whom they trust and respect not only to advance their agendas but also to nourish their intellect. What is not always appreciated is that these relationships and connections are at risk when a leader no longer leads. Former leaders often suffer the loss of close confidantes, supporters and colleagues, and the extensive networks they used to access. They may no longer see and enjoy the company and stimulation of the people they were accustomed to being with on a daily basis. Their executive team no longer features in their daily schedule; the office staff are not there every morning with a warm hello; they no longer enjoy shared jokes and stories on a regular basis.

The loss of relationships goes beyond colleagues, direct reports and work friends. The connections leaders enjoy at every level of leadership provide them with the ability to open doors, to access people who are more powerful than they are, to associate with individuals and institutions that help advance their causes and issues. The prime minister of Canada can access the president of the United States; CEOs of major corporations can access the prime minister and ministers; department heads can access the CEOs of their respective organizations; school principals can access the superintendent of the school system; vice presidents of corporations and deputy ministers can access the president or minister, respectively; board chairs can access the CEO; deans can access the president of the university.

This ability to interact with thought leaders and decision makers distinguishes leaders from others in the organization. Their phone calls are returned; their requests for meetings are accepted; their queries are answered. Access to key individuals and networks brings with it intellectual stimulation, global connections and personal recognition. Yet, this access is short-lived, as it often ceases when the leader steps down; the doors no longer open as easily or as frequently.

SAMARASEKERA:

When I arrived at the University of Alberta it had few links with India. Given India and Canada's shared democratic traditions and India's large youthful population, I decided to make India a priority country and visited annually. My first visit was momentous.

The University of Alberta had awarded Prime Minister Manmohan Singh an honorary degree, and the former chair of the U of A board, Jim Edwards, had developed strong ties with the prime minister and arranged for me to meet him. I was ushered into a large but unpretentious room in his official residence Lok Kalyan Marg that was overlooking beautiful gardens with peacocks strutting about majestically. I expected to have a 20-minute meeting and had rehearsed endlessly what I hoped to ask him. The prime minister arrived with no aides and to my surprise spent 45 minutes with me. He was warm and engaging, and I had to remind myself I was speaking to the leader of the world's largest democracy of over a billion people. Following this propitious meeting and over the ensuing 10 years, U of A built strong ties with India, its schools, universities, private sector and government. For me it was a life-changing experience—I could not have learned as much about India's people, culture and promise any other way.

A few months after stepping down, it struck me that I would not have access to remarkable leaders and influential thinkers. I could not expect to engage with individuals who were shaping their communities, countries or the world. I was now on the outside and had to be content with being a spectator, watching the news unfold remotely—a realization that was tinged with some sadness.

PIPER:

When I stepped down as a director of the Bank of Montreal after 10 years of serving on the board, I was unprepared for the sense of loss I would experience. I had served responsibly, attended the regular meetings in Toronto, chaired a committee and spent hours on early morning conference calls that began, in my time zone, at 5 a.m. It was like a weight being lifted from my shoulders. I was ready to step down. I was pleased that I would not be making monthly trips to Toronto, and I relished the thought that I would not have to spend endless hours reading reams of material, sitting in airports, eating on the run, sleeping in hotel beds and coping with jet lag. And yet, what I totally underestimated was what I would lose by relinquishing my directorship.

Several months after leaving the board, I became aware of how much I missed my colleagues, all amazing individuals, and the intellectual stimulation that went far beyond the boardroom. I recognized that I was possibly not going to see these people again, and even if I did, it would be only a brief encounter. It was as if I was disconnected to a part of the country that had provided me with friendships and exposure to key national and global issues. It saddened me to know that these cherished relationships were at risk.

Who Am I?

Former leaders are often unprepared for the loss of attention: no longer do people covet being with them; they often find themselves standing alone at a reception with no one to talk to; they are no longer acknowledged when boarding a plane or eating in a restaurant; and their requests for communications are often ignored or overlooked. In short, their status has been diminished, and as a result they are denied the recognition or respect they previously received. Are former women leaders "forgotten" more readily than their male peers? Perhaps. All we know is that quickly after leaving office, we became invisible and often were ignored at public events.

And what about the loss of title? How many times have former leaders struggled to tell people who they are now that they no longer hold the title of president or vice president, CEO, chair, dean, executive director, deputy minister and so on? How do they complete forms and applications when asked where they work or what position they hold? Moving from being able to introduce yourself as the head of the department, or the director of X, to saying you are "retired" or "unemployed" is one of the most difficult transitions a former leader needs to make. One day you are the person in charge with business cards to prove it; the next, almost overnight, you not only do not have the keys to the office but also you have no position to call your own. Not that a title determines who you are, but it does signal your role in an organization, your position in society and your skill set and identifies who you are in relation to your peers. For leaders, more than anyone else in the organization, their identity is so tied up in their title, their role and the work they do that when they are no longer leading, they suddenly feel completely lost and adrift.

PIPER:

I have never gotten used to the question, "What are you doing now?" Embarrassed to use the R-word, or to suggest that I am not gainfully employed or extremely busy, I find myself immediately becoming defensive—reciting all the wonderful things I am now involved with and how exciting life is. It is as if I have to convince not only others but also myself that I am still in high demand and worthy of attention and respect. I feel as if I have to prove myself all over again.

After leaving UBC, I joined the Canadian delegation of the Trilateral Commission, an international think tank focused on global and political issues. Time after time, well-known international figures introduced themselves, waiting for my response as to who I was exactly and what title I currently held. I was confused and felt lost, as the only response

I could conjure up was, "I used to be . . ." which seemed so inadequate and irrelevant.

I continue to wonder why it is that I am so uncomfortable with this issue. Why have I lacked the nerve to admit I am retired or just doing what I want to do, rather than having to define myself in terms of either the position I held previously or a new appointment with an impressive title? I really haven't figured it out, other than to say the obvious, that society does not value people for just being who they are but rather assigns worth according to what individuals are doing and the positions they hold.

I become angry with myself when I admit my reluctance to say that I am not that busy, that I am just enjoying my days as they unfold, that I am not reporting to anyone and have no one reporting to me. I know that my life still has worth and that I am eagerly participating in the day-to-day rhythms of living a full life; slowly I am becoming more comfortable identifying myself as a grandmother in contrast to having a specific duty, title or position. I have learned the hard way that it takes time and nerve to redefine one's sense of purpose and to become comfortable with who you are rather than what you do for a living. I do believe, however, that women are better at accepting their new identity than men. Women have numerous interests they are committed to, whether it is volunteering, friends, fitness or hobbies, often making this transition easier for former women leaders than their male colleagues.

Lessons Learned

While experiencing a sense of liberation, former leaders also encounter a series of significant losses when they step down: the loss of status and identity, the loss of purpose, the loss of relationships, the loss of influence and voice.and the loss of support and routine, to name a few. These losses are real. And yet, they are often overlooked or go unrecognized when a leader is planning for retirement and living a life after leading. How does a leader anticipate these losses, and how does a former leader cope with the inevitability of the swings in mood and emotional upheaval they will experience once they give up their position of leadership? What are some of the pitfalls they should try to avoid immediately after forgoing their leadership duties? And what are some of the dangers specific to women leaving their leadership role behind?

1. The most important aspect of preparing for and coping with the losses associated with leaving a leadership position is recognizing that these losses will occur; that it is normal to experience some sadness or regret when leaving office in addition to the newly found sense of freedom. By recognizing that these losses are commonly experienced by all leaders stepping down, that what you are experiencing is normal rather than abnormal, you will be more effective in moving through this transition period.

2. The losses you will experience are in most cases short-lived and will diminish with time. While each individual's timetable differs, and no one journey is the same as another, there is a light at the end of the tunnel. By knowing that you are not alone in what you are experiencing and that it is normal to feel ambivalent about your post-leadership life, you will be much better prepared to face the changes you will inevitably encounter when you give up your position of leadership.

3. Knowing that your journey of recovery is not unique, you may find comfort and support in discussing your experience with other leaders who have gone before you. This form of disclosure requires significant trust in and respect for the individual you are confiding in, but these interactions can be extremely helpful in knowing that others have dealt with the same situations and have successfully moved on.

4. Be aware that your influence and voice have changed. No longer will people listen to you primarily because of your position. Focus on developing a new voice, based on thoughtful ideas and insightful interventions. Accept the fact that instead of being the leader, you are now one of many valuable contributors.

5. Work at redefining yourself by creating a new identity that goes beyond your leadership profile. Foster meaningful relationships and networks that build upon and extend

beyond those associated with your previous life. By accepting the fact that you are no longer in charge, you will be better able to carve out unique roles that will provide you with a new sense of purpose.

CHAPTER 14

Doing well or doing good

"How wonderful it is that nobody need wait a single moment before starting to improve the world."

—ANNE FRANK, *THE DIARY OF A YOUNG GIRL*

Women leaders are often faced with the dilemma of how they should spend their time, find new purpose and give of their expertise after stepping down from their leadership positions. They worry that their days will be empty and that they no longer will be in demand. Some have concerns that their financial needs will exceed their income; others wonder whether their phones will ring or remain silent; still others are uncertain about where they want to invest their time and effort. Should they consider another full-time position that builds upon their past experience, or should they be content focusing on travel, family, hobbies or personal needs? Should they make money by consulting, establishing a start-up company in an area they have always wanted to pursue? Or should they volunteer and give back to their community through contributing to nonprofit organizations, mentoring other colleagues or serving on government panels and commissions? Where and how do they continue to be intellectually engaged and stimulated? And what about corporate boards? Is this a possibility, and if so, how do you go about being appointed to such a board?

It is likely that you will eventually choose a mix of activities, so then the problem becomes determining the right combination of things and how to identify your commitments without compromising the most important aspects of this period in your life—personal freedom and time for yourself.

There are no simple answers to these questions, and these choices are clearly different from other previous career decisions. You don't have to commit to an all-consuming work schedule where you're on call 24 hours a day, seven days a week. No longer do you need to position yourself for a promotion or pay raise. Nor are you limited by your previous work experience or your formal education. This time in a female leader's life is unique in its opportunities and possibilities, opening up doors that permit her to remain engaged, intellectually stimulated and an active participant in her community; but it is also time-limited due to aging and potential health issues. In short, women want to make the most of the time they have left to do the things they were never able to do, experience things they never had the time for, stretch their minds and learn things they never studied and ensure that they have no regrets when the clock runs out.

As two former leaders who have struggled to find the right mix of fulfilling activities, we understand the challenge women leaders face in determining what their personal priorities are in their post-leadership lives, knowing that other factors may come into play, such as age, health, place of residence, family commitments and financial concerns. Despite sometimes differing in the choices we have made, we do believe there are some common issues that all former women leaders confront when determining the path they will follow after leading. Some are associated with the fears and myths around retirement; others are related to the realities of the current landscape for former leaders in general and women in particular. Nevertheless, this particular period in one's life is unique; clearly it is a time to spread your wings, find the nerve to try things that you have never explored, become engaged in areas you are passionate about or that align with your personal values and address the initiatives you believe have the potential to make your community or the world a better place.

Fear of Being Forgotten

Women leaders are not known for an overabundance of self-confidence, often doubting their abilities and second-guessing their decisions. They are worriers and are known to suffer from imposter syndrome, that is, the lurking suspicion that they are frauds, less competent than others around them, and that they will eventually be found out. Unfortunately, this self-doubt seems to be permanently wired, existing long after they have performed magnificently and have the respect and admiration of everyone around them. When they finally step down from their leadership position, this lack of confidence tends to continue to haunt them as they contemplate what is next.

One of the biggest fears of women leaders who are stepping down is that their phone will not ring, that they will drop off into the abyss and no one will reach out to them or invite them to participate, contribute or engage. The fear of being forgotten. Women are known to be afraid that their future after leadership looks empty, that their associates and colleagues will no longer value their talent and expertise, and that the opportunities to contribute will be limited at best.

Our experiences suggest that the fear of being forgotten is not grounded in reality, and there is little evidence to support this concern. The possibilities to become involved and stay engaged are numerous, and women are well-advised to shelve their worries and anticipate having a variety of opportunities to choose from. Women leaders are firmly in the driver's seat to determine what they do after they step down, when and how they become involved in their communities, choosing carefully those organizations and events that they want to participate in. You do not have to wait until your phone rings; as a leader, you have taken charge of your destiny throughout your life, and this is no different—*you* can determine what you want to do and how you are going to do it.

PIPER:

When I stepped down from the presidency, my husband and I decided we would take a sabbatical year at Oxford University. It was a wonderful time for us, providing us with a genuine break from our daily routines and putting distance between ourselves and UBC. I did, however, worry while we were away. I had no idea what I would do following my sabbatical year and was concerned that my phone would not ring—especially since I was out of the country. How would people reach me? If I was not physically present, attending dinners, receptions and conferences, would I drop out of sight and out of mind? Would I be forgotten? Should I not be promoting myself rather than going into hiding?

And yet, as I sought advice from former leaders who had gone before me, the universal suggestion was to take my time in determining what I wanted to do, to not jump at the first things that came my way: take a break from making any decisions at all and be patient. As such, the idea of taking a year *off* seemed to fit the bill, consistent with the advice of people I most admired and respected.

My phone did ring—international borders be damned. My fears of being forgotten were unfounded; instead, I was being approached by various individuals and organizations to consider joining them or contributing to their efforts. What my sabbatical year provided me, however, was a wonderful hiatus, an excuse to be able to say that I would not be available for a year, and if they were still interested after that period, I would give the request serious consideration.

What did I learn from this experience? First, whether you are approached or initiate contact yourself, there are endless ways and opportunities for you to pursue your personal goals and priorities after leading. And, second, don't jump too quickly; carefully reflect upon not only the array of possibilities but also your own personal desires—how much time you want to commit, what initiatives you are passionate about, whether you are prepared to travel and be away from home and how important your personal needs are, whether they be family, friends, intellectual stimulation or physical well-being. Finally, I learned that regardless of the leadership position you have held, whether you reach out to them or they reach out to you, people will be interested in having you join them to give of your expertise, talent and time.

Saying No

Saying no has always been difficult for women, as their sense of purpose has been defined by their willingness to assume responsibility, please others and to take on tasks. They often feel guilty when they refuse an invitation or deny a request. "Yes" has been their default response when asked to do something; saying no is viewed as being adversarial, uncooperative, disinterested or selfish.

As leaders, women have been known to assume the duties that are difficult or challenging in order to advance the cause or objectives of their organizations, taking on the responsibilities that no one else wants or that are seen as being the role of a woman: recording the minutes in a meeting, organizing the professional conference, hosting and entertaining the important but difficult associate or reporting out from a focus group. In fact, many women believe they have to say yes to the tough stuff and the drudgery if they want to get anywhere in their career; if they say no too often or to the wrong thing, they fear they may be seen as unambitious or less of a team player than their male counterparts. However, once they are no longer leaders, women need to shift gears and realize that their decisions about whether to say yes or no should depend on their personal priorities rather than preconceived ideas of what is appropriate for a leader or what is "women's work."

Women who have led should recognize that they will tend to underestimate the time commitment and what is involved with each individual invitation or request. When all of the acceptances are tallied, women often find themselves overcommitted and overwhelmed with their new responsibilities. They often report becoming involved in initiatives that they do not enjoy, resulting in the even more difficult decision to step down from a commitment.

We both have struggled to learn not only to say no but also how to do so gracefully. Saying yes is easy. In most cases, saying no is accompanied by guilt, along with a perceived need to present a reason for rejecting a cause or an invitation. Why do we think we need to give an explanation, other than we just do not want to do something? Women are well-advised to draw upon their nerve and turn down the things that no longer meet their newly defined sense of purpose; by doing so, they will free up their time, attention and resources to engage in life in a way that is truly meaningful and personally rewarding.

Getting on Board

Male leaders who retire commonly anticipate continuing to earn an income, leveraging their CEO or senior management experience into corporate board appointments and/or consulting contracts. It is generally accepted that if a male leader has distinguished himself in the business world, he will be rewarded by being asked to join a corporate board, often of a company that is headed by one of his male colleagues or associates. Former male CEOs can expect to enjoy five to 10 years of additional earning power as a result of their record of leadership—thereby doing very well financially post-retirement and continuing to derive purpose from the work they do.

Former women leaders should be able to anticipate a similar path if they so choose, but interestingly many relate that they either have not been asked to serve or that they were at a loss in terms of how to seek a corporate board appointment. If there is one question that we both are continually asked by women who are stepping down from leadership positions it is this: "How do I obtain a corporate board appointment?"

The reasons women are in need of direction and advice when it comes to securing board appointments are not complicated. First, some do not have a track record of experience that allows us to break into this new territory. Many corporate boards still require directors to have been CEOs, thereby disqualifying the many women who have held senior leadership positions but have not been a CEO. Second, most corporate boards have historically been dominated by men, with less than 25 percent of women directors, even in the large market cap companies. As a result, women have had neither the visibility nor the network of colleagues to assist them in obtaining seats at the table.

But times are changing. Because of the efforts of women's advocacy groups and the heightened recognition of the importance of diversity at the board level, more and more corporate boards are actively seeking women directors, realizing that the perspective women bring is invaluable. Catalyst research published in 2020 found that Fortune 500 companies in the United States with the highest number of women on their board outperformed those with the lowest numbers, with return on equity 53 percent higher on average. Best corporate governance practice highlights diversity, and shareholders are demanding gender balance. In reality, there has never been a better time to be a woman leader seeking a corporate board appointment. Our time has come.

We believe that it is no longer a matter of being able to obtain such an appointment; rather, the primary issue now is women knowing what they want and being extremely selective in what boards they choose to join—it is a matter of being careful what you wish for. Hence, the first step in joining a corporate board is to do your homework. Seek advice from those who have gone before you; review biographical reports on the other board members; study the proxies, financial statements and annual reports to determine the strategic priorities and financial status of the company; identify potential or real conflicts of interest; and, most important, do not be afraid to say, "Thanks, but no thanks" to any opportunity that does not align with your personal values, interests and goals.

Women are often too eager to accept the first invitation that comes their way because they believe the myth that it is difficult to obtain a board appointment. By being selective, by being thoughtful in assessing the opportunity, by recognizing that other possibilities exist, women will find their voice and earn respect—even before they join the board. Would you buy the first car you drove or purchase the first house you saw? Would you marry your first date? A leading woman director once said, "It is a lot easier to get on a board than to get off!" Not unlike a marriage—it's easier to commit to a relationship than to end a bad partnership. So our first suggestion is to be selective and choose wisely.

But what if you are not sought out for a board appointment? How then do women go about securing a position on the board? Don't despair. There is a method to the madness, and it includes the following steps: Do your research to determine what boards interest you and what boards you think you can contribute to. Once you have identified the boards you would like to join and have studied the companies' business models, financial statements and strategies, reach out to any of the directors you might know on each of these boards, with particular focus on contacting the chair of the governance and nominating committee, as well as the chair of the board. Inform them of your interest, your reasons for selecting this company, what expertise you can bring to the table and your availability, along with your willingness to wait until there is an opening. And, finally, make yourself known to the headhunting firms that are working with corporate boards to identify key individuals for board appointments. Gone are the days of boards appointing only their friends and colleagues; most corporate boards are now using professional firms to identify and assess candidates, with a particular emphasis on promoting qualified women. If you are known to these firms, you are more likely to be considered by them for future appointments. Women need to do what their male colleagues have done all along: be proactive in advocacy and have the confidence and nerve to risk rejection, while at the same time positioning themselves to be seriously considered and subsequently appointed.

SAMARASEKERA:

I was approaching my retirement from U of A when I started to worry about what I would do after I stepped down. Although I was already a director of Scotiabank, I wondered whether I would be invited to join another corporate board. My appointment to the bank board was partly due to where I lived. At the time Alberta was experiencing an economic boom as a result of the investment in the oil and gas sector; because the bank was interested in growing their customer base there, they wanted someone who understood the geopolitical dynamics and culture of the province and chose me.

Would I receive another invitation to join a corporate board? Seeking the advice of a male senior colleague who was the chair of two corporate boards and director of a third, I was surprised to learn that he had played a proactive role in obtaining these appointments. He shared with me that as he neared his retirement as a highly respected CEO, he had developed a strategic approach to secure his board positions. There was nothing passive in his method. He did not sit quietly waiting for his phone to ring. Instead, he had become his own advocate, actively presenting his case and making his availability known to a select group of boards to which he thought he could add value. He told me that after reviewing the proxy circulars and studying the strategies and financial positions of the companies he was considering, he narrowed his list to 10 with strong CEOs. He proceeded to write to the individuals he knew who were serving on those boards, directors he respected, stating his interest in joining their board and explaining why he had identified the specific company.

I was stunned. I would never have considered reaching out so directly, announcing my availability and interest and advocating for my appointment in such a bold manner. He assured me that it was appropriate for me to do so, that my leadership experience made me an attractive candidate for boards, especially those looking for more qualified women.

I took his advice and began to do some research on companies that might be a good fit given my background in mechanical engineering. At the top of my list was a company whose board included two individuals I knew and respected. After thinking about it for several weeks, I summoned the nerve to write to one of them expressing my interest in the company and a board directorship. Voilà, it worked! I received an enthusiastic response with an introduction to the chair of the board and the CEO. An in-person meeting with both of them followed to assess fit, and a month later, after they had conducted the appropriate due diligence, I was invited to join the board.

I learned from this experience that men have a long history of advocating for themselves, working the corners and making the case for their appointments. Why is it that men are comfortable in actively seeking what they desire, while women are reluctant? Is it that women fear rejection? Is it that we do not like asking favors or believe we should not promote ourselves or that modesty is the best policy? Whatever the reason, I am convinced that women who seek challenging professional opportunities after their tenure as leaders should take a page out of their male colleagues' book and conjure up the nerve and determination to strategically advance their own interests. Of course, you must have the appropriate experience and qualifications to obtain whatever you are after. But too often we are overlooked and passed by, not because we are unqualified to serve, but rather because we are hesitant or unwilling to make it known that we have both the desire and the ability to do something well. I learned a lesson I will never forget. Armed with a good case for how they can contribute, women can be successful in achieving the results they desire.

Being Different

Women university graduates now outnumber men, yet they remain underrepresented in leadership roles, especially when it comes to directorships on corporate boards. Gender diversity on boards is primarily a talent issue; tapping into the entire population for top talent rather than limiting the pool to only 50 percent of the population results in a larger group from which to draw. In addition, other benefits are derived through the diversification of boards. A report published in 2020 by Catalyst suggests mixed-gender boards experience fewer instances of fraud due to better risk management practices and increased engagement among members, which strengthens the environmental, social and governance performance of the board. While some reports have suggested the presence of women in the boardroom improves business results, these studies have largely been correlational rather than prospective predictive trials. As such, it is difficult to tease out whether the better business performance of companies with women directors is truly a result of the diversity factor or whether the companies that have appointed women are just more progressive and better managed overall than those companies without women directors. Rather than seek to justify the presence of women in boards solely through elusive evidence on improvements in business results, we believe a stronger argument may be made around the change that occurs in board culture when women are at the table.

For over a decade, boards have sought to increase gender diversity, and some progress has been made. In a recent Osler report on board diversity in Canada, women hold 31 percent of the board seats in S&P/TSX 60 companies and 21 percent in TSX companies, with 58.5 percent of the S&P/TSX 60 companies having adopted diversity targets.[30] Norway, Spain, Iceland and France all have laws requiring that women comprise at least 40 percent of the boards of publicly listed companies.[31]

As boards adapt and work towards achieving gender diversity, we predict that the corporate world will encounter an even greater challenge in achieving social diversity, including race or ethnicity, physical disability, geography, sexual orientation and age. Diversity and inclusion have risen to the top of the societal agenda after the recent protests on racial injustice and the impact of the Black Lives Matter movement, and are being broadly discussed in the media and the public and private sectors. Shareholders and stakeholders of corporations expect progress on the broader question of diversity to ensure the workforce, senior management and boards reflect society. This is our cultural landscape. We firmly believe that Canadian corporate boards will benefit and flourish by better representing the populations they serve. Whether it be global trends, contemporary social justice issues or geopolitical tensions, socially diverse boards will be better equipped to assist in aligning a company's strategic objectives with the realities and priorities of its employees, customers and shareholders.

In order to reap the benefits of social diversity, boards must create an egalitarian culture that values new backgrounds, various viewpoints and different perspectives, thereby enhancing "cognitive diversity."[32] Cognitively diverse directors who possess backgrounds relevant to the company's business and strategic plan, but who have no relationship with the CEO, board chair or other directors are more likely to ask tough questions and set the stage for other directors to express dissent and challenge the status quo, thus improving board governance and company performance.

Because we have served as directors on major Canadian corporate boards, we have experienced firsthand both the efforts boards are currently making to diversify and the subtle resistance to appointing directors who are "different." We have both worked to identify, advocate for and appoint diverse candidates to our respective boards—sometimes successfully, sometimes unsuccessfully. We have witnessed the fruits of diversification at the board table, including the leveraging of innovative ideas and processes, the willingness to question previously held assumptions and the contradiction of various inconvenient truths. While these changes may be hard to measure objectively, we are convinced that over time diversification of corporate boards will lead to better performance and increased accountability of the respective companies.

PIPER:

When I assumed the chair of the Governance and Nominating Committee of BMO, corporate boards were being challenged to adopt diversity targets and policies. The chair of the board, Rob Prichard, tasked me with addressing this issue and bringing forward recommendations on how we might as a board confront gender diversity.

Naively, I assumed that responding to this request would not be difficult and that the adoption of a progressive diversity policy would be straightforward. With Rob's wholehearted support, I recommended that the board act aggressively and set an ambitious goal of having a board composition in which each gender comprised at least one-third of the independent directors. Going even further, I advocated that the bank confirm its intent by approving a diversity policy that would be publicly available on our board website. In short, I was recommending the bank set a gender diversity quota.

While I obtained committee approval of the proposed diversity policy, I encountered some resistance when debating the policy at the board. The age-old arguments were put forward: this policy would hurt qualified women, who would view their appointment as being based solely on being female; the policy would be difficult to implement as there still were not enough qualified women to serve; because there were so few women CEOs of major corporations, and because many directors thought you needed CEO experience to qualify for a board appointment, women were therefore ineligible for consideration. I countered as best I could with statistics on women who had advanced degrees, on the numbers of women who had reached the highest levels of achievement and who had distinguished themselves in various fields. I argued the importance of having a diverse set of directors, who were more representative of our employees, customers and shareholders. I continued with new evidence that demonstrated women were the financial managers in their households and were acquiring wealth at a high rate. The world was changing, and women were a major factor in that change; the bank needed to embrace this change in order to prosper. Fortunately, the chair of the board, Rob Prichard, and the CEO, Bill Downe, both strongly supported the policy, and, after some debate, it passed.

Once the policy was established, it had immediate effect. When recruiting new directors, the policy was always front and center, driving who was being nominated and considered for vacant directorships. We charged the search consultants with bringing us the names of women who had all the qualifications we required. I am convinced that had the bank not adopted the policy and publicly committed to gender diversity, we would not have been as successful in appointing women to the board. I am proud of BMO and the role it has played as a leading example of how board policy can have a positive impact on achieving gender diversity. The challenge now is to build on this legacy and work towards addressing social diversity in all of its forms.

SAMARASEKERA:

A couple of years after I joined the Magna International board, I became engaged in the director search process as a member of the Corporate Governance and Compensation and Nominating Committee (CGCNC). Working with an experienced consultant, the committee identified technology expertise, especially software, as being an important skill set for the next director to possess. Magna International is the third largest Tier 1 automotive parts supplier in the world, and electronics, namely sensors and software, were strategic to the company's growth trajectory in the automotive market for the car of the future. The growing importance of diversity—social, gender, professional and geographic—was also top of mind and a requirement in our search. As a champion of diversity within the company, CEO Don Walker strongly supported our approach.

Following a board discussion around these priorities, we tasked the search consultant with identifying strong candidates who brought business acumen and professional expertise relevant to the company's financial and strategic plan. We also wanted to tap into talent pools outside our traditional networks and to consider candidates who had no ties to other board members or the CEO.

The board chair, Bill Young, and I reviewed the candidates with the search consultant and interviewed several strong contenders, including women with very diverse backgrounds. Our top choice was a woman of Asian heritage, an engineer who had held leadership positions in wireless and consumer electronics, as well as infotainment businesses, areas important to the car of the future. The board chair tasked me with presenting our recommendation to the board. This was not an easy exercise, as I was new to playing a leadership role on the board, and we were seeking to appoint an individual who was different from other previous appointees.

The entire process was an eye-opening experience. I learned how easily unusual candidates may be overlooked, especially if they have a nontraditional career background and have neither been a CEO nor served on other large corporate boards. It became evident that it is crucial to have the support of the board chair and CEO for appointing diverse directors, thereby changing the board culture.

We successfully onboarded our recommended choice. She is a valued board member and has consistently added expertise critical to the development of the car of the future. I appreciated the opportunity, as a woman of color, to take a leadership role in director selection. The mentoring provided me by the chair, along with the support of the CEO, resulted in my being appointed chair of the board's CGCNC.

While progress has been slow, I am pleased to note that, as a result of previous efforts by key male directors, such as Tom O'Neill, former chair of the Bank of Nova Scotia, more women are being appointed as corporate directors. As boards seek to diversify, it is essential that women corporate directors have the nerve to step up and lead by identifying and advocating for the appointment of qualified candidates who may be unknown, unrecognized and potentially overlooked or rejected because they do not possess the traditional qualifications.

Hard Work

Women tend to believe that the hardest aspect of being a corporate board member is securing a seat at the table. Nothing could be further from the truth. Getting on a board is easier than adding value to the board and earning the respect of management and fellow directors.

Being a corporate director in today's world is hard work—and it is even harder for women directors, who seldom have a wealth of board experience, are often in the minority around the table and whose performance is often being evaluated through a different lens than that of their male colleagues. Unfortunately, our more than 20 years of combined experience serving on corporate boards has revealed a disappointing trend: women directors have sometimes faltered by failing to gain the confidence and respect of their colleagues and as a result have not been able to contribute as effectively as they should.

Why is this? Our experience has been neither easy nor pretty. Both of us have struggled in terms of defining how best we can contribute and add value to the enterprise. We have worked extremely hard preparing for every board meeting only to feel intense dissatisfaction and disquiet with our own performance after the meeting. We have continually questioned our role, trying to better understand the reasons we were appointed and whether we were meeting the expectations for board members. Only after years of experience, hard work and self-doubt have we been able to define the manner in which we can contribute effectively. If only someone had told us what we now know after years of trial and error: the four myths that often undermine women's effectiveness as they embark on their corporate board experiences. We believe if these myths are blindly accepted, a woman's role as a corporate director will be compromised.

Myth 1: There is no such thing as a dumb question.

If we had a loonie for every time we have been told that the most important task of a board member is to ask questions, that there are no questions not worth asking and that there is no such thing as a dumb question, we would be extremely wealthy. Do not believe it. There *are* dumb questions, and the hard work of being a board member is figuring out the difference between an insightful, helpful question and one that is irrelevant, insignificant or trivial.

Me-too, or copycat, questions fall into the category of worthless interruptions. Micro detailed questions are a close second. The burden of becoming an effective board member lies in trying to look at the big trends, the macro picture; connecting the dots between data and strategy; and asking questions that can move the company forward rather than just take up air time. Listen to and learn how respected board members contribute to the discussions; think strategically about what questions you want to ask and why; and if your question focuses on clarifying a detail, pursue it with the appropriate member of management outside of the boardroom rather than asking it in the meeting.

Myth 2: Silence is golden.

No one wants a board member who dominates the debate or feels compelled to speak on every agenda item. When confronted with this type of director, it is easy to believe that silence is golden, that it is better to remain quiet and let others do the talking. While there are clearly times to listen rather than speak, there is no value in a board member who refuses to get into the fray or voice their opinion. A director is chosen to contribute; no one is paying you to remain silent.

Myth 3: Limit your interventions to those areas in which you are an expert.

Every director brings special expertise to the table and needs to be careful in terms of wading into areas that they know little or nothing about. Women directors are no different. Our experience, however, suggests that women directors tend to become easily pigeonholed, only intervening in their areas of expertise, traditionally fields such as human resources, marketing or communications. The best directors, we believe, are those who, in addition to commenting on their own area of expertise, also contribute significantly by constructively challenging management, questioning the strategic direction of the company, displaying sound judgment when assessing critical issues and applying intellectual rigor to the overall issues and initiatives that are being advanced. In the end, the job of an outstanding director is to be concerned about the entire business and to consider each issue as it is presented from the perspective of the overall strategic direction of the company, the expectations of the shareholders and the integrity of the enterprise.

Myth 4: You can go it alone.

Whatever you do, don't assume that you are ready for a board position just because you have been a leader. Find yourself a mentor, someone whom you respect and trust who will tell you when you are off message and guide you as you develop into being a strong and independent director. Ideally, your mentor is someone who has had extensive board experience—but more important, it is someone who wants you to succeed and is willing to give you honest feedback, as well as thoughtful encouragement.

In summary, corporate board membership is a fulfilling and stimulating post-leadership role, but it is also a demanding responsibility that involves hard, hard work—learning the business, earning the respect of other directors and management and adding value to the corporation through insightful, informed interventions and actions.

PIPER:

I was lost and overwhelmed. After attending my first several corporate board meetings, I was flailing, feeling grossly incompetent and unsure of what to do about it. What was my role? How could I contribute? What was I doing wrong? And, most important, how should I proceed to address my shortcomings?

The transition from leading an organization to being a team member exerting oversight of an enterprise is not easy, especially for those of us who have little if any experience in the corporate world. As I moved from being the CEO of a public institution to corporate board director, I was keenly aware of my basic unpreparedness for this new role. As such, I fell back to my default position—I needed to learn, study and take a course. In desperation, I approached each of my board chairs and asked if I might register for professional development aimed at educating directors of corporate boards. With their support, I completed two outstanding courses, at Wharton and Harvard business schools, geared to board members of large market cap companies. It was one of the best things I did; each course entailed several full days of classes, tutorials and lectures. Preparing for the discussion of case studies was hard work, but in the end, gave me the confidence and knowledge I required for my corporate board journey.

But it did not end there. I worked tirelessly to prepare for each board and committee meeting, but still felt unsettled afterwards, knowing I could and must do better. Then I found a mentor, a fellow board member, whom I worked with to receive more feedback and suggestions on how I could contribute more effectively. Clearly helpful, but still not enough.

After my first year on the BMO board, I received my first annual peer evaluation from the other board members. I felt I had just taken a cold shower; reading the confidential feedback on my performance, I was disheartened. Not only were my scores below the average of all the board members but also the specific comments were difficult to read. My overall peer rating was 2.08 compared with the average for all members of 2.20, with a range from 1.79 to 2.57. I was not the lowest ranked director, but I have never taken criticism well and knew I could do better. When meeting with the board chair, I found the nerve to ask him to help and advise me, to make suggestions on what I should be doing and what I should not be doing. These discussions were difficult but critical in assisting my development as a corporate board member. Over time I was rewarded. My scores went up, the comments from my peers improved and my confidence grew as I slowly learned the ropes and how I might add value to the board's discussions and deliberations.

Doing Good

Women are good at doing good. We are born with the doing-good gene: the need to be of assistance, helping and taking care of others, volunteering our time to make our families and communities healthy, safe and secure. We are nurturers and believe we have a responsibility to lend a hand wherever we are needed. We are the ones who look after the children, assist in the care of aging parents, bake the cookies for community events and organize the walkathons. Doing good is in our DNA, and our mothers, grandmothers and great-grandmothers have shown us the way—being the mainstay of the church, mosque or synagogue, the local schools and hospitals, and working tirelessly for community causes they believed in.

Women differ from men on this count, as the role models for men have traditionally stressed *doing well* rather than *doing good*—working outside the home to provide for themselves and their families—leaving the doing-good role to women who remained at home. Even though women are now sharing the doing-well role with their male counterparts, and men are clearly assuming more doing-good roles, women are still hardwired and conditioned to do good, driving them to volunteer and advocate for causes.

Women who have been leaders are no different. Many of us assume that when we step down, we will finally have the bandwidth to devote our talents, resources and energy to the causes we hold dear. The commitment to do good is not at issue for former women leaders; rather, the challenge lies in determining which causes and organizations they will devote their time to.

There is no shortage of opportunities to do good. Any woman who has led will be inundated with requests for her time; charitable and not-for-profit organizations in particular are keen to have a high-profile woman with a strong network at the helm. Would she be willing to chair the board of this foundation or that? Could she organize a fundraiser for mental health or a women's shelter? Would she be willing to sit on the board of the symphony or the children's creative theater? What about being on the executive committee of the annual hospital charity event or joining the annual walk in support of cancer research? All great causes; all worthy of your time, talents and money. But how do you decide which causes to support, which will align best with your skills and values and the extent to which you can get involved without being spread too thin?

Our experience has shown that it is extremely easy to overcommit (as both of us did), which only results in not being able to give as effectively as you would like and sometimes becoming engaged with causes and organizations that, while worthy, do not necessarily reflect your key personal priorities.

Here is our simple advice: Think long and hard about what you want to give your time and money to, and identify the causes you most care about. Be realistic about the time any one cause will require. If they say you will have to attend only four meetings a year, do not believe it. Triple it. And remember that in most cases the causes you choose not only require your time but will also entail a significant donation of your personal funds. Almost all nonprofit organizations depend on private dollars, and if you become involved you must be willing to lead by example—giving as generously as you can to the organizations you support.

PIPER:

I knew I wanted to give back, and I wanted to make a difference in an area that I was passionate about but had put off participating in when I was president. For 10 years I had been on a crusade for UBC to educate students to be global citizens, believing that Canada and Canadians must play a critical role in helping to make the world a better place. As I reflected on the various opportunities to do good upon my retirement, I realized that my personal behavior had not been aligned with my rhetoric; that is, I had done little or nothing to become a global citizen. What had I done to address global poverty or the inequities women in the developing world face? How was I translating my words into actions?

With that as a backdrop, I jumped at the chance to join the board of CARE Canada, an international development and humanitarian relief agency recognized for its role in reducing global poverty and eliminating gender bias to empower women and girls throughout the world. I have come to believe that we will only achieve peace and well-being in our local communities if we contribute, especially as privileged women, in assisting those less fortunate around the globe: to ensure girls everywhere receive an education; that women are able to live safe and secure lives, have access to health care and family planning and work at meaningful jobs; and that men are encouraged to treat women as equal partners in society.

My involvement with CARE Canada has not disappointed me; I have received far more from this remarkable organization than I have given. Over time we have been able to establish the Vancouver Council for CARE—a powerful group of like-minded women, many of whom I otherwise would not have known and who share the commitment of being responsible global citizens. It has been a wonderful journey for me personally to be associated with an amazing NGO and to be able to put my beliefs into action.

I have also realized that in addition to giving my time and advocating for global concerns, I have needed to step up and put my money where my mouth is. I have been fortunate, as a woman in the Western world, to have had access to advanced public education and health care and to have had opportunities to do meaningful work and earn a living as my career evolved. I understand that these freedoms and privileges have been supported by others who have gone before me, who fought for women's rights and equity in the workplace; hence, my desire to give back and to assist those who follow, especially less advantaged women, requires not only my gift of time but also my gift of dollars.

———

In summary, this is a wonderful time for former women leaders. Their time and expertise are incredibly valuable and present an opportunity to give back to the community that has supported them throughout their time as leaders. We suggest that you jump in wholeheartedly, enjoy giving of yourself and your resources, remembering these wise words: "We make a living by what we get, we make a life by what we give."

Creative Choices

The careers of leaders generally follow predictable paths that build upon their skills, educational background and experience—moving methodically up the organizational ladder to the top rung as leader. Rarely do potential leaders think outside the box about other opportunities to apply their skills and talents. The road to leadership can, in fact, present boundaries that exclude other career possibilities; developing as a leader becomes a full-time job, and the role itself becomes all-consuming. However, when a leader steps down, a world of creative professional opportunities opens up, offering intellectual enagagement that could be both deeply satisfying and financially rewarding: consulting contracts; speaking engagements; advisory positions in law, accounting or headhunting firms; serving on expert panels or commissions; the list goes on. Former women leaders would be well-advised to think broadly in terms of envisioning new roles they might take on. By connecting with other women leaders, consulting with other retired leaders and engaging with individuals in your networks, you may be surprised by how many new and creative choices to stay engaged exist.

SAMARASEKERA:

A few months before I was to retire from U of A and move back to British Columbia, the managing partner of the international law firm Bennett Jones invited me to lunch to ask if I might be interested in serving as a senior adviser in their new Vancouver office. Given my engineering background I was intrigued that I was being invited to take up an advisory role in an international law firm. What could I possibly contribute without any formal legal training? When I asked what my role would be, he pointed to their public policy group, which comprised retired lawyers, economists and senior officials in government, both civil servants and politicians, all of whom provided the firm and clients with a wide and varied perspective on the ever-changing public policy landscape. Still, I needed to be convinced that the fledgling office could benefit from my experience as an engineer and past university president before I accepted the position.

I have often wondered whether a male colleague would have questioned his worth or the role he might play if receiving the same offer to serve. I am convinced that most men would have jumped at the request, never questioning why they were being approached; I as a woman, on the other hand, needed to be certain that I could offer something of value before agreeing to serve in a role so very different from any I had previously held.

At first I had no idea how law firms operated, and it was difficult to figure out what my role was and what I could possibly do to advance the firm. Over the past five years the firm has grown considerably, and I have slowly defined how I can be of value. I have mentored young associates on balancing work and family, introduced the new managing partner from Toronto to leaders in the Vancouver community, engaged in strategic planning and business development, hosted roundtables for associates and clients on public policy related to oil and gas, higher education and innovation.

Making my part-time position both meaningful and effective has required creativity and initiative on my part, with a constant appraisal of where I can make a difference. I learned that asking for advice, building relationships with the Bennett Jones team in Vancouver and the public-policy group across the country were important first steps, along with familiarizing myself with the company's strategic plan and growth potential. Acting as an ambassador and opening doors for the firm in the community were also appreciated. Reflecting on this unusual assignment, it is evident that there are creative choices for post-retirement work, which may not be obvious but are definitely worth exploring. I have enjoyed being a member of a growing office in Vancouver and having a new community of colleagues. Former women leaders would be well-advised to scan the landscape for such opportunities, be open to them when they come along out of the blue and seek counsel on how best to contribute.

Lessons Learned

Women leaders upon leaving their leadership roles will have numerous opportunities to fill their time. Whether they decide to make money by leveraging their past experience or to contribute to special causes through volunteering—or a combination of both—will be up to them. Choosing how to spend these precious years is a luxury that wise women will seize upon, recognizing that they will have the good fortune to engage in things they were never able to do when leading. The following suggestions may assist women in defining a new sense of purpose while they still have the energy and health to contribute to society in meaningful ways.

1. Recognize this time in your life is limited. When considering how best to spend this time, conduct an honest inventory of the important things in your life: Do you need to make money? What are the causes you deeply care about? How much time do you need to yourself? How will you continue to be intellectually stimulated and involved?

2. Do not fear that you will be forgotten. If your phone does not ring, be proactive and reach out to others to make it known you are available to contribute to the things you are most interested in.

3. When considering corporate board membership, be intentional and highly selective in terms of the boards you might join. What business are they in? What financial and strategic issues are they confronting? Who is the CEO, and who are the other board members? Where might you add value? Not all boards are equal. Remember: it is easier to get on than to get off.

4. Recognize that being a corporate director entails a great deal of hard, hard work. Seek all the help you can find, including identifying a mentor, taking any courses that might be helpful, welcoming constructive feedback from your peers and board chair and working hard to understand the business.

5. Once you have succeeded in obtaining a board seat, attempt to identify and advocate for the appointment of other directors who are eminently qualified but may be overlooked because they are different from the traditional appointees. Take a leadership role in assisting boards to achieve gender and social diversity.

6. Doing good comes naturally to women. Identify the causes you are passionate about and actively seek opportunities to contribute to them. Acknowledge that doing good takes a great deal of time, often well more than you estimate; be very careful not to overcommit yourself.

7. Be aware that in addition to giving of your time, doing good normally requires that you also give of your financial resources. Be prepared, according to your personal situation, to put your dollars into the causes you have selected to support.

8. Think outside of the box. Do not limit yourself to roles that are generally associated with your previous career or educational background. Remember that your leadership experience has prepared you to contribute to a variety of organizations and areas that you have not been formally educated in. By being creative about your choices, you will be surprised by the new opportunities that may present themselves to be stimulated and engaged, to stay connected to others and, perhaps, to continue earning an income.

CHAPTER 15

Building relationships: better the
second time around

"The best and most beautiful things in this world cannot be seen or even heard, but must be felt with the heart."

—HELEN KELLER

"The spectacles of experience; through them you will see clearly a second time."

—HENRIK IBSEN

Georgia O'Keeffe once said, "Nobody sees a flower—really—it is so small—we haven't time—and to see takes time like to have a friend takes time."[33] How true that is. Friendships are hard to see clearly. We often take them for granted, thinking they will flourish on their own. But like flowers that sometimes go unseen and require a deliberate effort to notice and time to nurture, friends require time—and lots of it. This time commitment is one of the things that distinguishes real, meaningful relationships from passing encounters.

Women leaders tend to develop relationships based on the goals and objectives of the organizations they lead rather than on personal choice.

They are generally limited to cultivating friendships and associations that advance their company or institution, seeking out individuals who will assist in moving them forward—colleagues, other leaders, politicians, government officials, donors, power brokers, members of the media and thought leaders in the community. Little time, if any, is available to develop personal relationships with the people they most like being with, including family members and special friends. Even when they are with friends or family, their minds are often elsewhere, thinking about what has to be done, clocking the time remaining before they have to return to work.

Not only does the lack of free time hinder the types of relationships that leaders can maintain when leading, but also the ability to honestly share and reveal to others who they are, and what they are feeling is greatly affected, too. Leaders are prohibited from disclosing certain things to others—confidential information, trade secrets, personnel decisions or strategic initiatives, for instance. And it's a small leap for them, or others, to believe that it is inappropriate to disclose certain aspects of themselves—their position on a controversial issue, political affiliations or the deepest emotions they are experiencing. Leaders are required to be masters of discretion; they become so accustomed at this point in their lives to withholding certain information that by extension they soon find themselves unable to appear vulnerable at all.

Psychologists stress the importance of personal authenticity in establishing true friendships, trusting the other individual enough to honestly reveal to them who you really are. Without that level of trust and authenticity, the relationship may be nothing more than fun and entertaining. A true friendship must not only be satisfying but also safe and secure, developing so that both people feel they are truly seen and understood. However, leaders' relationships are most often the products of their leadership role rather than who they are as individuals; hence, the limitations imposed by their position and responsibilities often interfere in gaining the trust and affection of others.

Women in particular put high value on relationships and are generally better at cultivating and managing them. But female leaders are not immune from the dampening effect leadership roles have on personal connections. They must put the needs of the organization before everything else while they are responsible for leading it. It is common for women leaders, once they have stepped down, to feel a void because their close personal relationships have withered on the vine—sacrificed at the altar of their commitment to lead—and to crave meaningful connections once again. Former women leaders must consciously work at reestablishing the relationships they have allowed to lapse or seek out new relationships that better fill their current needs or both.

Becoming intentional in establishing meaningful alliances, based on personal needs rather than professional goals, is a challenge and takes enormous amounts of time and energy. Being there for individuals who once again or for the first time play an important role in your life can be all-consuming: showing up for their birthdays and anniversaries, demonstrating empathy when they have problems, making time for lunch or coffee and visiting them when they are under the weather. We both have struggled with fully understanding the importance friends and family play in our new lives, and we have had to work at consciously committing our time and attention to people we enjoy being with rather than people we *have* to be with. And, as difficult as it has been, we have sometimes had to extricate ourselves from those relationships we no longer value.

Our view is that during this new life phase, there is probably nothing more important than determining who you want to spend time with, who you are prepared to share your vulnerability with and to whom you will give of yourself—not only to make your life more meaningful but also to provide them with the support, care and love they require.

While time has passed, and people may have changed, reestablishing relationships and reconnecting with family and old friends can be particularly rewarding. Children have matured, grandchildren are growing up and friends have aged and are facing many of the same issues that you are. By acknowledging you are being given a second chance to relate to these important people, you are in a unique position to give of yourself in ways that were impossible when leading. Life is clearly better the second time around.

PIPER:

When I stepped down, I knew I needed to invest in new relationships. I was aware that I had failed to develop fulfilling and sustainable friendships over the previous several decades as I moved forward in my various leadership positions and that I had unwittingly limited the little time I had to being with family rather than with friends. Where would I even begin?

As with most things I have taken on, I recognized I had to be intentional; that making friends would not just happen, that it would require purposeful actions and that I needed to take the task seriously. As crazy as it sounds, the first thing I did was make a list of 10 women I wished to cultivate to be my friends. These were women whom I knew but didn't really know; women I had admired from afar; women I wanted to spend more time with. To this day, that list is pinned to the bulletin board above my desk, and I check it occasionally to see how I am doing.

Once I'd prepared the list, I went about my work—reaching out to these women, one by one, arranging coffees and lunches, yoga sessions and walks. I was serious about cultivating these new friends because this sort of thing didn't come naturally to me anymore: calling; scheduling time; and then committing to building and sustaining a relationship based on trust, discussing and sharing ideas, stories, issues, world problems and family concerns and just being myself. Has it worked? I can categorically say it has. All of my women friends are different; they have had different experiences and are on different life journeys . . . but all of them are special. And over the past several years, we have come to not only enjoy each other's company but also to cherish our time together. Do they know they are on my list? Not really. But I do. And that list keeps my feet to the fire, reminds me daily that it is my turn to reach out, makes me pick up the phone to connect and continues to guide me in honoring the relationships I hold dear.

Heart and Mind

Friends come in all shapes and sizes, ages and backgrounds. We need and want friends of all kinds: friends from our childhood, friends from university, friends from our work environments, friends we have acquired through our children and friends we are aging with. Friends touch our hearts and keep us grounded, share with us the highs and lows of life, know us intimately, finish our sentences for us and are there when our children are born and our parents die. They confront us when we are wrong and catch us when we falter. Close friendships develop when there is true reciprocity—a give and take. Friends of the heart uplift you and nourish your emotional well-being, and you do the same for them. We believe women naturally form these close friendships more easily than men. Why this is the case we are not certain. Is it a result of our upbringing, our capacity for nurturing or just a result of our need to have close relationships? Whatever the reason, we view it as a positive attribute that can be strengthened with time and dedication.

We also need friends who push us intellectually, who engage with us in serious conversation, who share books and articles with us and who question our opinions on world issues—friends of the mind. These are friends with whom we can have *intellectual intimacy*, where we are free to express ideas and opinions without fear of being judged or misinterpreted. They share an interest in debate with the intention of advancing their understanding and yours about complex issues. You seek them out because you value their opinions, wisdom, experience and curiosity. They are fun to be with, as they spark new ideas and enrich your mind.

These two categories of friends—heart and mind—play different roles at distinct times and in different situations in our lives, but they are not mutually exclusive. You may find your friend of the heart and friend of the mind in one and the same person. However these roles are expressed among your good friends, having both the heart and mind stimulated and refreshed by our relationships is essential.

We have both been fortunate over the years to have friends who have satisfied and continue to satisfy both of these needs—friends who are dear to us because they fill our emotional concerns, and friends we cherish because they are our intellectual companions. When we stepped down from our respective leadership roles, we reinvigorated some of these relationships and sought out and developed others. We have been fortunate in being able to fulfill these important aspects of our lives, but we also know these special relationships need to be constantly nurtured and invested in if they are going to sustain us through our new life journeys.

SAMARASEKERA:

When I stepped down, I returned to Sri Lanka frequently to see my mother. With the luxury of time, my trips home were no longer frantic exercises in cramming obligatory visits to members of my extended family into a few days. Instead, I felt a yearning to recapture moments of my childhood now that I had time to think and reflect. I reached out to close childhood friends from Ladies' College, with whom I had had infrequent contact over the 40 years since I had left the island.

My friends in Colombo never failed to host a lunch or a dinner when I returned, and we reverted to being teenagers again, picking up where we left off without missing a beat. There were hoots of laughter at the mention of a teacher who reprimanded us for silly behavior or on recounting the time we found ourselves in the principal's office for a more serious misdemeanor. We reveled in memories of our old flames and agreed that they married the wrong women. We lamented the idiosyncrasies of the men we married. We were able to reminisce about what had made the difference in our lives and careers, recalling the seasons of adversity and joy candidly. Friends who knew us before we had husbands, children or careers allow us a rare glimpse of ourselves in our youth.

I have spent most of my adult life in Vancouver, where my children were born and developed many close friendships with women who are first and foremost friends of the heart, although our friendship has never failed to enrich the mind. Many of these friends are parents of my children's friends or people I met serendipitously and with whom I sensed an instant connection. These are friends with whom I have shared life's ups and downs, who have been essential to my emotional well-being. We have been there for each other when there has been a death of a spouse or a parent, a divorce or a cancer diagnosis.

Upon returning to Vancouver from Edmonton, I made a special effort to reconnect with my old friends. We were in a new season of our lives. Our children had married and were having children of their own, so our time together was less about parenting and more about grandparenting, aging and finding novel ways to enjoy our newfound freedom. We traveled to places near and far, taking a cruise on the Danube, spending two weeks in Sri Lanka, a weekend in the Canadian Rockies or on the ocean in Victoria. The deep roots of our relationships did not wither and die while I was absent for a decade in Alberta.

I have also sought new friends with whom there are natural connections, namely Sri Lankans who have immigrated here and raised children. In my early years, I deliberately avoided becoming part of an expat community of fellow Sri Lankans, as I wanted to befriend people of other cultures and ethnic origins. But now it's different: I have a broad enough social circle that I can rekindle my roots without sacrificing diversity. I have been drawn to many other people from all walks of life, whose company I seek because they enjoy the same things I do, sharing book clubs, cooking groups and mah-jongg sessions.

How does one cultivate friends of the mind after retirement? This, too, takes deliberate effort. Upon returning to Vancouver, I reconnected with several academics I knew from my earlier days at UBC and with women I had met at a national retreat for women. As a result, I joined the Vancouver Roundtable, which meets every Tuesday to hear from an interesting speaker or discuss a contemporary issue. The group consists of retired leaders, former judges, academics, members of the media and other public figures from the arts community. I leave mentally stimulated after every one of these lunches.

In reflecting on friends of the heart and mind, I am struck by how quickly my life has passed by. I have a new determination to find joy and meaning in these later years. My friends and I are conscious that time is of the essence, and we are more intentional in how we spend it.

Family

How often do we hear leaders say they are leaving their position "to spend more time with family"? We dislike this phrase for two reasons. The first deals with truth telling. Everyone knows that this phrase is generally nothing more than a euphemism, a generic statement that says little and is difficult to refute. There is nothing wrong with leaving a position of leadership to become your child's primary caregiver or to deal with a troubled teen or take care of an elderly parent—but this is rarely the case. In most cases, the truth more likely lies in a mutual agreement between the leader and their board that it is time for a change due to questionable performance, the inept handling of a crisis or an inability to deliver agreed upon outcomes. Why not just say it like it is? You are looking for new opportunities, the organization's direction is shifting, it is time for renewal and new leadership. By using family as the excuse and disguising the real reason for their departure, leaders run the risk of not being heard, permitting rumors to abound and allowing others to define the reasons behind their decision to step down.

The second reason we dislike this statement is that it suggests that leaders are either unable or unwilling to give their families the attention and time they deserve while they are leading. We believe that even in the most demanding jobs, it is possible to spend time with family. A leader's immediate family often provides them with the comfort, support and unconditional love they need to confront the demands of their positions, and their families keep them grounded and humble when they most need to be.

Is this a gender issue? Are women leaders more able and determined to ensure their families remain in their lives than their male colleagues are? We have observed male leaders who have refused to take time off when a family member has died or become extremely ill, have traveled extensively for long periods of time away from their loved ones and have attended every evening event that presented itself. We were often surprised by their decisions to put work responsibilities ahead of family commitments. When faced with similar circumstances, we did not make the same choices. We believe most women leaders view their immediate family as high priority, assuming responsibility for everything that affects their health and well-being, honoring family traditions and celebrations. We also believe women do not leave those responsibilities at the door when leading; instead, it has been our experience that, while they may ask others to assume some of these responsibilities and may not spend as much time as they would have done before leading, they do not abdicate their positions as partners, wives and mothers when they become leaders.

Still, there is no question that the demands of leadership take a toll on the relationships female leaders have with their family; so how then do they continue in their family roles when they cease leading? Does their role in the family differ after they step down? What does this new relationship look like, and how do former women leaders adapt to their new family roles? These are questions we have grappled with in our own post-leadership years.

It also needs to be said that one of the great joys of those years is the relationship we have with our grandchildren. We both are grandmothers of four grandchildren; we both live in the same city as they do; we both cherish our roles as grandmothers and know we are blessed to have these special children in our lives and this concentrated period of time to share with them. All the books will tell you that a grandparent's role is to impart wisdom to their grandchildren, but nothing could be further from the truth. In fact, it is just the opposite. Our grandchildren impart wisdom to us, expand our thinking, ask the unthinkable and share the sense of mystery they experience when exploring their worlds. Because of the challenges, disappointments and unresolvable issues we both had to deal with when leading, we are jaded, skeptical and sometimes cynical, seeing the world with all of its warts rather than reveling in its mysteries and beauty. Enter the grandchildren. Their most precious gift is their ability to reawaken the sense of wonder we have lost. It is not unusual for them to question why the clouds are floating in the sky, where the stars come from, how a bird flies and what heaven really is. No one else poses these questions or shares these kinds of thoughts. No longer CEOs, we have chosen instead to be chief joy-maker for our grandchildren. In the process, they have helped us rediscover joy.

PIPER:

My family has always been important to me. It has defined who I am, given me my core values and principles to live by and provided me with love and support throughout the years. I was very fortunate to have had an amazing childhood and benefited enormously from being embraced by not only my nuclear family but also a loving extended family of grand-parents, uncles and aunts and numerous cousins. I was the beneficiary of not only the family itself but also the understanding that family, more than anything, sustains you in both the good and the bad times.

As an adult with a husband and two children, I knew inherently my job was not only to build a strong family unit but also to depend upon them to provide me with the sustenance, confidence, love and under-standing I needed to be personally fulfilled. Although I bucked the trend by choosing a full-time job outside the home at a time when most of my women friends remained at home to raise their children, I refused to compromise my family commitments. With the support of my husband, who took on more than his share of the family responsibilities, my family remained front and center in my life. Almost all of our free time was spent with our nuclear family, forgoing other relationships and friend-ships, to devote our time and effort to our marriage and our children. As I assumed more and more responsibility as a leader, the amount of time I had to give to my immediate family may have diminished somewhat, but the commitment to them was as strong as ever.

When I stepped down from leading, I began to recognize that while I was connected to and supported by my nuclear family, I was estranged from my extended family: my siblings and their partners and their children and grandchildren. Because I was the only family member who had moved away from our birthplace and because my experiences had differed significantly from theirs, we had grown apart over the years, coming together only for larger family events such as funerals and weddings and the occasional reunion. I rarely kept in touch with them in between.

One day I woke up, post-retirement, and felt lonely. There was something missing in my life. I was aware that not only was I aging but also that my siblings were growing older, that time was limited, and that I needed to reach out and reestablish our relationship before it was too late. It was a matter of intent; the desire to connect and rekindle the love we had shared as children and young adults was overwhelming. What has followed has been phone calls to connect with each of my siblings; cards, photos, letters and emails informing them of what is happening in my life; regular family reunions; remembering birthdays and anniversaries not only of my siblings but also of their children and grandchildren.

It has not been hard, but it has required patience and perseverance, along with understanding and tolerance. We do not always agree on certain political and social issues; we see the world sometimes through different lenses; our life experiences have been dissimilar; but what we share is a love that prevails regardless of the things we disagree on. I have worked at finding common ground: the values we hold dear, the family memories we share, our commitment to one another and our children and grandchildren. I know inherently that they love me and my family, that they would do anything for me and I for them and that they accept me for who I am regardless of my faults and our disparities. I also know that if I were still leading, we would have remained apart. I am grateful for the time I have remaining to reestablish my connection to those family members who had drifted away from me. It has truly been one of the joys of my retirement years. Blood is definitely thicker than water.

When I retired, I realized that my children had undergone significant changes in the decade I had been away in Alberta. They had completed their education, married and were having children of their own. During my leadership years I saw them infrequently, as they were busy with their life in other parts of Canada. When we met, I don't recall thinking about how they were maturing as adults, as I was too preoccupied with my leadership responsibilities; our conversations were focused on their careers.

When I returned to Vancouver, I was fortunate that both my children were settled there. I saw them through new eyes, as I was no longer simply a parent, but found myself relating to them as adults and in some ways as a friend. I was proud of who they had become and respected and admired their spouses; I had to now establish a relationship with them as couples, along with my children's in-laws. The word *mother-in-law* conjures up all kinds of stereotypes and stories, and I needed to define what kind of in-law I was going to be. In essence I had to build a matrix of new relationships, being sensitive to family dynamics.

It's one thing to meet your children and their spouses on a fly-in visit, but it is quite another thing to see them weekly at family dinners and to be regularly in and out of their homes. I can no longer tell them what to do or impose my views and have had to learn how to engage in debate with them tactfully. Every subject from parenting to politics, global issues to climate change, taxation to health care has been on the table. And believe me, the discussions get heated!

It was an adjustment to be a member of a clan and not the leader of the tribe. I had to get used to no longer being the authoritative figure in their lives. I am now simply mother. Furthermore, roles are slowly being reversed, where instead of me advising them, they have begun to give me advice on health and lifestyle! This has been a momentous transition and not without its drawbacks. I have learned that while a career is a source of much satisfaction, it is your family that gives you true joy. Family calls for sacrifice, unconditional love and support in the ups and downs of life and eventually being available in ways one could not be when one was a leader.

Lessons Learned

Leaders have no shortage of relationships. They are in constant contact with their peers, associates, assistants, staff and people in the community. They spend countless hours attending meetings, receptions and conferences, where the majority of their time is spent interacting with their professional acquaintances and colleagues. With the exception of their families, they have little time to foster true friendships based on who they are as a person rather than the position they hold. As a result, old friendships may wither on the vine as the leader devotes the large proportion of her time in pursuing and developing relationships that advance her leadership goals and the organization.

That situation changes dramatically once a leader exits her leadership position. No longer is she sought after by the people who wanted to have a relationship with her when she was leading. No longer does she attend the meetings, receptions and conferences where those relationships were cultivated. She now has the time she lacked when leading to develop other meaningful relationships that will support her in this next phase of her life. Who she decides to spend time with in this critical period is one of the most important decisions she will make in her retirement years. We believe the relationships that are established post-leadership are in many ways the cornerstone to a former leader's sense of purpose and happiness in their life after leading.

1. Recognize that the focus of your relationships changes dramatically after you have ceased leading. No longer do you relate to people based on your role as leader. Instead, you must intentionally determine which people in your life you want to seek out and establish meaningful relationships with.

2. When determining who the key people in your life are, identify individuals who can support your emotional needs and stimulate you intellectually. In some cases they will be the same person; in others, they will differ.

3. Think carefully about your family relationships. Has your role changed within your nuclear family, such as evolving from being a parent to being a friend and/or confidante to

your children? Has your family increased to include new members, such as grandchildren and sons- and daughters-in-law? Is there a desire to reconnect with extended family members, and if so, how will you deal with the issues that might keep you apart?

4.   Be sensitive to the fact that time is finite. As you develop your new relationships or reestablish old friendships, be aware that you are aging and that the opportunity to develop meaningful relationships will not come again.

5.   If you do have grandchildren, consider how you will nurture this intergenerational relationship. Recognize that you are not their parent and, hence, must give up certain amounts of control that you have become used to having as a leader. In addition to you being important in their lives, be aware that today's grandchildren, if listened to, can reignite in you a sense of wonder that may have dissipated as a result of your leadership experience.

CHAPTER 16

Super-aging: the joys of old age

"Aging is not 'lost youth' but a new stage of opportunity and strength."

—BETTY FRIEDAN

Current research suggests that women may anticipate several decades of a vibrant physical and intellectual life after retiring. While there are no guarantees as to how long any one person will live or remain active, more and more women are facing years, if not decades, of good health after stepping down from their leadership position, living an average of six to eight years longer than men.[34] Their lives as they age will differ considerably from those of their mothers and grandmothers and will include activities and pursuits that their forebears would never have even thought about, let alone taken part in. It is not unusual for women well into their eighties to be both mentally and physically fit, playing tennis weekly or jogging daily, while still being intellectually alive by participating in forums, discussions and panels.

Although there is a large amount of literature on becoming a "super-ager," the emphasis of this research is largely on how to live longer, while preventing dementia and other age-related health issues. Our interest in super-aging is somewhat different; rather than stressing the aim of living longer, we believe the goal should be how to live better regardless of the length of time you have. While the two objectives may go hand in hand, we think the distinction is important. We have characterized living a better, fulfilling life as "Aging with Joy" and have identified four critical aspects of joyous aging: intellectual engagement, active living, spiritual consciousness and discovering joy in your life.

Compared with women in general, former women leaders face unique circumstances and opportunities in their years after leading. Despite having connections and relationships that keep them engaged mentally and intellectually and are more likely to have the financial means to support them as they age, they must recommit to looking after themselves after many years of worrying solely about their organizations or institutions. Many women leaders also have difficulty in developing and listening to their spiritual needs and conscience, never having had the time or interest while they were leading to think about the big questions of life and to ponder what is next. And perhaps most difficult for women who have always been on the go is the need to slow down to discover and relish the joy in their lives.

We have worked extremely hard at identifying what we want and need to do as we age, recognizing that charting this course is not always easy. We know that growing old is inevitable, that we cannot turn the clock back or cling to youth, and while we want to be as healthy as we can be, that in itself does not drive our behaviors. Neither of us wakes up every day thinking about what we must do to live to be 100. Instead, we aspire to be happy, to find joy and meaning in our remaining years, to gain wisdom and find a new sense of purpose.

Aging with delight is not a given. Like most things worth striving for, it requires intention and effort. Slowing down, committing time to discover a new philosophy of life and finding joy in the little things may not come easily to women leaders who have been going full tilt for their entire career. For us, this new way of living has required a conscious effort to define a new pattern of day-to-day behavior, including the establishment of routines, habits and goals that are very different from those we had as leaders. After a life of leadership, defining a new identity and sense of purpose does not occur immediately or easily—but with patience, nerve and perseverance we have been able to relax into aging with joy and to find fulfillment in things we never imagined when we were leading.

Mind Games

Women leaders who have spent much of their lives being mentally engaged and intellectually stretched rarely want to dial down the level of mental stimulation after leading. However, when one is no longer a leader it is not easy to replicate the exposure to people who have new ideas that call into question one's opinions. How do you find a forum to debate issues for which there is no right answer or find intractable problems to solve when one is out of the fray? Pundits who advise older adults to play bridge, complete a *New York Times* crossword puzzle every day or play sudoku to keep their mind active are offering well-intended solutions to stay mentally engaged. Yet these exercises are hardly satisfying to an individual who spent every hour of their day, even when sleeping, imagining the future of their organization or figuring out how to move their company forward to win market share in a competitive world.

Numerous studies support the thesis that staying mentally active by playing chess, reading widely and having debates with friends are good for the brain. We are not proposing that former leaders ignore this research, but instead suggest that these activities could become routine and insufficient to ensure they will be a "cognitive super-ager." Obviously, genes play a significant role in staying cognitively young, but an article in the May 2017 issue of *Harvard Women's Health Watch* points to research that sheds light on what else contributes to this phenomenon. Neurologist Dr. Bradford Dickerson and his colleagues have been studying super-agers for several years, identifying people in their seventies and eighties who are mentally and physically compa-rable to individuals who are decades younger. Their results suggest that embracing very challenging mental activities may be the key to preserving brain function, including learning the language of your favorite translated book so you can read the original, joining a theater group, writing poetry, creating original origami sculptures, becoming proficient in a musical instrument or learning to use new computer software. A common theme of their advice is to seek experiences and learn skills outside your comfort zone; experiences that continually stretch the mind are key to cognitive super-aging.

SAMARASEKERA:

When I was approaching retirement, I had a meeting in Ottawa with Jeffrey Simpson, an author whom I admired. He was a member of the Trilateral Commission and wanted to know whether I would allow my name to be considered for membership in the Canadian group. The Trilateral Commission brings together leaders from business, government, academia, the press and media who share a belief that human progress is advanced by the rule of law, international rules-based systems, democratic government, human rights, free enterprise and freedom of speech. How could I say no?

This invitation was an honor, but there was one problem. What did I really know about geopolitical and social issues? During my years as a leader, I had time for only a cursory review of national newspapers and international journals. How could I credibly contribute to discussions at the Trilateral Commission? I accepted the invitation with trepidation.

I remember feeling outside my comfort zone at my first meeting. In attendance were Canadian leaders from federal and provincial governments, universities, media and business, as well as international leaders from large global companies, foreign heads of state, academics, members of the intelligence community, award-winning journalists and others. I remember being seated at one meeting next to General David Petraeus, former commander of the International Security Assistance Force in Afghanistan. I was in awe and at first struggled to find words to introduce myself, but soon enough we were in an engaging conversation that I could never have imagined having.

At each meeting—whether in Washington, Ottawa, Mexico City, Paris or Singapore—I was being stretched to think more deeply about major geopolitical issues, and I learned as much from the questions being asked by participants as I did from panel presentations. I resolved to explore more deeply at least one issue that had been discussed at every meeting, and I subscribed to global magazines such as the *Economist* and the *Financial Times*. I soon realized that no one has all the answers, and the purpose of these meetings was to question, to debate and to advance our collective understanding. It was a strenuous exercise for the mind, grappling with complex issues in real time, as the world unfolded unpredictably. My time on the Trilateral Commission has been invigorating and rewarding. Being outside my comfort zone is the mental stretch I need at this stage of my life.

Staying Young

Aging is inevitable. While no one succeeds in turning back the clock, some people seem to weather growing older better than others. Research points to diet and nutrition, genetic makeup, ethnicity, physical and emotional fitness and mental agility as key elements of healthy aging.

Women are generally better than men at attending to the primary factors that affect their health as they age, such as diet, exercise and annual medical checkups. They go for their mammograms, have their teeth cleaned twice a year, hire a personal trainer or join a fitness club, watch their weight and avoid junk food. Many women will lean especially hard into retaining a youthful appearance with Botox treatments, face-lifts and spa and salon visits, erasing obvious signs of aging such as gray hair and wrinkles. Unlike men who are often perceived as more handsome when they become older, women face double jeopardy in that not only are they becoming less spry, but also they live in a society that tends to value youth over maturity in women. Millions of dollars are spent every year by women seeking the holy grail of looking younger than their age. For many women there is no greater compliment than telling them they look like they are 50 when they are actually 70.

We believe that staying young at heart is about one's outlook on life rather than attempts to live longer or remain youthful in appearance. While we do aspire to be healthy and look reasonably put together, our main concern centers on how we can stay as actively engaged and personally fulfilled as possible in the years we have left, and that depends to a great extent on being open to learning new skills, pushing yourself to try things you have never before experienced and adopting new ways of behaving. Aging with joy is all about attitude.

As one ages it is easy to fall behind, to not keep up, to refuse to learn new skills or adapt to changing trends. We all know people who are unable to stay abreast of new products or technologies when they get older, let alone social trends. They tend to hearken back to the "good old days" and yearn for the past. On the other hand, we also know people in their seventies and eighties who are well informed about current events, have youthful friends, are fun to be with and are always willing to do something that is daring or different. Some have sky dived or learned to water ski for the first time or started a gardening or catering business. These are behaviors that not only take nerve but also reveal a positive mindset, a determination to stay young by experiencing and learning new things.

Having nerve as you age is not easy; it requires work and persistence to stay current. As difficult as that may be, and while it is not a given that remaining actively engaged and trying new things will extend your life, we firmly believe that a positive attitude and an open, inquisitive mind are critical elements in countering the effects of aging.

SAMARASEKERA:

I do not enjoy exercise—visits to the gym, though necessary, are boring and tedious to me. I find myself looking for every excuse to avoid going. One evening at a dinner party, my sister-in-law described how much she was enjoying line dancing. I was intrigued. Studies have shown that dancing improves brain function, especially memory, and reduces depression. The complex mental coordination that dancing requires helps develop new neural connections. A 2003 study in the *New England Journal of Medicine* examined the effects of 11 different types of physical activity, including cycling, swimming and tennis, and found only dance reduced the risk of dementia. In essence, dance provides aerobic benefits, along with social interaction and mental health dividends. I was sold— dancing was a path to staying fit, sane and young! And it sounded like a lot more fun than going to the gym.

I scoured community center websites for line-dancing sessions, and the only ones I could find at convenient times were being offered in Mandarin, which I do not speak. I convinced myself that I could simply watch the other dancers and learn the steps, so I summoned my nerve and enrolled. When I attended my first session at the community center, I was not surprised that the class consisted entirely of East Asian women. Needless to say, I stood out like a sore thumb. Even the teacher was perplexed about why I was there.

At first I struggled, as I am not really that well-coordinated. The last time I had engaged in dancing was as a teenager. Trying to follow the steps was like trying to walk and chew gum at the same time! One of the women watched me flail and suggested I go on YouTube to find the dances and practice. Other women in the class made me feel welcome, confessing that they, too, had struggled at first. The teacher began to feel comfortable with my presence when she realized that it did not matter to me that the class was in Mandarin and encouraged me by commenting when she saw real improvement.

Attending line-dancing classes has been far more than staying fit, sane and young. It has been a culturally transformative experience, as I am immersed in a group of women I normally would not have known. I join them at their annual Christmas lunch at a Chinese restaurant and am struck by their generosity and joy. Only in Canada could I stay young by line dancing to country and western music with women of Asian ancestry!

Spiritual Consciousness

Spirituality can be interpreted in a variety of ways, but perhaps the unifying theme is the recognition of a feeling or belief that there is something greater than the individual, that there is something more to being human than just our physical existence. It involves seeking a sense of peace and developing beliefs around the meaning of life and your connection with others. Spirituality can also involve pursuing a purpose that embodies a set of values, principles and tenets that gives meaning to your life and provides you with the overarching guidance for your decisions and actions.

There are as many different ways of expressing your spiritual consciousness as there are people, and spirituality has been practiced since time immemorial in various ways, including prayer, meditation, chanting, breathing, mindfulness, listening to music and celebrating your natural surroundings. People find spirituality in nature, in the mystery of the universe, in museums or concert halls, in God and organized religion and in places of worship.

Many are attracted to Buddhism with its teachings of compassion, detachment from material wealth and karma in which present actions have consequences in this life or the next. Others turn to Christianity, centered around one true God who is righteous, who has endowed us with free will and a knowledge of right from wrong, with love and forgiveness of sin being the route to spirituality and eternal life. Similarly, other religions—whether it is Judaism, Hinduism, Islam and Sikhism—lay out paths to higher consciousness and well-being through adherence to spiritual practices. On this continent, the Indigenous peoples practice spirituality through a deep connection to nature and a reverence for the Earth and its environment. And then there is spiritual consciousness, outside the context of organized religion. The practices of meditation and mindfulness, for example, have attracted a devoted following, providing many people a source of grounding, peace and comfort, as well as values and beliefs to live by.

Most leaders have little time to practice spirituality or to think about its role in the human condition. Those who do tend to keep their beliefs to themselves since the practice of spirituality is a personal choice not deemed appropriate for sharing in the day-to-day world of business. Retiring from a demanding life of leadership, women are free to explore their spiritual beliefs; at a time when their own mortality looms larger, the meaning of life after leading needs to be defined and their desire to live in peace and harmony becomes increasingly important.

Since stepping down, we have grappled with our own beliefs and have embarked on our personal spiritual journeys, becoming increasingly aware of the link between spiritual, mental, emotional and physical well-being. We have chosen two very different paths to practice our spirituality, but we believe there is much to be gained by any pursuit of spiritual consciousness, including a deeper understanding of the purpose and meaning of life.

SAMARASEKERA:

Standing at the grave of my partner, watching his casket being lowered into the ground over two decades ago, I was overcome with a vast sense of sadness, emptiness and futility. It was 20 below freezing in the small prairie town of Rosalind, Alberta, when he was laid to rest after suffering a massive heart attack at the age of 54. It was a dark time as I tried to make sense of life and its purpose. I was raised a Christian but had never found my faith deeply comforting, as I had not really delved below the surface.

A cousin who visited me from Australia while I was in the depths of despair suggested I read *Mere Christianity* by C.S. Lewis, a legendary Oxford professor who became a Christian after being an atheist. I was blown away by the power and simplicity of his intellectual arguments supporting the existence of God, because he, too, had grappled with unbelief. Much of what he wrote about was familiar to me—the central tenets and beliefs of Christianity—but was it true?

As compelling as Lewis's case was, I wanted to know whether there was evidence to back it up. What did scientists think? I was fortunate to meet Dr. Francis S. Collins when I was Vice-President, Research, at UBC, a distinguished scientist who led the Human Genome Project. I was surprised to learn that he, too, became a Christian after reading *Mere Christianity*. Dr. Collins lays out his rationale in his book *The Language of God*, where he discusses the big bang, evolution and the laws of nature as signposts for God. I know that these deep questions of God and spirituality will never be easily resolved, but grappling with them is part of the human condition.

While my own spiritual journey began long before I took on leadership roles, I cannot say that I spent any time really thinking much more about my journey towards Christianity while leading. When I stepped down, the meaning of life, human suffering and death all came to the fore. Not long after I retired, my mother was diagnosed with terminal cancer. One of my closest friends discovered she had pancreatic cancer with a few months to live. A young couple I knew well were grappling with the death of their child, killed in a tragic accident. Good people to whom bad things were happening. Through all this I have had to reexamine what it means to be a Christian.

Upon retiring I joined Christ Church Cathedral in Vancouver and found a group of believers with shared values that reflect the times we live in. The church is exemplary in its practice of Christianity, with its embrace of the LGBTQ community and practices of reconciliation with Indigenous peoples. I have learned since retiring I can improve my capacity for what are termed "fruits of the spirit": love, joy, peace, patience, kindness, goodness, faithfulness and self-control. The mountains are more beautiful, the sunsets more breathtaking and life is more precious than ever. I have found joy in the smallest of experiences, and I have given up trying to control all the details of my life. I worry less and have indeed found the "peace that passeth all understanding" when life throws curveballs.

Three years ago I stood by my mother's grave and watched her casket being lowered. As I did when my partner died, I felt great sadness that I would not see her again or hear her voice in this life. However, gone was the emptiness and sense of futility that I had felt back then. My mother died a devout Christian. I knew where she was going and was comforted that I would see her again. Whether this view is relevant or not to how each of us lives in the here and now, spiritual consciousness that leads to comfort in adversity is helpful to women leaders grappling with issues of aging, ill-health, loss of a partner and death. More importantly it is a source of peace, joy and gratitude for the gifts we do have, which is extremely relevant to how we live our lives in the moment.

PIPER:

I am not sure that I am spiritual. I am neither religious, nor do I believe in a higher being. I attended Sunday school as a child, but I do not have a history of praying or practicing specific religious traditions; I am not overly concerned with death. And yet there are certain aspects of life that remain mystical to me and are unexplainable through scientific reasoning or rational thought—the beauty of our universe, the emotional rush that comes with loving another person and the origin of life itself.

I have been brought up to believe that reason provides the foundation for rational thought and critical thinking, permitting us to distinguish fact from fiction. My life has been spent problem solving, analyzing and integrating information to identify answers to critical issues and thorny problems. Never more so than when I was leading. I relied upon my critical thinking skills to guide me in everything I did, not only in terms of solving problems but also in developing key initiatives to benefit the institution. It was in many ways a skill that I prided myself on.

Yet, like most people, I have had to deal with disappointments in life that defy reason. Most recently I have been haunted by the question, "Why do bad things happen to good people?" My life has been complicated by my husband's diagnosis of Parkinson's disease, a progressive neurological disorder that affects every aspect of one's existence. There is no clear reason for why some people get this debilitating disease; it is neither genetic nor linked to specific behavioral or environmental causes, making the diagnosis even more difficult to accept.

My first reaction, when he received the diagnosis, was to approach the issue in the same manner as I did everything else in my life: think hard enough about the problem, analyze the facts and craft a solution. This time, this very logical approach took me only so far. All the thinking and analysis in the world, while helping me understand and manage the disease, did not solve anything. It could neither provide me with a cure nor the answer to why my husband, who is a wonderful person, had this disorder.

I did not dwell on the problem when I was leading. I was too busy to worry endlessly about the situation, and he was in the early stages of the disease and was not that severely affected. I wrongly assumed an answer would come when we required it, still thinking we would conquer whatever we had to face in the future by rationally thinking about every possible aspect of the disorder. We carried on as if everything was almost normal.

Things changed dramatically when I stepped down from the presidency. His condition was worsening, and I had more time to experience the impact of the disease not only on his life but also on mine. I slowly began to realize that no matter how hard I thought about the problem, no matter how well we coped with his disability, I was unable to make sense of the situation. Why him? Why now? Wasn't this the time in our lives when we should have been enjoying a healthy, carefree existence?

I knew I needed help in dealing with this challenge at this particular time in my life. Enter Sheryl Sandberg and her book *Option B: Facing Adversity, Building Resilience, and Finding Joy*, which discusses how to move forward after life's inevitable setbacks. Following the sudden death of her husband, Sandberg recounts how she was able to recover and rebound from this life-shattering event and find strength in the face of adversity. Her message is powerful: everyone experiences things that are not explainable, and in order to be resilient during times of adversity, you need to forgo trying to understand or reason why and accept that life is uncertain and entails both good and bad events that cannot be easily explained or rationally interpreted.

She points out that most of us believe our lives will unfold in a predictable fashion, a plan A that we are seeking and striving for. Her major message is that it is not uncommon for unknown and unpredictable events to occur that interfere with plan A, that throw us off course and that, if not dealt with, can result in anger and a life of regret. She argues that we all must learn, hard as it is, to let go of plan A, to adapt and not become preoccupied with why our initial plans must be abandoned as a result of things we have no control over—that by letting go and moving on, we arrive at plan B.

Easier said than done. What was our plan B? Over time and with hard work I have begun to forgo plan A and follow a new path. I have found that I can be sad without being angry; that I can begin to accept life as it is, without resenting the loss of what I had previously thought my life should be. Most important, I have discovered that I need to accept the fact that I cannot solve every problem by just thinking about it and coming up with the answer logically. Rather, I have had to acknowledge that there are aspects of life that are mysterious and unexplainable, detours in our plan A that need to be accepted as part of the life journey without trying to rationally understand or fight them.

Sandberg also importantly notes that there is a continuum of mysterious things in life—everything from the difficult aspects, such as death, illness and environmental disasters, to things that bring us joy, such as nature, love and the birth of a newborn child. She suggests that one way to remain in touch with the positive mysteries of life and raise your spiritual consciousness is to regularly acknowledge the wondrous positive forces in your life: a good deed, a kiss and hug from your grandchild, an inspirational poem. You will be better able to accept the negative mysteries by recognizing that your life also has positive qualities even in the face of adversity. She recommends that you stop and note on a daily basis the one or two events that have brought grace and gratitude into your life. And so, while it might seem like a crutch, I have tried her recommendation and now have a small notebook that sits on my bedside table. Three or four times a week, I record the two or three mysterious things that I am grateful for that occurred that day. In some way, I think it resembles how I would pray if I were religious: a recognition of those things that I am not responsible for but that occur mysteriously in my life and elicit my gratitude.

It has been hard work. Am I totally accepting of the difficulties we experience from time to time? Am I never angry or discouraged? Of course not. But what I have found is that by acknowledging that there are some things that are out of my control, things that are unexplainable and mysterious, I am able to not only build resilience in the face of adversity but also create a sense of tranquility in life where there might have been only anger and resentment before. Is this a spiritual consciousness? I am not certain, but it definitely differs from logic, scientific explanation or rational thought. It calms me, brings me inner peace and permits me to celebrate all the good things in my life while accepting the more troublesome aspects. In many ways it answers the question for me: "Why do bad things happen to good people?" They just do . . . and it is not our job to explain why.

Finding Joy: The Hummingbird Effect

"Aging with joy is a little like the hummingbird effect—allowing for the unexpected and unpredicted moments that can change us. It goes like this. As flowers developed colors and odors, they attracted insects that were able to extract pollen. Over time flowers added sweet nectar to their pollen, becoming more attractive not only to insects but also hummingbirds. To get at the nectar, hummingbirds had to evolve to fly like insects, flapping their wings swiftly up and down to 'float' in midair. An unexpected development that was neither planned nor predicted—the hummingbird effect."

—STEVEN JOHNSON, *HOW WE GOT TO NOW*

Such is the discovery of joy in life—unpredictable and fleeting, joy appears when least expected: a baby's soft sweet smell, a gorgeous sunset that lights up the western sky, the first cup of coffee taken on your deck early in the quiet of the morning, fresh sheets on the bed, the exuberant sound of an opera aria, a handwritten letter from a loved one.

Joy is found in the most unusual places and the most unexpected situations. It can result from a conscious action, such as giving of yourself to another person or cause, or it can occur unconsciously through observing or witnessing something totally unanticipated. It can be felt directly or vicariously, through personal experiences or through the accomplishments of those you care about. It can come with gifts given to you or gifts you give to others. It is hard to explain or describe accurately, and it is often impossible to connect it to the event that actually triggers it. But one thing is certain: when you experience it, you know it—the warm glow, the stillness and silence that accompany it and the gratitude you feel.

Leaders, because of the demands of their position and the singular focus of their attention, are often too preoccupied to notice joyful moments. It takes time to experience joy; it takes awareness of the things around you to notice the warmth of the sun, the hush of a snowfall or the sense of fulfillment that accompanies a deed or act done for others. Without noticing or being attuned to these amazing aspects of life, the human experience of joy is forfeited. Joy is all about connection—with a moment, with others, with yourself—and women, who typically seek and crave connection to a greater degree than men, may suffer more from its absence when they are leading.

When women stop leading they seek to reignite the joy in their lives, to become reconnected to the people, happenings and situations that lift their spirits and allow them to celebrate life—life as it is, not as it was or will be; life as it presents itself, not as it is remembered or anticipated. Joy requires living in the moment and not being preoccupied about what needs to be done, what has already happened or what tomorrow will bring. By taking in the natural beauty and splendor that surround us as well as the people who play meaningful roles in our lives but who often go unnoticed, joy will occur and provide a new sense of purpose and meaning to your life.

We have found that slowing down has been one of the most challenging things we have had to do after leaving our leadership positions. It is not easy to accept the fact that you do not have to be busy every moment in the day to be personally fulfilled; that you do not always have to be on the go, seeing people, answering emails and honoring commitments in order to be successful and happy in life. In fact, we believe it is just the opposite: being still, finding quiet moments in your day, listening to the sounds of nature, thinking about what you are able to do for others to celebrate them—these are just some of the things that can be done to invite joy back into your life.

PIPER:

My mother was a birder. From the time I was a child and watched her feed the sparrows from our kitchen window until I saw her in her seniors' residence observing the chickadees and cardinals that came to her outside feeder, I was aware that birds were important to her. And yet I did not share her fascination or love for these feathered friends. I was too busy. Preoccupied with other things in my life, I did not see what she saw in these creatures.

Only after I stopped leading and moved into a condo perched four stories above the ground did I discover birds—birds that soar by my windows in the light of the early morning, birds that warble at dusk and dawn and birds that flit about the flowers and shrubs in our neighborhood. One bird in particular captured my attention and eventual adoration—the hummingbird. So small, so glittery, so magical, so beautiful. I have become addicted to hummingbirds, feeding them with sugar water perfectly concocted, planting red flowers in my planters to attract them and becoming mesmerized when they appear outside my window. What is it about these tiny creatures that makes me catch my breath and wonder at their beauty? Simply put, they bring me joy. Hard to describe, hard to understand, hard to define; but every time a hummingbird appears at my feeder, I am joyful. It really does not matter what is going on in my life—rain or shine, bad days or good, difficult times or happy— the hummingbird brings simple joy to my heart, making me stop and take stock of everything in my life that I am grateful for.

How different my life is now than when I was leading. Then, watching and observing hummingbirds, let alone feeding and attracting them, was the furthest thing from my mind. Not only did I not have the time to stop and admire, but also I had no interest in finding joy in the simple things in life. It is hard to explain, but my life now is less complicated, more introspective and more joyful.

Another joyous surprise: my sewing machine—the whirring of its motor, the slippery feel of the material moving through the feed dog, the letting go of concerns and basking in the harmony of the moment all bring me joy. I have always loved to sew but never had the luxury of just appreciating the simplicity of the activity. While I made numerous Halloween costumes and doll clothes over the years, I rarely if ever had the time or desire to sew just for the sweetness of the experience.

Even better, I have discovered the joy of making something I had never sewn before—quilts. Self-taught, I have worked hard at acquiring the skills necessary to make quilts of all colors, patterns, sizes and descriptions—baby quilts, lap quilts, bed quilts, throw quilts. And, to my delight, I now know that the best part of quilting is giving the quilt away as a heartfelt gift to good friends on special occasions: the birth of a grandchild, a 50th wedding anniversary, a sweet 16 birthday, a house-warming gift or an expression of gratitude.

I am extremely fortunate to have found joy in the most unexpected places in my life after leading: never in my wildest dreams would I have thought I would find it in hummingbirds and quilts. Like the humming-bird, I have evolved—changed my ways, slowed down, learned new skills and developed the capacity to gather the sweet nectar out of life.

Lessons Learned

How women leaders choose to live their lives after leading involves not only decisions around their health and fitness but also conscious choices to define a new sense of purpose, develop mental strength, find a level of spiritual consciousness and rediscover joy in their lives. Super-aging does not automatically happen. It requires intention, nerve and hard work, including the establishment of new routines, habits and goals. We believe that by accepting the inevitable fact that we are all getting older and focusing on four critical aspects of super-aging—intellectual engage-ment, active living, spiritual consciousness and discovering joy—former women leaders will be able to redefine themselves to find happiness and fulfillment long after leading.

1. Consciously work to stretch your mind. Seek out opportu-nities, people, groups and associations that encourage you to think differently, expose you to new ideas and issues and allow you to focus on areas of concern that you normally would not have contemplated.
2. Recognize that by stretching your mind, you will experience a level of discomfort and unease that ensures your brain is working overtime. Unless it makes you somewhat uncom-fortable, you are most likely not expanding your mental capacity.
3. Seek out new skills. By doing things you have never done before and cultivating new ways of experiencing life, you will

remain young in terms of the way you see and experience the world.

4. Think about the spiritual side of life, the things you cannot explain by applying reason and critical thinking. Consider how you can best stay in touch with your own spiritual consciousness to enrich your life and bring yourself peace and a new sense of calm.

5. When confronted with adversity, an inevitable occurrence in life, consider letting go of your previous hopes and life plans and adopting another approach to accept and adapt to new circumstances as they unfold.

6. Work at being still, slowing down and listening to and seeing all the wonder around you. Take time to acknowledge the good things in your life that bring you joy.

CONCLUSION

"While I may be the first woman in this office, I won't be the last."

—KAMALA HARRIS

Being the first women to lead our respective organizations was exhilarating. We were given the unprecedented opportunity to demonstrate how women leaders can make a difference and be true to themselves by having the nerve to step up and assume the responsibility of leading. We were honored to have had the chance to leave a mark on our universities and to work with amazing colleagues and associates to advance our agendas. But as U.S. Vice President Harris notes, it is not good enough to have been the first; our job as women leaders goes far beyond our own leadership experience. We must now lend a hand to assist other women to become leaders—leaders at every level, in the public and nonprofit sectors, in government and business, in all areas of pursuit. We must ensure that our time as leaders was not a fluke, not an arbitrary occurrence, not a one-off event. Our job is to make certain that other women will follow and accept the call to lead in their personal and professional lives.

This purpose drives our determination to share not only our experience but also the lessons we learned over the years, including the importance of cultivating, exercising and living with nerve. While our stories and ideas are not unique or all-encompassing, they do highlight some of the key components of the leadership journey for women. We believe a broad range of factors contribute to developing the nerve to lead—everything from how a girl becomes a woman to the role education plays, relationships with others and many more. It is critical that we women shed our reluctance to lead; that we take stock of everything that has prepared us to lead; that we recognize opportunities to lead for what they are, no matter what stage of life they occur; and that we have the confidence and nerve to answer the call to lead when it comes.

How a woman leads may differ from how her male colleagues do, but she is no less effective. And the act of leading does not end once a leader walks away from her formal position. Women clearly continue to lead as they age, having the nerve to be themselves, contributing to causes and issues they care about and discovering the freedom that comes with the validation of who they really are and what they truly value. In fact, we now realize that this may be the most important aspect of women leading—that we take charge of our lives, determine who we want to be and give of ourselves and our talents in the interest of the things that matter most in our lives.

Nerve plays a unique role in forging a woman leader and in empowering her to lead throughout her life. Without nerve, women run the real risk of failing to seize an opportunity to exert themselves actively in the pursuit of their life goals. Nerve is the basis for women to be free and choose for themselves how and when they will lead. Nerve underpins every phase of their leadership journey, permitting them to act on their convictions, develop their own style of leadership and defy convention when it stands in the way.

Georgia O'Keeffe was a remarkable woman for her era—one of the first North American female artists who made her mark by painting what she wanted to paint. She actively chose not to paint as others painted. She did not paint typical portraits or still-life representations. Nor did she study with the masters in Europe or the Impressionists of the time. No, she had the nerve to pack her bags, move to New Mexico and paint skulls, flowers and southwestern landscapes. She had the nerve to find her own voice and lead as a pioneering woman in the man's milieu of art, to express herself as she wanted, to paint differently despite criticism and rebuke. And that is our wish for women leaders of today: that they find the nerve to determine what and how they want to paint; to lead with nerve and confidence, knowing that they are as capable as any man; and that by bringing their unique perspectives and talents to their leadership positions, they will paint a different picture of what is possible for future generations of women to come.

NOTES

1   Adams, "Birth Order," 411–439.
2   Black, Grönqvist, and Öckert, "Born to Lead."
3   Steinberg, "Making of Female Presidents," 89–110.
4   Madsen, "The Experience of UAE Women," 75–95; Ganesan, "What Do Women Leaders Have in Common?"
5   Peters and Rosenthal, *Speaker Nancy Pelosi*, 203.
6   Freedman, *Eleanor Roosevelt*.
7   Sommers, "A Necessary Option."
8   Reyes, "Effects of Overparenting."
9   Bell, "Out of the Beaten Track." Engraving of quote can be found at Bell Labs.
10   Indiana University, "Men Do Hear."
11   Robbins and Coulter, *Management*.
12   Schein, *Organizational Culture and Leadership*.
13   CultureIQ, "How to Have Successful Leadership Transitions."
14   Gillmor, *Fred Terman at Stanford*.
15   Zenger and Folkman, "Research: Women Score Higher."
16   Fisher, "The Natural Leadership Talents of Women."
17   Broadus, "Small Beginnings."
18   *Merriam-Webster*.
19   Coats, "Grit and Grace."
20   Kets de Vries, *Global Executive Leadership Inventory*.
21   Ibarra and Obodaru, "Women and the Vision Thing."
22   Spiridigliozzi, "The Leadership Theories."

23   Rane, "What Causes Women Not to Succeed."

24   Lazard, "Here's the Truth about False Accusations."

25   Smith, "Wanting to be Liked."

26   Shekshnia and Osnes, "Why the Best CEOs Are Already Thinking."

27   Kellner, "What Is the Retirement Age for Women?"

28   Lanning, "Time for Myself."

29   Hochschild, *The Time Bind.*

30   MacDougall, et al., "Report: 2020 Diversity Disclosure Practices."

31   Mensi-Klarbach and Seierstad, "Gender Quotas on Corporate Boards: Similarities and Differences in Quota Scenarios."

32   Landaw, "How Diverse Is Your Board, Really?"

33   O'Keefe, "About Me."

34   Kellner, "What Is the Retirement Age for Women?"

REFERENCES

Chapter 1

Adams, Bert N. "Birth Order: A Critical Review." *Sociometry 35*, no. 3 (September 1972): 411–439. doi.org/10.2307/2786503.

Black, Sandra E., Erik Grönqvist, and Björn Öckert. "Born to Lead? The Effect of Birth Order on Non-Cognitive Abilities." *National Bureau of Economic Research*, Working Paper No. 23393 (May 2017): 4. doi.org/10.3386/w23393.

Ganesan, Sharmilla. "What Do Women Leaders Have in Common?" *The Atlantic* (August 17, 2016). theatlantic.com/business/archive/2016/08/what-do-women-leaders-have-in-common/492656/.

Hennig, Margaret, and Anne Jardim. *The Managerial Woman.* New York: Doubleday, 1976.

Madsen, Susan R. (2010). "The Experience of UAE Women in Developing Leadership Early in Life." *Feminist Formations 22*, no. 3 (September 2010): 75–95. doi.org/10.1353/ff.2010.0014.

Steinberg, Blema S. "The Making of Female Presidents and Prime Ministers: The Impact of Birth Order, Sex of Siblings, and Father-Daughter Dynamics." *Political Psychology 22*, no. 1 (March 2001): 89–110. doi.org/10.1111/0162-895X.00227.

Chapter 2

Freedman, Russell. *Eleanor Roosevelt: A Life of Discovery*. Boston: Clarion Books, 1993.

Peters, Ronald M., and Cindy Simon Rosenthal. *Speaker Nancy Pelosi and the New American Politics*. Toronto: Oxford University Press, 2010.

Sommers, Christina Hoff. "A Necessary Option." *The New York Times* (September 6, 2016). nytimes.com/roomfordebate/2011/10/17/single-sex-schools-separate-but-equal/a-necessary-option.

Woolf, Virginia. *A Room of One's Own*. London: Hogarth Press, 1929.

Chapter 3

Reyes, Zoe. "The Effects of Overparenting on Children." PsychCentral (December 30, 2015). psychcentral.com/blog/the-effects-of-overparenting-on-children#1.

Slaughter, Anne-Marie. "Why Women Still Can't Have It All." *The Atlantic* (July/August 2012). theatlantic.com/magazine/archive/2012/07/why-women-still-cant-have-it-all/309020/.

Chapter 4

Bell, Alexander Graham. "Out of the Beaten Track." An address to the graduating class of the Friends School in Washington, D.C., May 2, 1914. See also "Discovery and Invention by Alexander Graham Bell." *The National Geographic Magazine*. Vol. 26, no. 6 (June 1914): 650.

Hewlett, Sylvia. *Forget a Mentor, Find a Sponsor: The New Way to Fast-Track Your Career*. Boston: Harvard Business Review Press, 2013.

Kennedy, Pagan. "How to Cultivate the Art of Serendipity." *The New York Times* (January 2, 2016). nytimes.com/2016/01/03/opinion/how-to-cultivate-the-art-of-serendipity.html.

Chapter 5

Kay, Katty, and Claire Shipman. *The Confidence Code: The Science and Art* of *Self-Assurance—What Women Should Know*. New York: Harper Collins, 2014.

Chapter 6

CultureIQ. *How to Have Successful Leadership Transitions*. CultureIQ Blog (August 15, 2018). cultureiq.com/blog/how-to-have-successful-leadership-transitions/.

Ducasse, Patrick, and Tom Lutz. *Assuming Leadership: The First 100 Days*. Boston Consulting Group, Inc: 2003. unida.com.tr/haberDosyalar/723077188-assuming-leadership.pdf.

Indiana University. "Men Do Hear—But Differently than Women, Brain Images Show." Science Daily (November 29, 2000). sciencedaily.com/releases/2000/11/001129075326.htm.

Robbins, Stephen P., and Mary A. Coulter. *Management*. Eighth edition. New York: Pearson Prentice Hall, 2005.

Schein, Edgar H. *Organizational Culture and Leadership*. Fifth Edition. New Jersey: Wiley, 2017.

Schlesinger, Arthur M. Jr. *The Coming of the New Deal: 193335, The Age of Roosevelt, Volume II*. New York: Mariner Books, 2003.

Chapter 7

Broadus, E.K. "Small Beginnings." *Saturday and Sunday*, Toronto, 1935. As cited in the Dictionary of Canadian Biography, "Biography of Edmund Kemper Broadus," Volume XVI (1931–1940). biographi.ca/en/bio/broadus_edmund_kemper_16E.html.

Fisher, Helen E. "The Natural Leadership Talents of Women." In *Enlightened Power: How Women are Transforming the Practice of Leadership*, edited by Linda Coughlin, Ellen Wingard, and Keith Hollihan, 133–140. San Francisco: Jossey-Bass, 2013.

Gillmor, C. Stewart. *Fred Terman at Stanford: Building a Discipline, a University, and Silicon Valley*. Redwood City, CA: Stanford University Press, 2004.

Munir, Zarina B.A., A. Mat, Nur Liana Kori, R.A. Aziz, and Lailatul F.A. Hassan, L.F. "How Women's Leadership and Rewards Would Influence Women's Power in an Organization." *International*

Proceedings of Management and Economy, IPEDR vol. 84 (2015): 125–132. ipedr.com/vol84/015-E30003.pdf.

Welch, Jack. *Winning*. New York: Harper Collins, 2005.

Zenger, Jack, and Joseph Folkman. "Research: Women Score Higher Than Men in Most Leadership Skills." *Harvard Business Review* (June 25, 2019). hbr.org/2019/06/research-women-score-higher-than-men-in-most-leadership-skills.

Chapter 8

Brown, Brené. "The Power of Vulnerability." TED Talk. 2010. brenebrown.com/videos/ted-talk-the-power-of-vulnerability/.

Coats, Cari H. "Grit and Grace: A Power Combination for Women Leaders." *Forbes* (August 12, 2019). forbes.com/sites/forbescoachescouncil/2019/08/12/grit-and-grace-a-power-combination-for-women-leaders/?sh=5b111428404a.

Ibarra, Herminia, and Otilia Obodaru. "Women and the Vision Thing." *Harvard Business Review* (January 2009). hbr.org/2009/01/women-and-the-vision-thing.

Kets de Vries, Manfred F.R. *Global Executive Leadership Inventory (GELI)*. New Jersey: Pfeiffer Wiley, 2004.

Rane, Zulie. "What Causes Women to Not Succeed at the Highest Level?" Medium (June, 15, 2019). zulie.medium.com/what-causes-women-to-not-succeed-at-the-highest-level-a6c02ac3c432.

Spiridigliozzi, Ginamarie. "The Leadership Theories that Lie Behind Indra Nooyi's Vision for PepsiCo." Foundations of Leadership (Dobbs) (June 3, 2018). sites.psu.edu/leaderfoundationsdobbs/2018/06/03/the-leadership-theories-that-lie-behind-indra-nooyis-vision-for-pepsico/.

Chapter 9

Brown, Brené. *Daring Greatly: How the Courage to Be Vulnerable Transforms the Way We Live, Love, Parent, and Lead*. New York: Avery, 2012.

Grounds, Jessica N., and Kristin Haffert. "Do Women Lead Differently During a Crisis?" Business Culture, NBC News (May 8, 2020).

anbcnews.com/know-your-value/feature/do-women-lead-differently-during-crisis-ncna1200506.

Krakauer, Jon. *Missoula: Rape and the Justice System in a College Town.* New York: Knopf Doubleday, 2016.

Lazard, Lisa. "Here's the Truth about False Accusations of Sexual Violence." The Conversation (November 24, 2017). theconversation.com/heres-the-truth-about-false-accusations-of-sexual-violence-88049.

Chapter 10

Sandberg, Sheryl. *Lean In: Women, Work, and the Will to Lead.* New York: Knopf Doubleday, 2013.

Smith, Kurt. "Wanting to Be Liked is Not the Same as Needing to Be Liked." PsychCentral (March 21, 2020). psychcentral.com/blog/wanting-to-be-liked-is-not-the-same-as-needing-to-be-liked#1.

Chapter 12

Kellner, Gail. "What Is the Retirement Age for Women?" Retirable (June 15, 2020). retirable.com/advice/lifestyle/retirement-age-for-women.

Shekshnia, Stanislav, and Gry Osnes. "Why the Best CEOs are Already Thinking About Their Exits." *Harvard Business Review* (October 31, 2019). hbr.org/2019/10/why-the-best-ceos-are-already-thinking-about-their-exits.

Chapter 13

Hochschild, Arlie R. *The Time Bind: When Work Becomes Home and Home Becomes Work.* New York: Metropolitan Books, 1997.

Lanning, Kate L. "Time for Myself, Time for Others: Gender Differences in the Meaning of Retirement." *Sociology Honors Project.* Paper 36. Sociology Department, Macalester College (2012). digitalcommons.macalester.edu/soci_honors/36.

Chapter 14

Catalyst. "Quick Take: Women on Corporate Boards." (March 13, 2020). catalyst.org/research/women-on-corporate-boards.

Landaw, Jared L. "How Diverse is Your Board, Really?" *Harvard Business Review* (June 11, 2020). hbr.org/2020/06/how-diverse-is-your-board-really.

MacDougall, Andrew, John M. Valley, and Jennifer Jeffrey. "Report: 2020 Diversity Disclosure Practices—Diversity and Leadership at Canadian Public Companies." Osler (October 5, 2020). osler.com/en/resources/governance/2020/report-2020-diversity-disclosure-practices-diversity-and-leadership-at-canadian-public-companies.

Mensi-Klarbach, Heike and Seierstad, Cathrine. "Gender Quotas in Corporate Boards: Similarities and Differences in Quota Scenarios." *European Management Review*, vol. 17, issue 3 (Fall 2020): 615–631.

Chapter 15

Fisher, Alice. "The Bitter Sweetness of Becoming a Grandparent after 70." Sixty and Me (May 24, 2019). sixtyandme.com/the-bitter-sweetness-of-becoming-a-grandparent-after-70/.

O'Keefe, Georgia. "About Myself." *Exhibition of Oils and Pastels*, January 22–March 17, 1939. Georgia O'Keeffe Museum. okeeffemuseum.org/wp-content/uploads/2015/03/taketimetolooksource.pdf.

Chapter 16

Collins, Francis S. *The Language of God: A Scientist Presents Evidence for Belief.* New York: Free Press, 2007.

Harvard Women's Health Watch. "What does it take to be a super-ager?" Harvard Health Publishing (May 2017). health.harvard.edu/healthy-aging/what-does-it-take-to-be-a-super-ager.

Johnson, Steven. *How We Got to Now: Six Innovations That Made the Modern World.* New York: Riverhead Books, Penguin Random House, 2014.

Kellner, Gail. "What is the retirement age for women?" *Lifestyle.* June 14, 2020.

Lewis, C.S. *Mere Christianity*. New York: Harper Collins, 2001.

Sandberg, Sheryl. *Option B: Facing Adversity, Building Resilience, and Finding Joy*. New York: Knopf Doubleday, 2017.

Verghese, Joe, Richard B. Lipton, Mindy J. Katz, Charles B. Hall, Carol A. Derby, Gail Kuslansky, Anne F. Ambrose, Martin Sliwinski, and Herman Buschke. "Leisure Activities and the Risk of Dementia in the Elderly." *New England Journal of Medicine 348* (June 19, 2003): 2508–2516. doi.org/10.1056/NEJMoa022252.

ACKNOWLEDGMENTS

W riting this book has taught us more about ourselves, and our leadership journeys, than we could have ever imagined. By questioning why we ended up leading, the factors that propelled and supported us as leaders and how we have redefined our lives after leading, we discovered new insights and interpretations that had remained hidden until we were compelled to recount and explain our own experiences. The most significant part of this discovery process was the identification of key people—people who inspired and supported us, people who picked us up when we faltered, people who cheered us on and encouraged us to excel and people who assisted us in the telling of our stories.

Starting with our families, both nuclear and extended, parents and grandparents, siblings, children, Emily, Hannah, Dinesh and Anji and grandchildren, we know we never could have accomplished what we did without their unconditional love, encouragement and unquestionable commitment to our success. We thank our sisters, daughters and daughter-in-law, who pushed us to dig deep, lent their voices to our discussions and advised, criticized and reflected upon what we were writing. Most important, Martha is enormously grateful to her spouse, Bill, and Indira to her former partner, Sam, who both took pride in our accomplishments, assisted immensely in sustaining our families while we led and encouraged us to tell our stories.

We would like to acknowledge the individuals who served as our mentors and sponsors, including Dick and Sylvia Cruess, David Johnston, Hubert Lai and Rob Prichard, who were especially helpful in reviewing certain points, issues and conclusions. Our women friends and associates, who throughout our journey provided us with daily examples of women leading at every level, in every area, in all pursuits, deserve special recognition. Without these lifelong friendships, we would not be who we are today.

The universities that played such an important role in selecting us to lead and entrusting us with their academic programs and futures— the University of Alberta, the University of British Columbia and McGill University—were essential in providing us with the means and support to lead at a time when few women had gone before us. We will be forever grateful to these institutions for taking a chance on us, and we express our appreciation to the boards of governors, senior teams, academic colleagues, staff, alumni and students who challenged and inspired us along the way.

And to the businesses who embraced us, despite our lack of corporate experience. To the Bank of Montreal, Bank of Nova Scotia, Shoppers Drug Mart, TransAlta Corp., Grosvenor Americas, Magna International, Stelco, TC Energy and Bennett Jones—all of which have taught us how to lead in a completely different environment than the academic milieu and given us the benefit of the doubt over and over again—we extend a sincere thank you. We received much more than we gave by working with and learning from remarkable CEOs and management teams, as well as numerous talented and experienced corporate directors.

Our respective associations with CARE Canada and various nonprofit organizations provided us with the opportunity to do good and focus on the areas we deemed important as we redefined ourselves after leading. And, as a result of the contributions we are making to education through our roles on the boards of York House School, Crofton House School and St. George's School, we have been able to explore how single-sex education is playing a new role in defining leadership in the 21st century for both boys and girls.

And, of course, we are thankful for all the assistance we received from our agent, Robert Mackwood at Seventh Avenue Literary Agency, along with Jennifer Smith from ECW Press for her advice and guidance, and

Karen Milner, Rachel Ironstone, and Samantha Chin for their magnificent editing and proofing of our manuscript. These experts trusted us to tell our stories as we saw fit.

In the end, however, our most sincere gratitude must be extended to each other. What a marvelous experience we have had working together; learning about and from each other; working day after day, listening to each other's voice and making sense of our collective experience. Together, we tackled the issues we believe to be important, challenged each other and found the nerve to disclose some of our most authentic feelings, insights and interpretations. We are certain that had each of us attempted to write this book solo, we would have failed. How lucky we are to have each other—underlining that nothing of import is ever accomplished alone.

INDEX

focus, prior to exit, 207–9
forgotten, fear of being, 227–28
Frank, Anne, 225
Franklin, Benjamin, 23
Friedan, Betty, 263
friends vs. peers, 103–7, 108. *See also* relationships

G
Gairdner Foundation, 181–82
Gardner, Howard, 182
gift horses, 79–80
going first, 92–94, 107–8, 281
Goldenberg, Eddie, 147
good, doing, 242–44
grandchildren, 256–57
grit and grace, 131–52; introduction and lessons learned, 131–33, 151–52; developing grit, 133–37; exhibiting grace, 137–41; partnerships and, 144–47; relationship with the boss, 147–51; vision and, 141–44
Grounds, Jessica N., 153–54

H
Haffert, Kristin, 153–54
Harris, Kamala, 92, 281
Hennig, Margaret, 9
Hewlett, Sylvia Ann, 67
honeymoon period (first hundred days), 85–87
Hôpital Sainte-Justine (Montreal), 134–35
Houghton, Michael, 146

household responsibilities, 193–94, 215–16. *See also* children
hummingbirds, 275, 277

I
Ibsen, Henrik, 249
identity, loss of, 220–22
India, 140–41, 219–20
Indian Institute of Technology (IIT) Bombay, 140–41
innovation, 25. *See also* curious learning
INSEAD, 141
intellectual intimacy, 253. *See also* mental engagement

J
Jardim, Anne, 9
Jobs, Steve, 111
Johnson, Steven, 275
joy, 275–78

K
Kay, Katty, 74–75
Keller, Helen, 249
Kennedy, Pagan, 59–60
Keohane, Nannerl O., 65

L
Lagarde, Christine, 75
lame-duck period, 205–6
leadership: introduction and conclusion, 1–4, 281–83; balance, 191–99; as born vs. bred, 7–21; compensation, 125–26, 213–14; crisis

Trilateral Commission, 221–22; vision, 142–44
plans, best-laid, 34–38, 39, 273–74
post-leadership lives, 225–48; introduction and lessons learned, 225–26, 246–48; corporate boards diversification, 233–38; doing good, 242–44; fear of being forgotten, 227–28; saying no, 228–29; securing corporate board appointments, 230–33; unexpected new opportunities, 244–46; working hard on corporate boards, 238–42. *See also* loss; super-aging
pregnancy, 48–50
Prichard, Rob, 235–36
protocol, 185–87
public personae, 171–89; introduction and lessons learned, 171–72, 187–89; likeability, 176–79; physical appearance, 172–76; protocol, 185–87; public speaking, 180–82; taking a stand, 182–85

Q
questions, asking, 239

R
recognition, 125–27
reflection, self-, 18–20
relationships, 249–61; introduction and lessons learned, 249–51, 260–61; with boss, 147–51; emotional and intellectual intimacy, 252–55; external partners, 144–47; family, 255–59; friends vs. peers, 103–7, 108; loss of associates, 218–20; Piper's intentionality post-presidency, 251–52; between women, 38, 122–25. *See also* family; marriage; talent
reluctance, 73–81; introduction and lessons learned, 73–74, 80–81; confidence gap, 74–77, 227; fear of leading, 74, 77–78; gift horses and, 79–80
resiliency, 17
retirement. *See* exits; loss; post-leadership lives; super-aging
Roosevelt, Eleanor, 27–28, 73, 153
Roosevelt, Franklin D., 86
Roosevelt, Theodore, 157
Rutnam, Mary (née Irwin), 11

S
sabbaticals, 227–28
Salcudean, Martha, 68
Samarasekera, Indira: in the arena during a crisis, 159–61; background, 2; at Bennett Jones, 245–46; best-laid plans, 37–38; Board of Governors at U of A and, 149–51; cancer diagnosis,